Mastering the Fujifilm X-E1 and X-Pro1

AUTHOR

Rico Pfirstinger studied communications and has been working as a journalist, publicist, and photographer since the mid-80s. He has written a number of books on diverse topics, from Adobe PageMaker to sled dogs. He produced a beautiful book of photographs titled *Huskies in Action*. He worked as the department head for the German Burda-Publishing Company and served as chief editor for a winter sports website.

After eight years as a freelance film critic in Los Angeles, Rico now lives in Germany and devotes his time to digital photography and compact camera systems.

Rico Pfirstinger

Mastering the
Fujifilm X-E1 and X-Pro1

rockynook

Rico Pfirstinger
rico@ricopress.de

Publisher: Gerhard Rossbach
Project Editor: Maggie Yates
Copyeditor: Aimee Baldridge
Layout and Type: Anna Diechtierow
Cover Design: Anna Diechtierow
Printer: Sheridan Books, Inc.
Printed in USA

ISBN 978-1-937538-31-6

1st Edition 2013
© 2013 by Rico Pfirstinger

Rocky Nook Inc.
802 East Cota St., 3rd Floor
Santa Barbara, CA 93103
www.rockynook.com

Copyright © 2013 by dpunkt.verlag GmbH, Heidelberg, Germany.
Title of the German original: Das Fujifilm X-E1 Handbuch
ISBN 978-3-86490-065-5
Translation Copyright © 2013 by Rocky Nook. All rights reserved.

Library of Congress Cataloging-in-Publication Data
Pfirstinger, Rico.
Mastering the Fujifilm X-E1 and X-Pro1 / by Rico Pfirstinger. -- 1st Edition.
pages cm
ISBN 978-1-937538-31-6 (pbk.)
1. Fujifilm digital cameras--Handbooks, manuals, etc. 2. Photography--Digital techniques--Handbooks, manuals, etc. I. Title.
TR263.F85P46 2013
771.3--dc23
2013022946

Distributed by O'Reilly Media
1005 Gravenstein Highway North
Sebastopol, CA 95472

WELCOME!

Do you really need a second handbook for cameras like the Fujifilm X-Pro1 and X-E1? Doesn't the owner's manual already cover everything? Unfortunately, it doesn't.

That's not to say that the owner's manual is useless; it documents all of the camera's functions briefly—including many features that I (and probably a majority of other photographers) won't ever use. What's really missing is background information, along with practical tips based on experience: What's the best way to activate a function? Which settings should you use in different circumstances? Why is the camera exhibiting a certain behavior? Which functions don't work the way you would expect them to, and how should you handle them?

This book in no way makes the owner's manuals of your camera, lenses, and accessories superfluous. You should definitely read them, because this book picks up where the manuals leave off. It condenses the knowledge and experience I gained in more than two years of groundwork, during which I collected a wealth of information from Internet forums and many other sources. While I was researching, I also shot thousands of images with all of the cameras of the Fujifilm X series.

This handbook includes personal experiences, tips, and background information—not only from me, but from other photographers as well. Since the X-Pro1 and X-E1 are very similar in functionality and operation, most of the things that are discussed in this book apply to both cameras. The major difference between the two is the hybrid viewfinder of the X-Pro1. Don't worry; I will be sure to clarify if a feature or topic applies to only one of the cameras. As far as the sensor, internal processing, and image quality are concerned, the two cameras are virtually identical and deliver interchangeable results. Hence all sample images are representative for both the X-Pro1 and the X-E1.

I'm assuming some basic photographic knowledge on your part. Your X-E1 or X-Pro1 is probably not your first camera, and you hopefully are already familiar with concepts like aperture and shutter speed.

If you still need to learn the basics, there are many excellent books (including some from this publisher) for building the knowledge and skills to fill this gap.

I hope you enjoy reading this book and shooting with your X-Pro1 or X-E1!

Rico Pfirstinger, September 2013

Figure 1: Have no fear: this book will ▶ help you master your X-Pro1 or X-E1. Both cameras are very versatile and can be used for a wide array of applications—from reportage to studio, just for fun, or for professional assignments. This image was shot with a single Profoto strobe and an X-Pro1 with a standard 18–55mm kit zoom lens. The RAW file was processed with Apple Aperture 3.4.

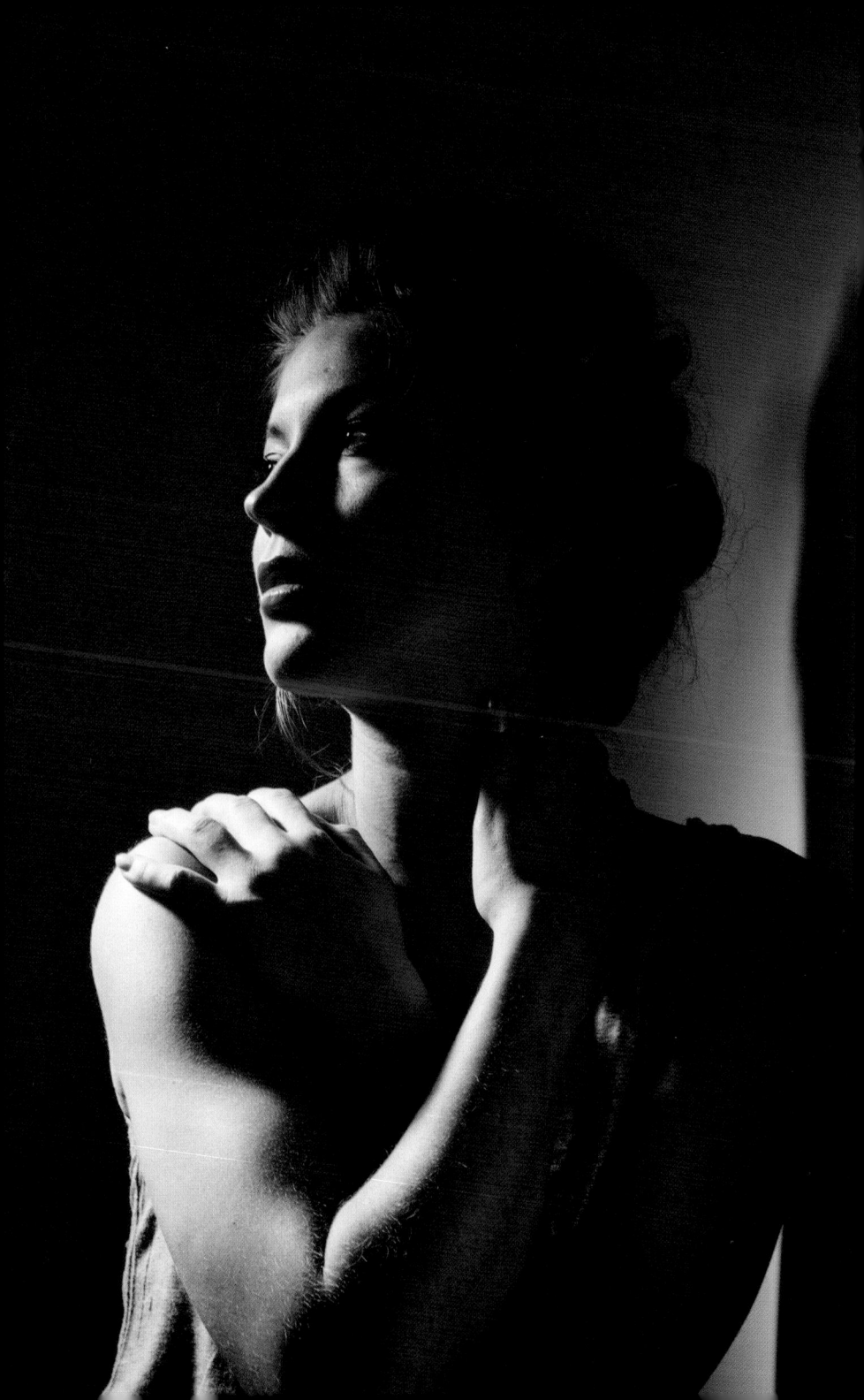

Contents

AN OVERVIEW OF THE X-MOUNT SYSTEM

The mirrorless Fujifilm X-mount system comprises several camera bodies as well as a host of additional components available from Fuji and several third-party vendors.

INTERCHANGEABLE LENSES
In addition to using a variety of X-mount autofocus lenses from Fujifilm (Fujinon) and Zeiss, you can attach current and older lenses from manufacturers such as Canon, Nikon, Contax, and Leica with the help of adaptors. A Fujifilm adaptor will enable you to use the Leica M system, and adaptors from other manufacturers like Kipon and Novoflex expand your lens mount options even further.

FLASH UNITS
Unlike the X-E1, the X-Pro1 doesn't come equipped with a built-in flash, but you can choose from three different system flash units designed for both cameras (and other Fuji camera models) that feature automatic TTL flash exposure capabilities. Or you can avail yourself of flash equipment from other manufacturers while shooting in manual mode.

ACCESSORIES
Do you wear glasses? If so, a diopter ring for the X-Pro1 could make a big difference for you. With its help, you'll be able to get the most from the X-Pro1's unique hybrid viewfinder without needing your glasses.

Do you plan on traveling with your camera system? Then you'll need replacement batteries and a handy power adaptor. And how about an additional handgrip that allows you to get a better hold on your camera while shooting?

I'll also cover several other hardware issues in the pages that follow, such as: Which memory cards should you use? Which filters should you affix to your lenses? How do you update the firmware for your camera and X-mount lenses? And how do you keep troublesome dust and dirt particles from compromising your camera's X-Trans sensor?

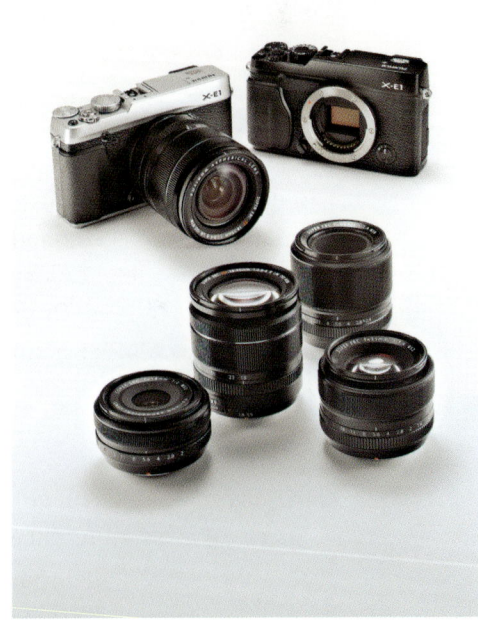

Figure 2: Silver and black versions of the Fujifilm X-E1 with a selection of zoom and prime lenses.

1.1 THE CAMERAS

Before we get started with the actual operation of your
X-Pro1 or X-E1, we should take a quick look at the camera's buttons, dials, menus, and connections to become
familiar with the terminology that will be used throughout this text.

OVERVIEW OF THE CONTROLS

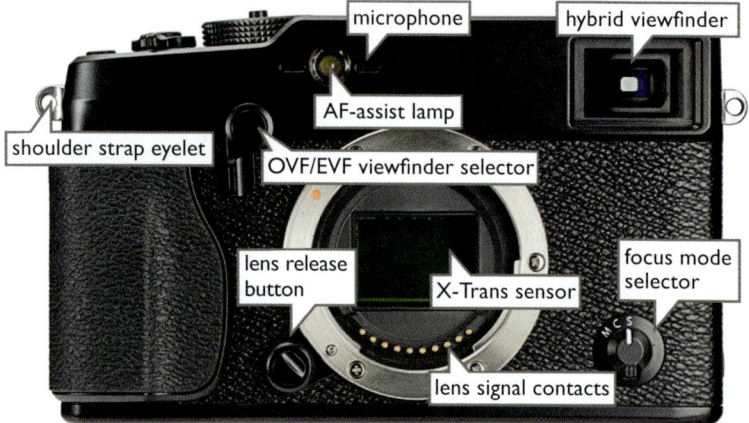

Figure 3: **X-Pro1 frontal view:** Hybrid viewfinder, shoulder strap eyelet,
focus mode selector, lens release button, lens signal contacts, X-Trans sensor,
OVF/EVF viewfinder selector, AF-assist lamp, microphone

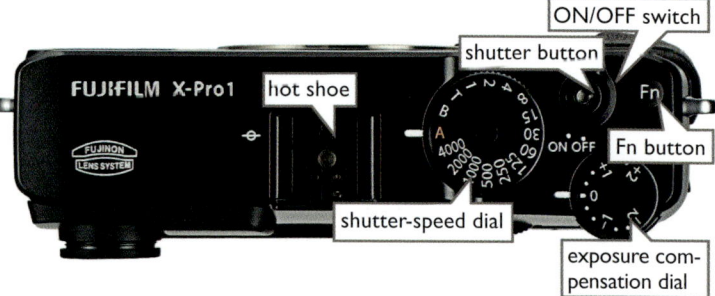

Figure 4: **X-Pro1 top view:** ON/OFF switch, shutter button with mechanical
cable release thread, Fn button, exposure compensation dial, shutter-speed
dial with dial release, hot shoe

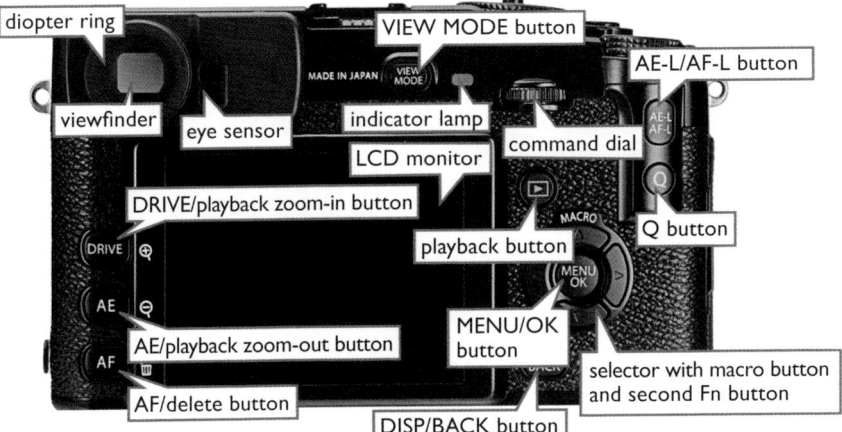

diopter ring

VIEW MODE button

MADE IN JAPAN / VIEW MODE

AE-L/AF-L button

viewfinder

eye sensor

indicator lamp

LCD monitor

command dial

DRIVE/playback zoom-in button

AE-L AF-L

Q

MACRO

DRIVE

Q button

playback button

MENU OK

AE

AE/playback zoom-out button

MENU/OK button

AF

selector with macro button and second Fn button

AF/delete button

DISP/BACK button

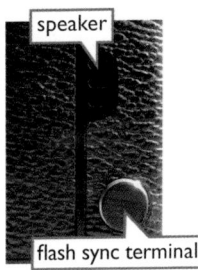

speaker

flash sync terminal

Figure 5: X-Pro1 back and left side view: Viewfinder with diopter ring, eye sensor, LCD monitor, VIEW MODE button, indicator lamp, command dial, AE-L/AF-L button, Quick Menu (Q) button, playback button, selector with macro button and second Fn button (arrow down key), MENU/OK button, DISP/BACK button, AF/delete button, AE/playback zoom-out button, DRIVE/playback zoom-in button, flash sync terminal, speaker

The selector enables you to navigate through the camera's menus and to control various features, such as the selection of the autofocus frame. You can confirm your selections either by pressing the MENU/OK button or by pressing the shutter button halfway down.

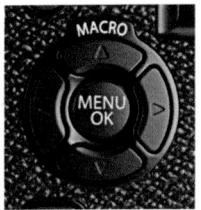

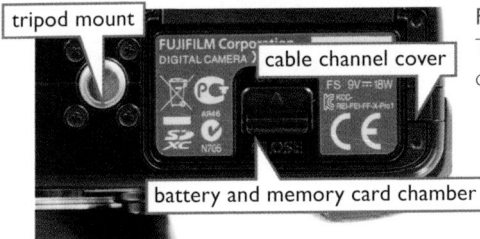

tripod mount

FUJIFILM Corporation
DIGITAL CAMERA

cable channel cover

battery and memory card chamber

Figure 6: X-Pro1 bottom view: Tripod mount, battery and memory card chamber, cable channel cover

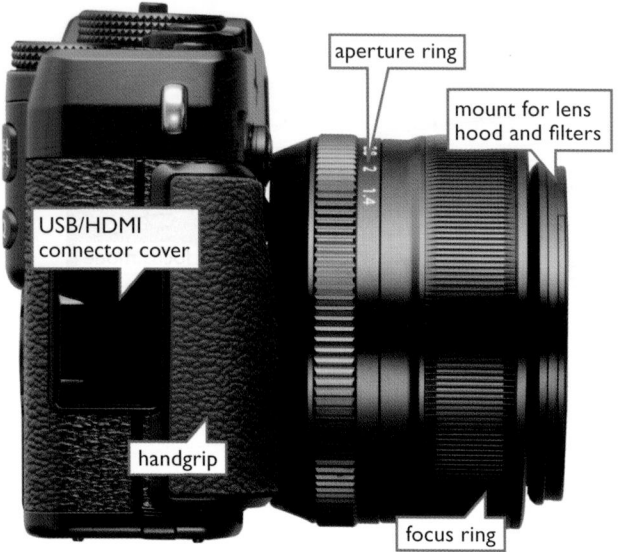

Figure 7: **X-Pro1 right side view (with 35mm f/1.4 lens):**
USB/HDMI connector cover, handgrip, aperture ring, focus ring,
mount for lens hood and filters

Figure 8: **X-Pro1 right side view:**
Open connector cover revealing
HDMI and USB ports

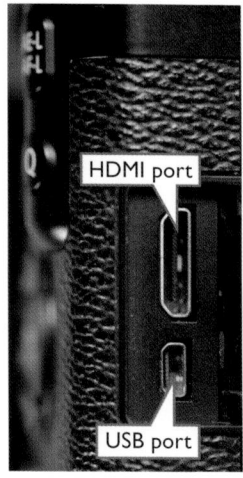

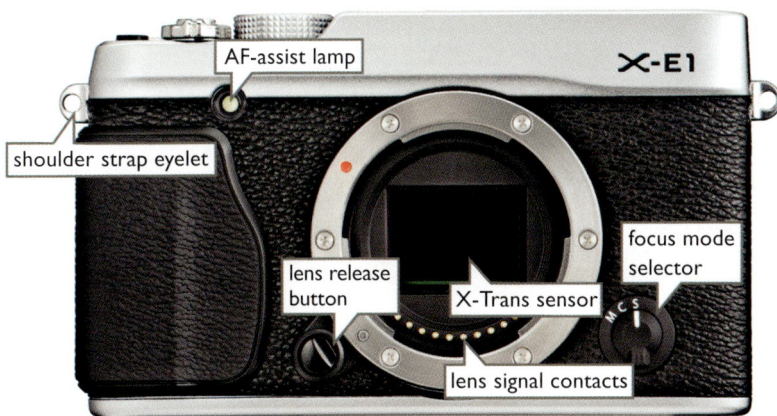

Figure 9: X-E1 frontal view: Shoulder strap eyelet, focus mode selector, lens release button, lens signal contacts, X-Trans sensor, AF-assist lamp

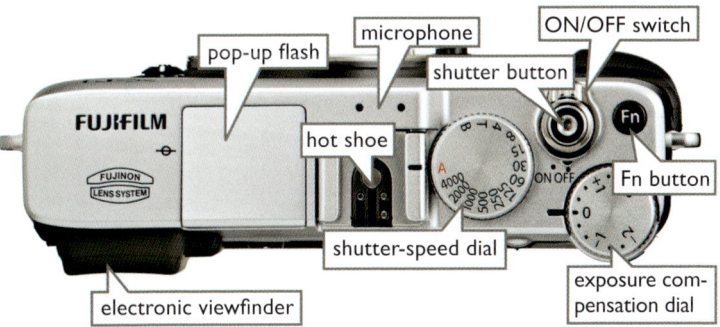

Figure 10: X-E1 top view: Electronic viewfinder, ON/OFF switch, shutter button with mechanical cable release thread, Fn button, exposure compensation dial, shutter-speed dial, hot shoe, pop-up flash, microphone

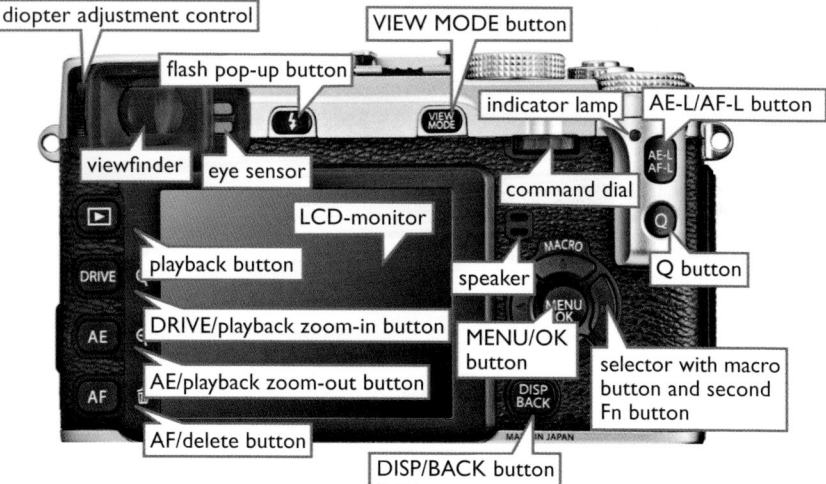

Figure 11: **Figure X-E1 back view:** Viewfinder with diopter adjustment control, eye sensor, flash pop-up button, LCD monitor, VIEW MODE button, indicator lamp, command dial, AE-L/AF-L button, Quick Menu (Q) button, playback button, selector with macro button and second Fn button (arrow down key), MENU/OK button, DISP/BACK button, AF/delete button, AE/playback zoom-out button, DRIVE/playback zoom-in button, speaker

The selector enables you to navigate through the camera's menus and to control various features, such as the selection of the autofocus frame. You can confirm your selections either by pressing the MENU/OK button or by pressing the shutter button halfway down.

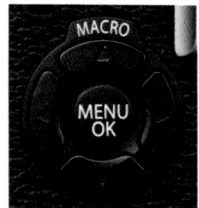

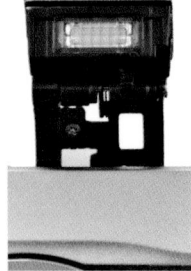

Press the **flash pop-up button** to release the tiny built-in flash. Once you do not need the flash, gently push it back into the camera body with your finger until it locks in place.

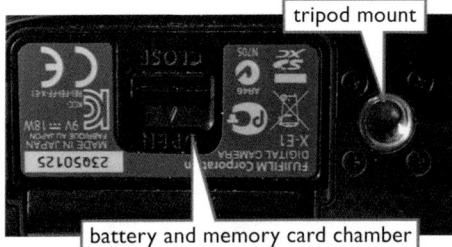

Figure 12: **X-E1 bottom view:**
Tripod mount, battery and memory
card chamber

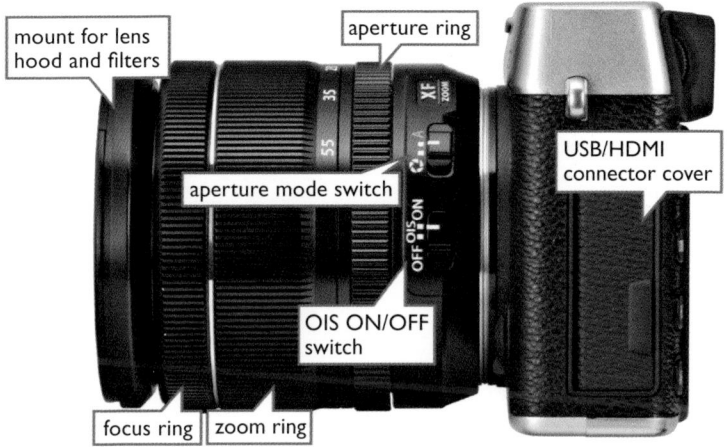

Figure 13: **X-E1 left side view (with 18–55mm kit zoom lens):**
USB/HDMI connector cover, OIS (optical image stabilization)
ON/OFF switch, aperture mode switch, aperture ring, zoom ring,
focus ring, mount for lens hood and filters

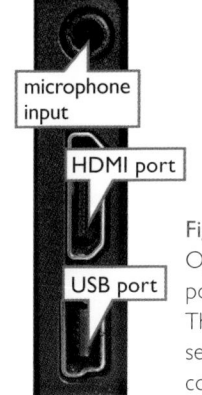

Figure 14: **X-E1 left side view:**
Open connector cover revealing HDMI
port, USB port, and microphone input.
The USB and microphone ports also
serve as electronic remote shutter release
control ports.

COLOR CODES FOR THE LED INDICATOR LAMP

The indicator lamp next to the VIEW MODE button on the X-Pro 1 and near the AE-L/AF-L button on the X-E1 conveys the following information:

 Solid Green: The autofocus has identified a target and has it in focus.

 Blinking Green: Warning—the image might be blurry, out of focus, or poorly exposed. You can, however, still snap the exposure.

 Blinking Green and Orange: The camera is saving images, but you can continue to shoot.

 Solid Orange: The camera is saving images, and you are momentarily not able to take additional shots.

 Blinking Orange (X-E1 only): The built-in flash is charging and will not fire when the picture is taken.

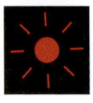 Blinking Red: There is a lens or memory error.

CAMERA MENUS

By pressing the MENU/OK button, you can view the camera's menus on the monitor or in the viewfinder. The X-Pro1 and X-E1 have three types of menus:

- **SHOOTING MENU:**
  The shooting menu—characterized by the color red—contains functions that directly affect how you will capture images. These include ISO settings, dynamic range options, various image settings (white balance, color, sharpness, contrast, etc.), AF mode, button assignments, and several photographic assistance features (grid lines, AF-assist lamp, AF frame corrected for parallax, etc.).

- **SET-UP MENU:**
  The blue set-up menu is where you will define the general configuration of your camera. For example, you can clean the sensor, format your memory card, and adjust various settings, including selecting your preferred language and setting the date and time.

- **PLAYBACK MENU:**
  The green playback menu is the shortest of the three. Its purpose is to allow you to manage your saved exposures. Since most photographers prefer to take care of that on a computer, this menu may be of limited use to you.

Press the MENU/OK button to access the camera menus. All three menus will never be displayed at the same time. The shooting menu and the set-up menu are accessible while in *shooting mode*. In *playback mode* (after you've pressed the playback button on the back of the camera), you will be able to access both the playback and the set-up menus. To switch back to *shooting mode* during *playback*, simply press the shutter button halfway.

The selector keys allow you to navigate through the various menu options by moving up, down, left, and right. In addition, the numbered tabs along the left side of the menu make it easy to jump quickly from one page of a menu to another.

HIGHLIGHTED VS. SELECTED

When I refer to a *highlighted* menu option in this book, I am describing the process of navigating to a particular entry, but not actually selecting it or activating the particular setting or feature. A menu option that has already been *selected* is indicated with a bar next to the active feature.

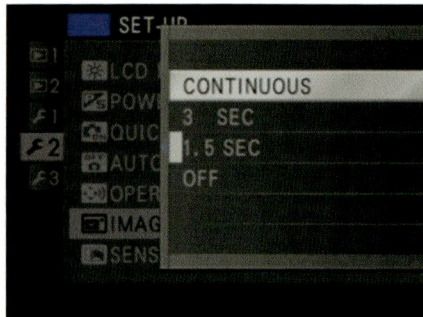

Figure 15: **Highlighted vs. selected:** In this illustration, the menu option CONTINUOUS is highlighted. The setting that is actually selected and active, however, is 1.5 SEC. You can use the MENU/OK button or the left selector key to activate a highlighted entry.

THE QUICK MENU (Q BUTTON)

Your camera has a fourth menu—the Quick Menu.

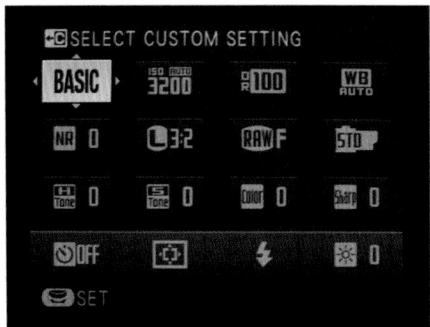

Figure 16: In shooting mode, you can open the Quick Menu by pressing the Q button. This menu allows you direct access to 16 of the most commonly used camera features: select custom settings (shooting profiles), ISO, dynamic range, white balance, noise reduction, image size, image quality, film simulation, highlight tone, shadow tone, color, sharpness, self-timer, AF mode, flash mode, and viewfinder/LCD brightness.

Use the selector keys to navigate to any of the 16 functions and then use the command dial to change the settings for the function of your choice. You can apply any changes you make in the Quick Menu with one of three buttons: you can press the Q button once again, press the MENU/OK button, or depress the shutter button halfway.

The X-Pro1 and X-E1 allow you to create up to seven sets of custom camera settings, or shooting profiles, which you can access with the Quick Menu. To create or alter a profile, hold down the Q button for a few seconds. This will bring you directly to the menu option EDIT/SAVE CUSTOM SETTING in the shooting menu, where you can either save your current camera settings as one of the seven profiles (SAVE CURRENT SETTINGS) or manually set and save values for ISO, dynamic range, film simulation, white balance, color, sharpness, high-light tone, shadow tone, and noise reduction for each profile.

While in the Quick Menu, you can use the command dial to cycle rapidly through the seven shooting profiles. As you do this, you will be able to see a live display of the settings of each profile. In other words, you not only see which of the seven profiles is currently selected, but you also see all of the settings that are associated with that profile. You can also use the predefined profiles as a starting point and then make adjustments to them in the Quick Menu. Any changes you make to the profile's basic settings will be indicated with a red dot.

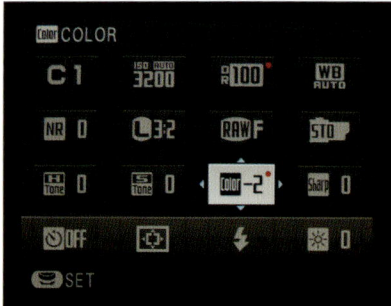

Figure 17: **Shooting profiles in the Quick Menu:** In this image, the *first shooting profile* is selected (C1), but the values for the *dynamic range* (DR100) and *color* (−2) have been manually adjusted. These changes are indicated with a red dot. They won't be saved with the shooting profile; they are active until you change them again or select a new shooting profile. To make permanent changes to a shooting profile, hold down the Q button for a few seconds or select EDIT/SAVE CUSTOM SETTING from the shooting menu.

Don't worry! I will discuss the various settings and features that I glossed over in the previous paragraph in greater detail later. For now, I want to emphasize that you can access the 16 most-used functions with the Q button and the Quick Menu instead of locating them in the traditional menus. All 16 features—and many more—can also be found on the conventional shooting and set-up menus.

UPDATING FIRMWARE

The X-Pro1 and X-E1 are novel cameras in many ways, and they also exhibit a few quirks. Users have many recommendations and wishes, and they would like to see the firmware (the control software) of the cameras and lenses further improved, the range of functions expanded, and the kinks debugged.

Fujifilm has heard a number of these requests, and they now offer a series of firmware updates that you can install on your own for the X-Pro1, the X-E1, and their lenses. You can determine the version of the firmware in your camera (and whichever lens you have attached to it at the time) by holding down the DISP/BACK button while turning the camera on. You can download firmware updates directly from Fujifilm at:

🌐 www.fujifilm.com/support/digital_cameras/software/#firmware

If you don't see the new firmware listed on the global Fujifilm firmware update site, there's a good chance your browser or Internet provider has cached an older version of that web page. In this case, just clear your browser cache or force your browser to reload and refresh the page by, for example, holding the Alt or Option key while clicking on Reload.

IMPORTANT

When downloading new firmware updates to your computer, make sure you don't have older firmware updates for the X-Pro1, X-E1, or other Fujifilm cameras in your destination folder when saving. File naming conflicts may cause your computer to save the new file under a different name, which your camera won't recognize and won't be able to install. Firmware files are currently named FPUPDATE.DAT for the X-Pro1 and FWUP0001.DAT for the X-E1. Updates for lenses are named XFUP00xx.DAT, with xx being a number signifying a specific XF lens. For example, updates for the XF35mmF1.4 R always bear the filename XFUP0002.DAT. Do NOT ever change these filenames!

FOLLOW THESE STEPS WHEN UPDATING YOUR FIRMWARE:

- Locate the latest firmware for your camera or lens on the Fujifilm website and download it to your personal computer. Unzip the file if necessary and then double-check that your computer hasn't assigned a name to the downloaded file that is different from the filenames mentioned above.

- Make sure that you have a fully charged battery in your camera.

- Connect an SD memory card to your computer. The card must have been formatted in your camera (SET-UP > FORMAT). If your computer has an integrated card reader, use it; otherwise, you will need an external card reader.

- Copy the FPUPDATE.DAT (X-Pro1) or FWUP0001.DAT (X-E1) or XFUP00xx.DAT file (when you're updating a specific lens) to the top directory level of the SD card.

- Use your operating system to properly disconnect the SD card from your computer. Make sure your camera is turned off, and insert the card into the memory card slot of your camera.

- If you are updating a specific lens, make sure this lens is now mounted on the camera. However, if you are updating the camera body, make sure no lens is attached to the camera while doing so.

- Turn your camera on while holding down the DISP/BACK button.

- Follow the directions on the LCD monitor and do not interrupt the update process. Do not turn the camera off before you receive confirmation that the process is complete!

IMPORTANT

The updating process can take several minutes, so it is important that your battery be fully charged before you begin. If your camera shuts down during the update, you may need to have it serviced by a professional.

Lenses and camera bodies often must be updated together. If you attach an updated lens to a camera body that has not yet been updated, the camera will detect this and indicate that a firmware update for the camera is needed. Conversely, the camera will indicate that a lens firmware update is needed if you attach a lens that hasn't been updated to a camera body with a newer firmware version.

RESTORING THE FRAME COUNTER

Updating your camera's firmware could cause its internal frame counter to reset to zero. If you would like to restore it to its previous position (or any other value of your choice), follow these steps:

- Insert your SD card into your computer and rename a picture that is saved on the card with your desired image number. For example, name the file DSCF2725. JPG instead of DSCF0001.JPG.

- Return the SD card to your camera and take a new exposure. This image will automatically be saved with the subsequent number in its filename—DSCF2726.JPG in the example.

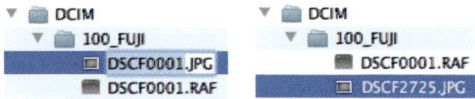

Figure 18: **What's in a name?** Well, whatever you want! By renaming an image file on your memory card in your computer, you can trick your camera into resuming its internal frame count where you want it to be.

This little trick obviously works for any situation in which you want to avoid unwanted or conflicting image numbers—for example, if you shoot with multiple cameras or you are using a camera that you normally don't use.

In these cases, reset the image counter by going to SET-UP > FRAME NO. > RENEW and then format the memory card by selecting SET-UP > FORMAT. Next, take a picture and change its filename (DSCF0001) on your computer to the number you prefer by using the steps described above. Then take a new exposure with this memory card.

While in the heat of the moment, don't forget to set the frame counter back to a continuous progression by selecting SET-UP > FRAME NO. > CONTINUOUS; otherwise, the frame counter will start numbering images from zero after you format your card the next time.

SD MEMORY CARDS

The X-Pro1 and X-E1 are compatible with SD, SDHC, and SDXC memory cards. You can safely ignore the claim that Fujifilm only guarantees the functional capabilities of SanDisk and (of course) Fujifilm brand memory cards— the cameras also work fine with the products of other manufacturers.

The X-Pro1 and X-E1 write RAW files in excess of 26 MB and JPEGs in excess of 3–5 MB, or in other words around 30 MB per RAW+JPEG exposure. When shooting continuously and producing six exposures per second, that adds up to 180 MB of data that can be captured within the span of a second!

The camera's buffer memory can fill up remarkably quickly—and it should be emptied (read: the data should be written to the memory card) just as quickly, so you can take additional exposures. I recommend at least a Class 10 memory card; if you use anything less, you're saving money in the wrong place.

Many of my colleagues and I go a step further. We only use the fastest SD cards available on the market today because the cameras in the X series can actually put this extra speed to use—our own and other tests have demonstrated this repeatedly. This advantage comes into play especially with the camera's automatic exposure bracketing, during which the camera is completely blocked (unnecessarily in my opinion) until all three bracketed shots are saved.

It all comes down to the *write speed* of the memory card. Watch out for deceptive marketing; sometimes the exceptionally fast speeds that are advertised really only describe the *read speed* of the cards.

Some of the fastest available SD cards read and write data with a nominal speed of 95 MB/s. I personally have had good experiences with models from *Panasonic* and *SanDisk*. Since these exceptionally fast cards aren't cheap, I generally use smaller capacity versions with 8 or 16 GB for my X-series cameras and make a habit of transferring my exposures to my computer regularly. When shooting with the maximum RAW+JPEG quality settings on your X-Pro1 and X-E1, a 16 GB card is good for about 500 exposures.

In addition to one or two of these super fast memory cards, I usually carry a few more affordable Class 10 cards that have a larger capacity (32 or 64 GB), which I use for data backup (bad things can happen) or in situations in which I have a greater need for capacity than I do for speed.

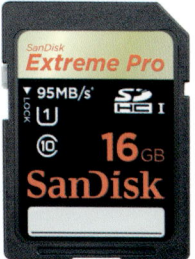

Figure 19: **The need for speed:** SD memory cards such as the *SanDisk Extreme Pro*, with a nominal read and write speed of 95 MB/s, are part of the basic equipment for many X-series camera users.

BATTERIES AND CHARGERS

The X-Pro1 and X-E1 use the same rechargeable lithium-ion battery, model NP-W126, which you can purchase separately at camera retailers—but at a steep price. Many photographers opt instead for (largely) identical and markedly less expensive alternatives from third-party manufacturers. You can find compatible models for a few dollars, but these bargain batteries don't always match the endurance of the original battery.

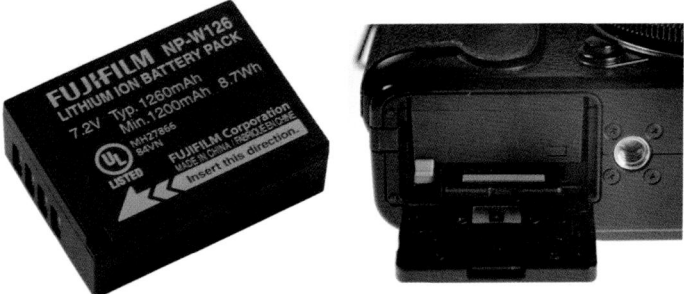

Figure 20: A Fujifilm original battery, model NP-W126, with a rated capacity of 1260 mAh. Compatible and less expensive models are available from other manufacturers in on- and offline markets. Not all models feature the practical gray arrow that indicates the correct orientation for inserting the battery (although you can solve the problem with a marker easily enough). Take care to match up the gray arrow with the gray battery latch and make sure to test whether the battery is in correctly by turning your camera on each time you replace it.

A fully charged battery is good for about 300 exposures. Consider this a ballpark estimate, though, because the actual charge-life of a battery depends on your personal settings and your habits as a photographer. For example, if you shoot with the optical viewfinder of an X-Pro1 (and switch off the LCD display on the back of the camera), the range of exposures per battery charge jumps up to 1,000.

Don't become a slave to your camera battery—it's better to get yourself a few spares. This will allow you to concentrate on your photography instead of worrying about how many exposures you can squeeze out of the remaining charge in your battery.

Unlike the X-E1, the X-Pro1 also features an energy conservation mode, which can be activated and deactivated by navigating to SET-UP > POWER SAVE MODE. Do yourself and your images a favor, however, and use this mode only in the direst of emergencies. It not only reduces the power consumption of your camera; it also limits the camera's capabilities. The autofocus works more slowly in power save mode, and the live histogram won't be available to you in the optical viewfinder. You're better off taking a second, third, or even a fourth battery with you instead of limiting your and your camera's ability to perform.

On the other hand, it can make sense to use the quick start mode of the X-E1 or X-Pro1, which you can toggle on and off at SET-UP > QUICK START MODE. The automatic turn-off feature is also advisable. With this option activated, the camera will automatically power down after a defined period of not being used. You can determine the length of time before the camera shuts off at SET-UP > AUTO POWER OFF.

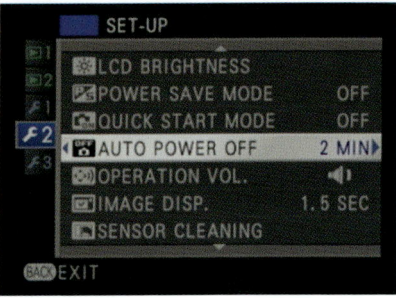

Figure 21: The power save mode, quick start mode, and auto power off features can all be found in the set-up menu.

I personally set the auto power off feature to two minutes, so my camera powers down after two minutes of not being used, which saves energy from being wasted. You can bring your sleeping camera back to life by pressing and holding the shutter button halfway down. As an alternative, you can use the ON/OFF button to turn your camera off and then back on.

The NP-W126 and its compatible brethren are not intelligent batteries, which is why you should take the camera's battery indicator with a grain of salt. As long as all three bars fill up the battery symbol, you don't have anything to worry about. When there are only two bars, the battery is already below half of its total charge, and when there's only one bar (the symbol will turn red at this point) it's time to swap out the battery as soon as possible.

TIP

While conserving energy is a popular concept, it only makes sense to do so with the X-Pro1 when it doesn't come at the expense of performance. For this reason, avoid using the camera's power save mode and opt instead to use the quick start mode and the automatic off feature.

The battery charger for your camera, model BC-W126, includes a conventional cable connection. When you're travelling, this means that in addition to the standard power cable, you can use other cables that fit into local power outlets. One useful travel option is the Apple World Travel Adaptor Kit. While this kit is actually designed for users with Apple notebooks and devices, you can also attach the small adaptor to the Fuji power supply unit and then plug your charger into a foreign power outlet.

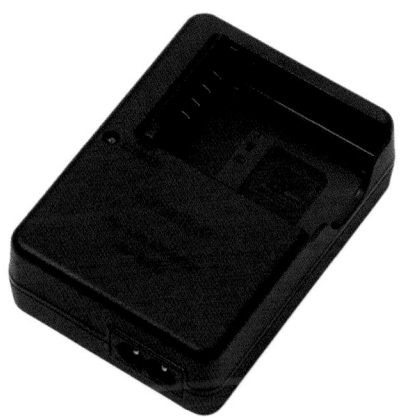

Figure 22: The original power charger, model BC-W126, features a standard power cable connection, which allows you to use the plug from the Apple World Travel Adaptor Kit, among many others—a feature that's especially convenient for foreign travel.

As is the case with batteries, it's wise to purchase a second charger. In addition to the original charger, there are various third-party offerings for this unit.

The BC-W126 includes a status lamp that glows green as long as the battery is charging. When the light goes out, it means that the battery is fully charged. A blinking status indicator is a bad sign—it indicates a battery or charger failure. When this occurs, unplug the charger from the wall and remove the battery. Insert another battery and check to see if the light continues to blink after you plug the charger in. If it does, your charger may be the source of the problem.

DIOPTER CORRECTION LENSES (X-PRO1 ONLY)

Retro cameras like the X-Pro1 are in some ways intended for an older crowd, which is why many retailers and prospective buyers find it all the more incomprehensible that the camera's viewfinder doesn't feature an integrated multilevel optical adjustment for photographers who wear glasses (luckily, the X-E1 features a standard diopter control dial next to its electronic viewfinder). Anyone who wears corrective glasses will need them while photographing, or will have to purchase a diopter correction lens with 19mm threads.

Fujifilm initially didn't offer a diopter lens as part of its line of accessories for the X-Pro1. Instead products by Cosina, a third-party manufacturer, were recommended. Aside from this reference, the owner's manual doesn't have anything to offer on the subject.

The X-Pro1's viewfinder features an internal setting of −1D. But what exactly does this information mean in practice?

The factory-provided diopter on the viewfinder is neutral—it is a simple piece of glass with no corrective optical effects. You could, in principle, remove the glass entirely, but that would allow dirt and dust to accumulate in your viewfinder more easily.

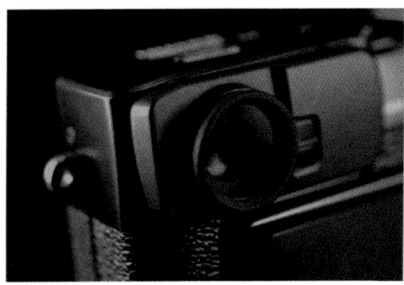

Figure 23: The diopter lens that comes with your X-Pro1 is an optically neutral piece of glass. Its rubber mount should protect eyeglasses from getting scratched if photographers press them up against it. Some X-Pro1 users lose the factory-installed, neutral diopter lens. To make sure this doesn't happen to you, check that the ring is screwed in tightly to the viewfinder on your camera so that it won't come undone by, for example, rubbing against your clothing when your camera is hanging around your neck.

Since camera viewfinders are designed for photographers with standard eyesight, we can assume that the neutral diopter lens (i.e., 0D) that comes with the X-Pro1 represents the normal case for people with normal vision. Experience shows that on this basis, farsighted people who wear reading glasses should use a diopter lens with the same correction value as the one they use for reading. For example, if you use a pair of reading glasses with a correction of +1D, you would be best off attaching a +1D diopter lens to your viewfinder.

You can attach Fujifilm's own corrective lenses to your X-Pro1, along with other offerings from Cosina and Zeiss, as well as various Nikon diopter lenses for its film F System. The threads are standardized; the only thing you'll need to do is make sure the lens has a 19mm thread diameter.

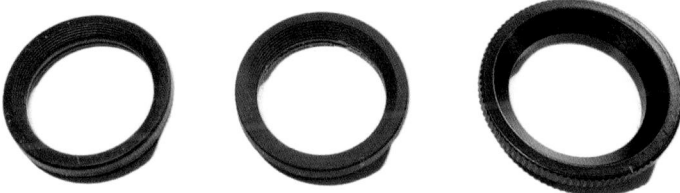

Figure 24: A selection of 19mm diopter lenses: Left, a neutral diopter provided by the factory; middle, a +2D diopter lens from Zeiss (also with a protective rubber ring); and right, a somewhat larger +1D diopter lens from Nikon without a rubber ring.

Diopter lenses from Fuji, Cosina, and Zeiss all have rubber rings around them, which is practical if you want or have to wear a pair of glasses while you use the lenses. Various Nikon diopter lenses are constructed entirely of metal. The upside of this, however, is that they feature a slightly larger inlet view, which some photographers will find beneficial.

People who wear gradient lenses or have complicated vision correction requirements should visit an optometrist with their cameras to discuss and try out different corrective lenses.

You can purchase diopter lenses from Fujifilm, Cosina, Zeiss, and Nikon at most specialized retailers.

IMPORTANT

The X-Pro1's optical and digital viewfinder displays are located at different virtual distances from the eyepiece. It is important that you use a corrective lens that gives you a sharp view of the images provided by both the digital and the optical viewfinder.

The naming standard for the corrective values of Nikon diopter lenses is slightly different from other manufacturers. With Nikon's lenses, you need to purchase a lens that has an advertised corrective value of 1D less than what you actually need. For instance, if you need an effective correction of +1D, then you should purchase a neutral Nikon diopter lens. To achieve a correction of +2D, get a Nikon diopter with a marketed value of +1D. This complication applies only to lenses manufactured by Nikon. With lenses from Fujifilm, Cosina, and Zeiss, the marketed and effective corrective values are the same.

THE X-TRANS SENSOR

The sensor inside the X-Pro1 and X-E1 is anything but ordinary. Though on paper it may not sound earth-shattering, behind its somewhat middling specs—APS-C format and 16 megapixels—is a level of quality that Fujifilm developed in order to bring the camera's image quality on par with the performance of larger full-frame sensors.

Figure 25: The heart of any
X-Pro1 or X-E1 is the
X-Trans sensor. Since dirt
and dust particles can
settle on the sensor over
time, it should be cleaned
occasionally.

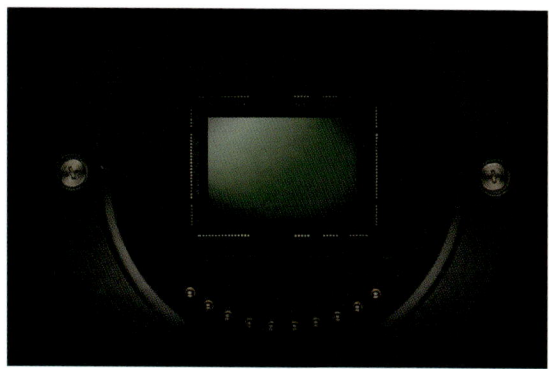

The sensor's most distinctive feature is the innovative structure of the color filter array over the sensor pixels. While conventional sensors employ a simple repeating 2x2 color matrix (the so-called Bayer array), the X-Pro1 and X-E1 feature a more complex 6x6 pattern of color pixels. The advantage of this color filter array is that it suppresses moiré effects, which have the potential to noticeably degrade the appearance of an image.

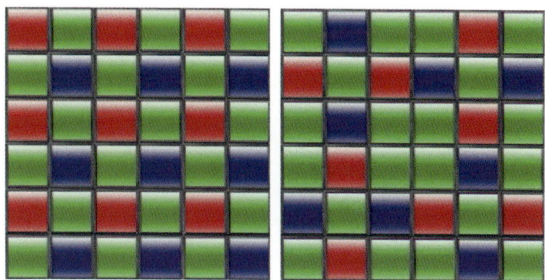

Figure 26: Left, Bayer sensor; right, X-Trans sensor.
While conventional Bayer sensors require a low-pass filter to suppress undesirable moiré effects, the sophisticated X-Trans color array needs no such filter. This increases the camera's resolution and allows it to produce excellent image quality for the sensor's size.

Camera manufacturers usually attempt to ward off moiré effects by installing a low-pass filter in front of the Bayer filter sensor. The disadvantage of this method is that the filter causes a noticeable loss of resolution. Fuji's alternative solution, the X-Trans sensor, combines both approaches: by eliminating the need for the low-pass filter, it achieves a remarkably high resolution, while the unusual color filter array effectively suppresses the appearance of moiré effects so that such problems occur only in rare instances.

One disadvantage of the unconventional sensor array is that not all external RAW converters are capable of interpreting the data. However, RAW support for X-Trans sensors has recently picked up and now includes major players such as Adobe (Lightroom, Adobe Camera Raw), Apple (Aperture, iPhoto), Phase One (Capture One Pro, Capture One Express), and ISL (Silkypix).

CLEANING THE SENSOR

Dust and dirt particles settling on the sensor is a fundamental problem for all digital cameras with interchangeable lenses. These particles can mar images by showing up as distracting spots in the light areas of an image (e.g., sky, clouds, walls).

Figure 27: **Color matrix:** ▶
The unusual color filter array of the X-Trans sensor initially made it difficult for RAW converter manufacturers to develop full support. This problem has since been resolved. This shot was taken with a preproduction X-E1 and a preproduction 18–55m kit zoom lens at f/2.8, and 1/250 second, at ISO 3200. The RAW file was processed in Adobe Lightroom 4.

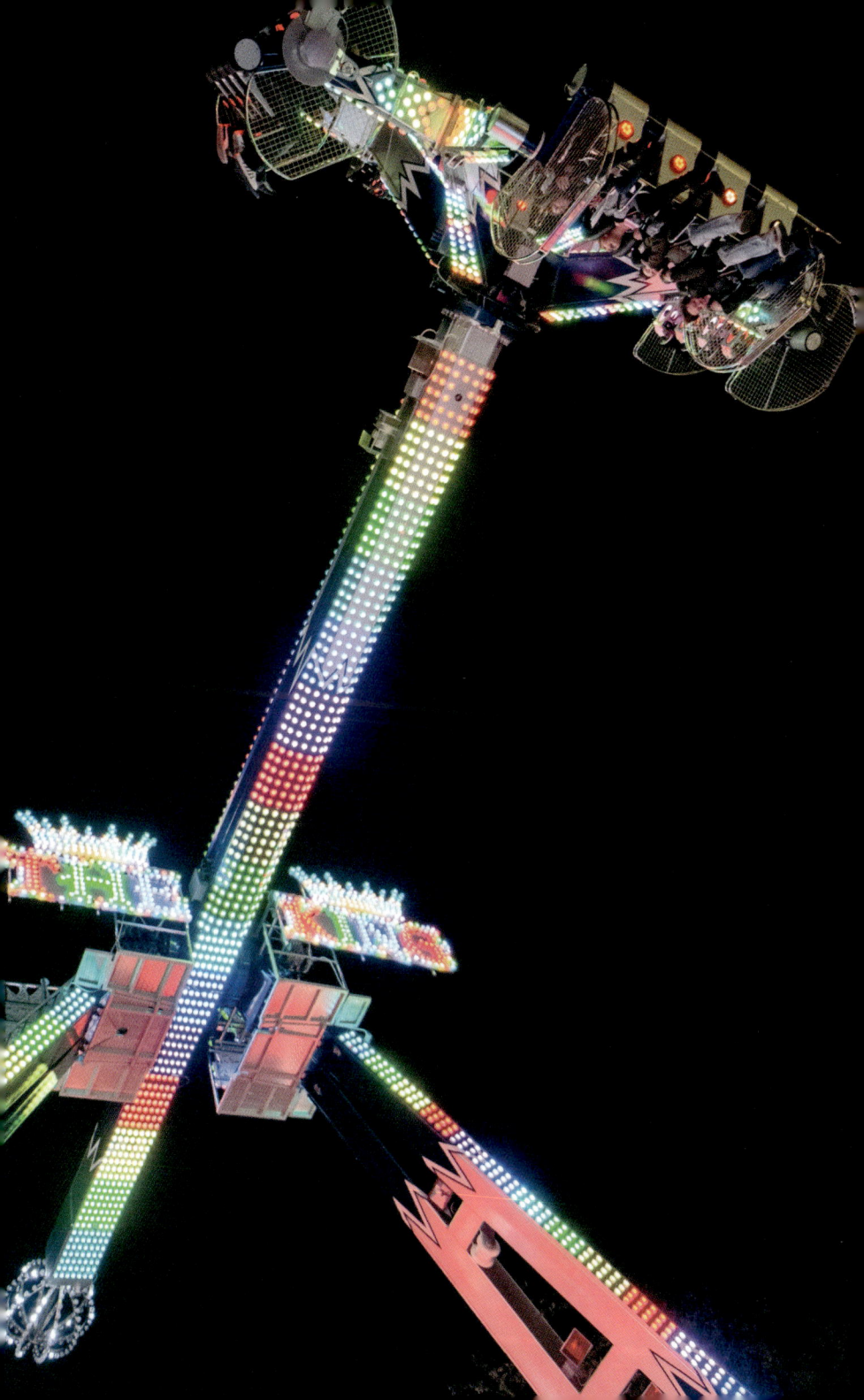

To minimize the effect of this problem, the X-Pro1 and X-E1 offer an integrated cleaning mechanism that runs when you turn your camera on or off. Navigate to SET-UP > SENSOR CLEANING to control this setting. You can choose to run the cleaning manually, by selecting OK, or you can choose to have the cleaning process run when you turn your camera on and/or off.

I have my camera set to clean the sensor both when I switch it on and when I turn it off—it's best to perform this function as often as possible. With the help of high-frequency vibrations, the dust particles shake loose from the sensor, which prevents them from becoming permanently attached. However, don't depend on the sensor cleaning function; if any dirt particles have set on the sensor, they're likely to remain stubbornly attached, even after you run the cleaning mechanism.

The most important strategy for maintaining a clean sensor is the active and passive avoidance of dust:

- Don't leave your camera open unnecessarily without a body cap or lens on.

- As much as possible, avoid changing your lens in dusty or dirty environments.

- When changing your lens, hold your camera pointed downward, not upward.

- When mounting a lens, make sure that the rear lens opening and optics are clean and free of dust to prevent dust from being transferred to the sensor inadvertently.

- Don't touch the sensor!

Even if you take diligent preventative measures, it's an unavoidable fact that the sensor of your camera will collect dirt or dust over time if you use it regularly. Don't deceive yourself—the question is not if, but when!

You can run the following test to check whether dust has already settled on your sensor: take an exposure of a blue or white sky, a bright wall, or a white piece of paper with a stopped-down lens (at the highest f-stop number possible). It's best to use the camera's automatic exposure bracketing feature (DRIVE button > AE BKT) and to manually set the lens to be out of focus. If you're shooting the sky, set the focus for a short-range shot; for a piece of paper, set the focus to infinity. If you then transfer your images to your computer and maximize the contrast, any flecks on your sensor should be readily visible.

Figure 28: This is how the sensor of my first preproduction X-Pro1 looked after three weeks of use in Asia. This exposure of a piece of white paper reveals (with the help of stark contrast settings on my PC) over a dozen flecks on the image sensor. That's something no amount of shaking and vibrating will remedy.

Using a cleaning bellows is one safe method of removing dust particles from the lens and sensor. Some photographers are particularly fond of the Super Rocket-air Blower from Giottos. This product features an air valve, which prevents dust from entering its bellows—the last

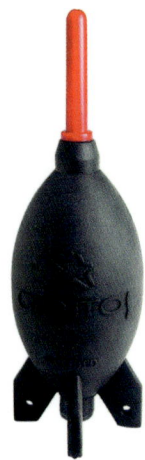

thing you want to do is blow extra dust into the camera's chamber. The goal is to loosen and remove the existing particles with a clean stream of air. For the best results with this tool, blow from below into the sensor chamber of your open camera.

Figure 29: **The Super Rocket-air Blower** from Giottos looks comical, but it effectively removes dust from cameras and lenses.

What about the flecks on the sensor that simply won't go away? I recommend Pentax's Sensor Cleaning Kit, which looks like a fruit snack on a stick. It is a specially coated cleaning head that collects dust from the sensor.

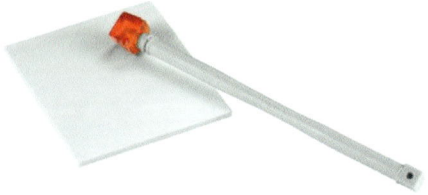

Figure 30: **Pentax's Image Sensor Cleaning Kit** includes a specially coated cleaning head that collects dust from the sensor. Every time you dab dust off of the sensor, you'll need to clean the head with a special piece of sticky paper that comes in the kit. To clean the entire area of the sensor, you'll need to blot off the cleaning head approximately six times.

Fuji depends (as do many other camera manufacturers) on products from Photographic Solutions for cleaning the sensor. Photographic Solutions is a U.S.-based company that makes a tool called a Sensor Swab, which is soaked in a cleaning solution called Eclipse and then wiped like a windshield wiper across the sensor—one side of the swab from left to right, and the other side from right to left. It's important that the swabs (which aren't cheap, to say the least) are used only one time and that each side of each swab is wiped across the sensor only once. Otherwise, the dirt and dust collected on the first pass can scratch the sensor on the way back.

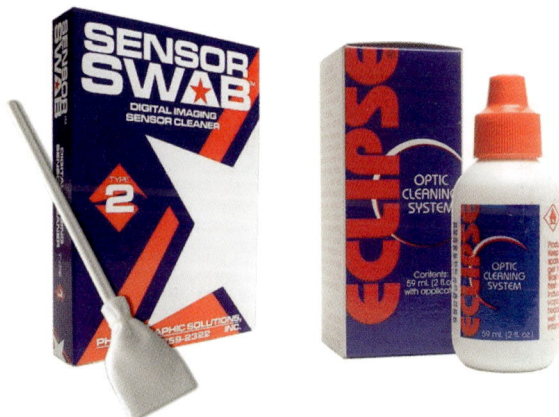

Figure 31: Fujifilm uses **wet-cleaning products** from Photographic Solutions. Sensor Swabs (for the X-Pro1 and X-E1 you'll need size 2) are moistened in Eclipse cleaning solution and wiped over the sensor once.

Specialist Torben Hondong, the service manager for Fujifilm in Germany, doesn't rely on just this standard solution (available for anyone to purchase in camera stores or online). More commonly, he replaces the original cloth on the swabs with special "cleaning wiper" cloths from Japan, which he finds work better because they smear less. In particularly difficult cases, he treats the affected area of the sensor with a drop of Zeiss Optical Cleaning Mixture. Hondong cautions, however, that this relatively aggressive solution is not recommended for home use.

That being said, it is usually possible to take care of the normal dirt and dust buildup on the camera sensor yourself, using products for DSLR cameras that are readily available in retail stores. The Canadian company Visible Dust offers a similar, more sophisticated line of products. They include swabs and cleaning solutions, at prices that aren't any higher than those of Photographic Solutions.

As a last resort for particularly stubborn sensor dirt that won't come out, you can always send your camera to be serviced.

1.2 THE LENSES

The ever-growing lineup of fully compatible X-mount lenses consists of several high-performance Fujinon and Zeiss fixed focal length lenses ("primes"), as well as several Fujinon zoom lenses. They all have electronic X-mount connections and autofocus (AF).

The camera's short flange back distance also makes it possible to connect countless lenses from third parties. Manufacturers such as Kipon, Metabones, and Novoflex offer adaptors that enable you to use lenses from dozens of other systems with your X-Pro1 or X-E1. In addition, Fujifilm offers its own adaptor for Leica M-mount lenses, which supports automatic adjustments made in-camera to correct distortions, vignetting, and color shifts (see section 2.10).

Information travels between the camera and X-mount lenses through electronic contacts. Even manual focusing (MF) is ultimately electronic. This "focus by wire" method is often criticized, since it operates with a small delay and does not provide the photographer with immediate feedback, unlike mechanical MF lenses. However, Fuji and Zeiss didn't actually design their AF lenses to have pure manual focusing capabilities. The intention is for the photographer to use the autofocus even in MF mode (by pressing the AF-L button) and to use the lens's focus ring for fine adjustments (with the help of a magnified image in the electronic viewfinder).

FUJINON XF18MMF2 R

The 18mm f/2.0 wide-angle lens is often considered a tool for reporting, partly because of its speed and compact design, which allow photographers to capture people and moments with relative ease, even in adverse circumstances.

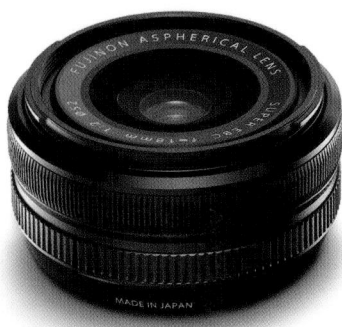

Figure 32: The Fujinon XF18mmF2 R wide-angle lens weighs in at just 3.5 ounces despite having a maximum aperture of f/2.0.

Because of a diminished sharpness around the edges and a need for digital distortion corrections by the camera or by your RAW conversion program, this lens is sometimes considered less than ideal for architecture and landscape photography.

This opinion must be qualified, though: figure 33 shows a landscape shot taken with the 18mm f/2.0 lens on March 21, 2012, in Bali. The RAW file was developed using a beta version of the free RAW converter RPP 64 with the V50 film simulation preset, and was polished off with Apple Aperture 3.2.

No automatic or manual lens corrections were undertaken during the RAW conversion or the finishing.

FUJINON XF35MMF1.4 R

The 35mm lens is the standard lens for the X-Pro1. If you want to buy only one lens (initially) for this camera, this would probably be it—and for good reason, because with a maximum aperture of f/1.4, it excels in low-light situations and offers excellent performance if you want to

Figure 33: Volcano in Bali: ▶
Exposure parameters: X-Pro1 preproduction camera, XF18mmF2 R preproduction lens, f/8.0, 1/400 second, ISO 200, automatic white balance.

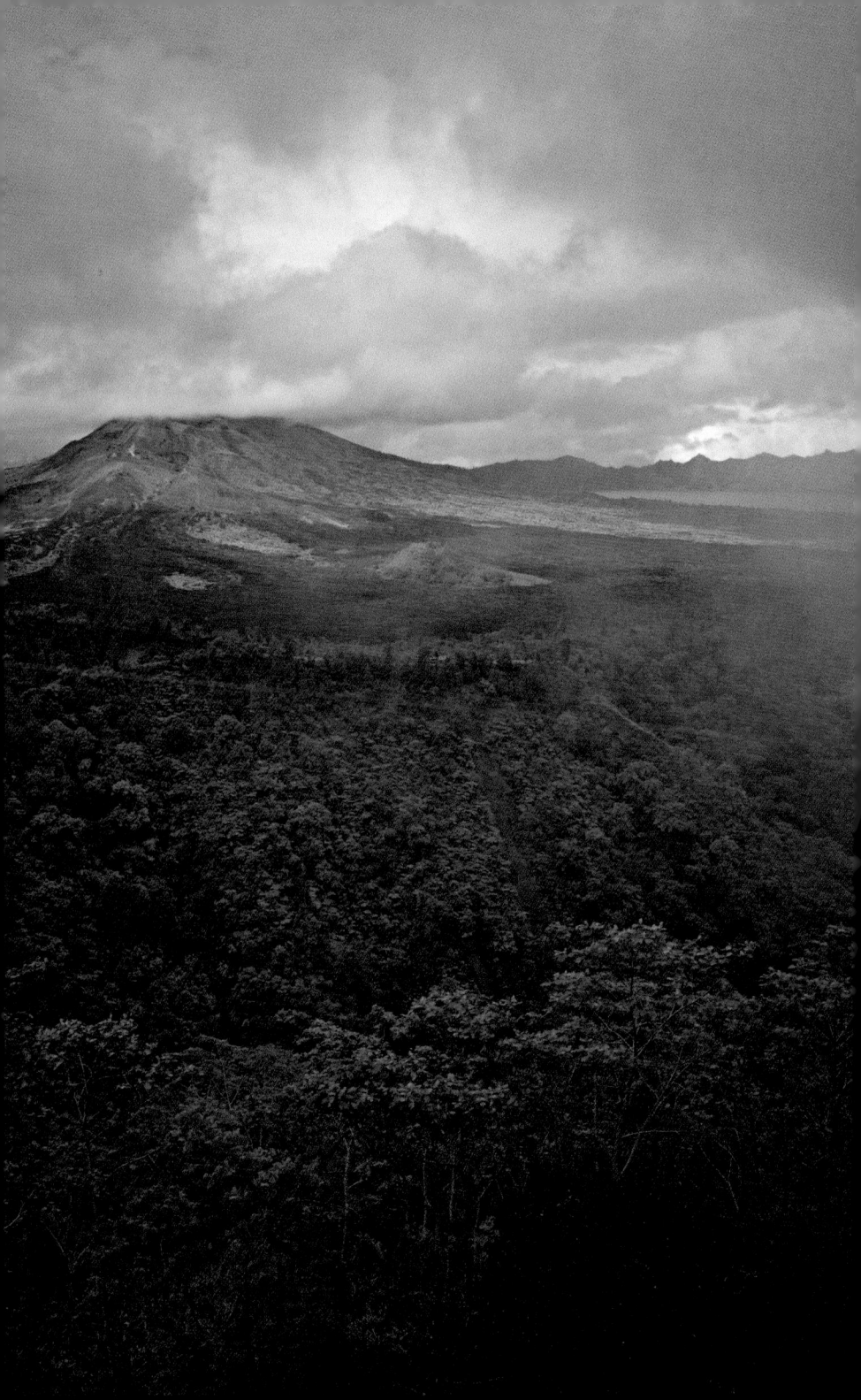

isolate a subject. It's also perfect in conjunction with the camera's optical viewfinder (OVF).

Even at maximum aperture this lens produces extraordinarily sharp and high-resolution images, and the value it brings for its price is exceptional.

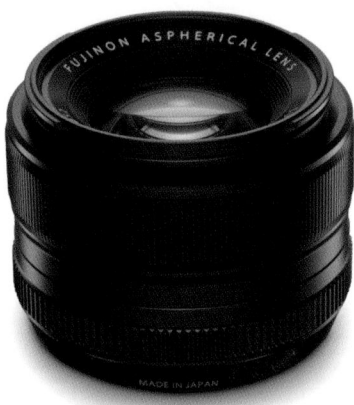

Figure 34: In terms of resolution and sharpness, the **Fujinon XF35mmF1.4 R** competes with more expensive lenses. Despite offering a large aperture, its 6.6 ounces make it a true lightweight.

Owing to its 35mm-equivalent focal length of 53mm, it functions as a great all-around lens but is sometimes considered not ideal for portrait photography.

I also have some reservations about this criticism. Figure 35 shows a portrait snapped on February 16, 2012, at the Warsaw Railway Museum with a preproduction 35mm lens. The RAW file was developed with Silkypix 4, and the image was finished with Apple Aperture 3.2.

The lighting in this exposure is a mixture of natural daylight (from the window on the right) and artificial light (from a studio floodlight in the back and on the left).

Figure 35: **Lady in Warsaw:** ▶
Exposure parameters: X-Pro1 preproduction camera, XF35mmF1.4 R preproduction lens, f/1.8, 1/1000 second, ISO 800, automatic white balance.

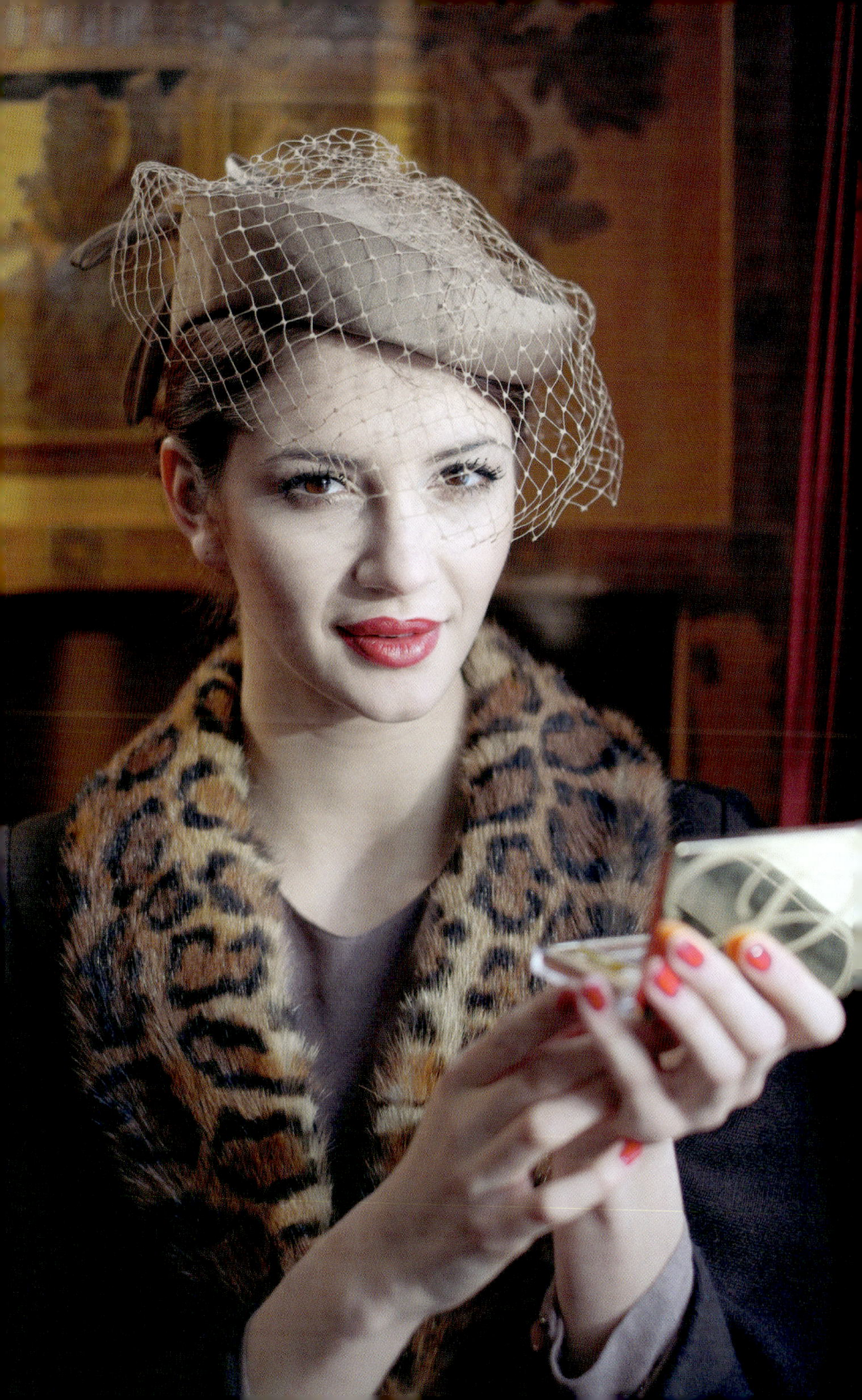

The camera's automatic DR setting settled on the extended dynamic range of DR400%. In other words, it underexposed the RAW file by two f-stops (see section 2.6).

FUJINON XF60MMF2.4 R MACRO

This modest telephoto lens, with its 35mm-equivalent focal length of 90mm, is actually better suited for portraiture, but Fuji sells it as a macro lens for closeup photography. Since it has a minimum focus distance of nearly 11 inches, however, one can't really speak of this as a bona fide macro lens.

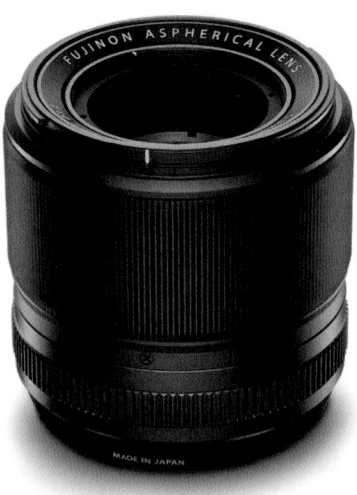

Figure 36: The **Fujinon XF60mmF2.4 R Macro** is the largest of the three basic lenses for the X-Pro1, but it still weighs only a little more than seven ounces. Since its inner tube extends and retracts when it's focusing, the lens has only a 39mm diameter filter thread. It comes complete with a sizeable lens hood.

Nevertheless, the 60mm lens is ideal for closeups. Even at its maximum aperture, it produces sharp and high-resolution images.

Figure 37: **Trusting butterfly:** ▶ Exposure parameters: X-Pro1 preproduction camera, XF60mmF2.4 R Macro preproduction lens, f/4.5, 1/125 second, ISO 800, automatic white balance.

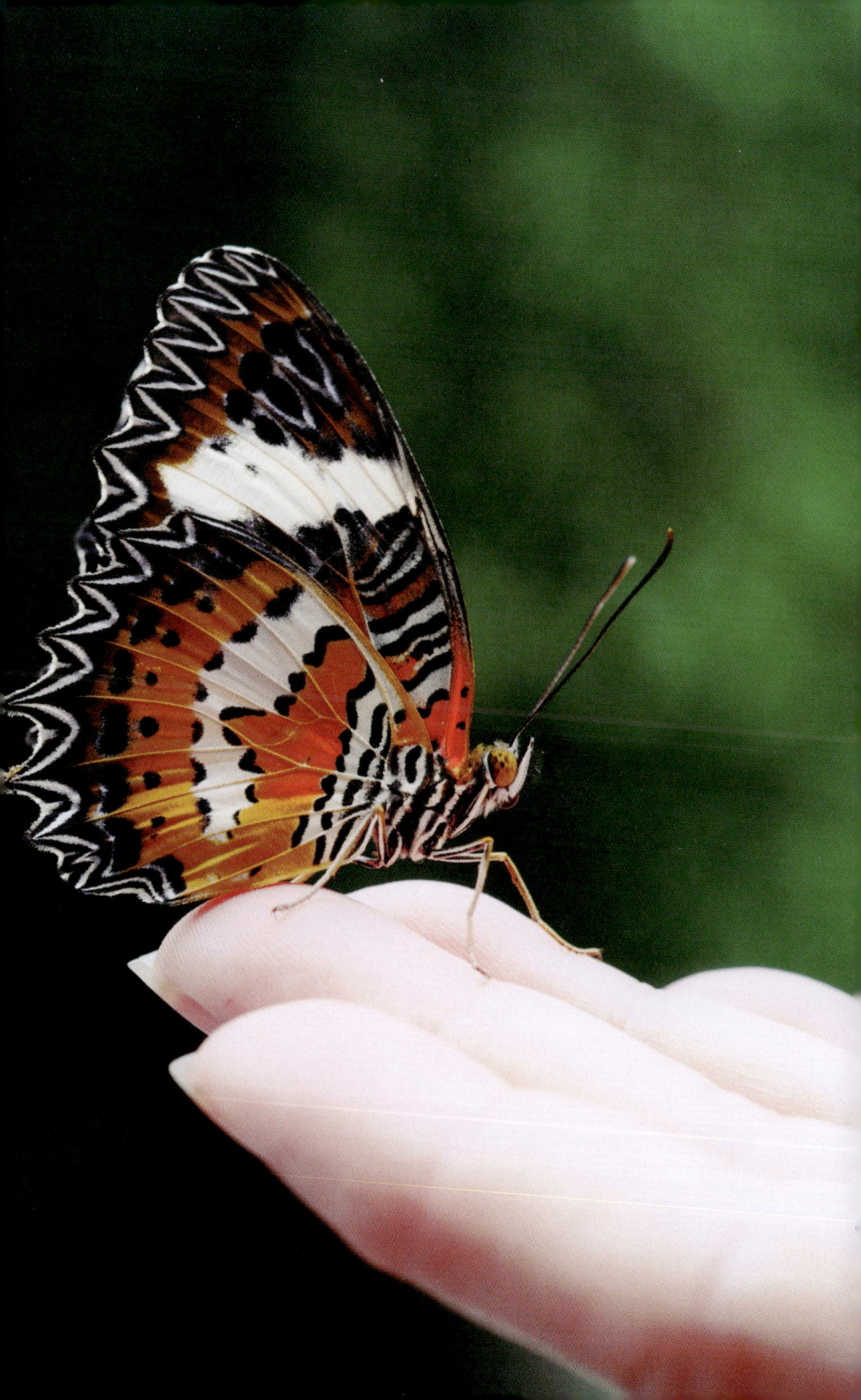

On the other hand, this lens is often criticized for its slow AF, which can be a hindrance for someone working quickly. As you may suspect, I also don't agree entirely with this judgment. I've successfully photographed nimble surfers on man-made waves as well as lively butterflies that alight on a blossom for no more than a second or two with this lens. In every instance, the lens acts quickly and precisely. You can learn more about using the AF in section 2.4.

Figure 37 shows a closeup from March 26, 2012, taken on the island of Sentosa in Singapore with the 60mm lens. The RAW file was developed with Silkypix 4 and finished with Aperture 3.2. This was a handheld snapshot using autofocus (with the smallest autofocus frame) on the head of a butterfly that landed for a moment on my companion's hand. The auto DR again opted to shoot at an extended dynamic range of DR400% (see section 2.6 for more on dynamic range).

TIP

To use filters with a 52mm diameter on the XF60mmF2.4 R Macro (which has a 39mm connection), you can purchase a relatively inexpensive 39-to-52mm step-up ring. To be able to attach this ring to the lens, you'll need to affix a spacer ring with a diameter of 39mm between the lens and the step-up ring. An easy solution for this is to find any old inexpensive 39mm filter from which you can remove the actual filter glass and just use the ring.

FUJINON XF14MMF2.8 R

A distinctive feature of the remarkably well-corrected XF14mmF2.8 R wide-angle prime lens is its focus ring with engraved distance and depth of field (DOF) markings—and hard stops at each end of the manual focus distance scale. In order to use the focus ring and see all markings, it has to be unlocked by sliding the focus ring backward. Once you do so, the lens and the camera will automatically enter MF mode. Slide the ring forward to relock it. This returns the lens and the camera back to the mode that's set on your camera's AF mode selector dial.

Figure 38: The XF14mmF2.8 R wide-angle lens is optically corrected and almost distortion-free, delivering results that are sharp from the center to the edges of an image.

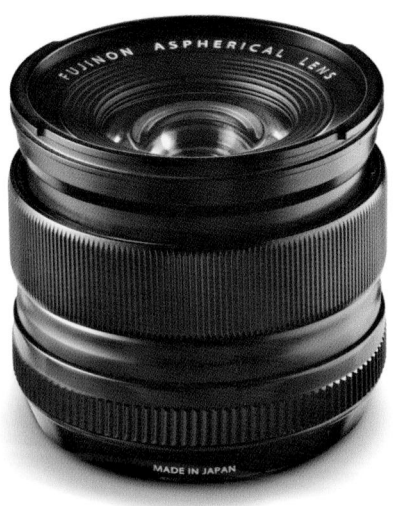

This high-end lens is special in other ways as well: the AF-L button will not focus the lens when the focus ring is set to MF mode. However, you can still use "one-press AF" by setting only the camera to MF and leaving the focus ring of the lens in its AF position. You also get two different scales indicating the depth of field and focus distance of a shot. Apart from the conventional digital distance/DOF scale in the camera's viewfinder or LCD, there's also the analog scale engraved on the lens.

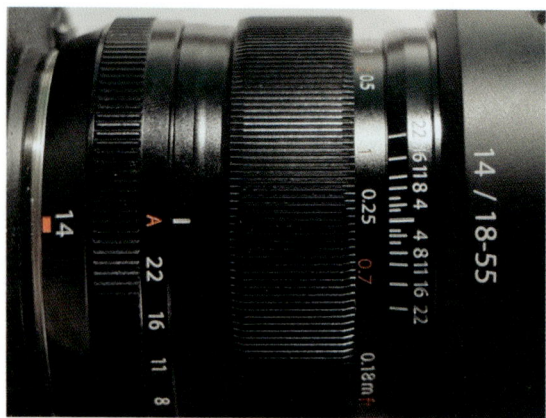

Figure 39: The XF14mmF2.8 R in MF mode, revealing
the analog distance and DOF readings.

However, the digital and analog depth of field scales do
not match. While the digital DOF scale is still based on
your camera's established, very conservative circle of
confusion (CoC) of about 0.005mm, the analog scale on
the lens barrel uses a less strict CoC of roughly 0.01mm.
The digital version of the scale is still available in autofocus modes, but it disappears once either the lens or the
camera is set to MF mode.

The 14mm lens is compatible with the optical viewfinder (OVF) of the X-Pro1, and the lens is also supported
by the camera's AF field parallax correction when used in
autofocus mode.

Figure 40: This impressive sample is ▶
courtesy of my dear colleague Mehrdad
Samak-Abedi from Berlin (*www.qimago.
de*). He shot it on May 30, 2013 with his
trusted X-Pro1, using a Hoya R72 infrared filter attached to an XF14mmF2.8
R lens. Exposure parameters: f/8, 2.1
seconds, ISO 400. The RAW file was
processed with Adobe Lightroom 4.4
and finished in Apple Aperture 3.4.

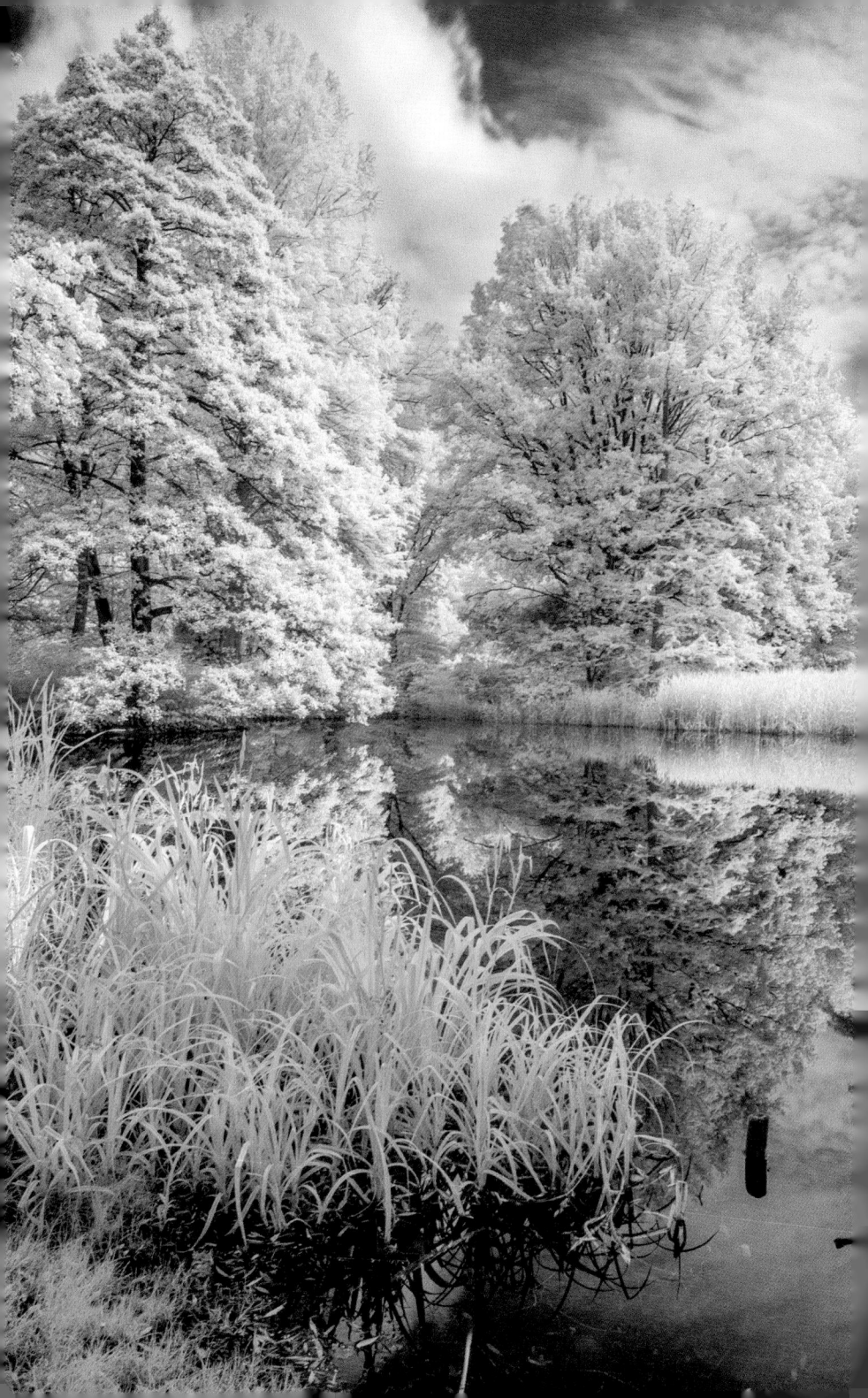

Using the XF14mmF2.8 R in manual focus mode may
be a mixed bag for some users: While most will appre-
ciate the traditional focus ring with its hard end stops
and engraved distance and DOF markings, offering two
different DOF displays based on two different circles of
confusion may confuse some less-experienced photographers. Of course, many users have asked Fuji for a
less conservative DOF scale (especially for zone focusing
purposes), so this was obviously a deliberate decision
to accommodate such wishes. You can learn more about
focusing techniques and depth of field in section 2.4.

FUJINON XF18–55MMF2.8–4 R LM OIS

One of the most pleasant surprises I experienced last fall
was shooting with Fujifilm's kit zoom lens for the then-
new X-E1, also known as the Fujinon XF18–55mmF2.8–4
R LM OIS. What a long and cryptic name! And what a
lens! It's certainly not your typical inexpensive, medio-
cre kit lens. Let's have a look at what each portion of the
cryptic name actually means.

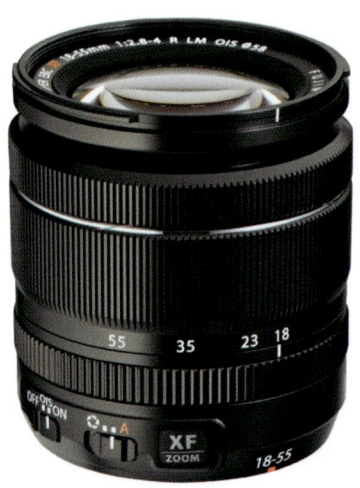

Figure 41: **The XF18–
55mmF2.8–4 R LM OIS**
kit zoom lens offers premium
quality in an affordable package.
It's the X-E1's standard kit lens.

XF means that the lens is part of Fuji's premium ("F" = Fine) lens lineup for X-mount cameras. (There's also a less expensive line of X-mount lenses named XC.) Aperture and focus are set through "fly-by-wire," but zooming with the zoom ring is fully mechanical.

18–55mm: This part of the name reveals the focal length range of the zoom. This lens offers any focal length between 18mm and 55mm, which corresponds to about 27–84mm in full-frame terms, or an angle of view between 79.1° at the 18mm end and 28.4° at the 55mm setting. Its 18–55mm range makes the lens fully compatible with the X-Pro1's optical viewfinder, which is optimized for lenses between 18mm and 60mm.

F2.8–4: These two numbers are the largest apertures (maximum aperture) the lens offers at the wide and long ends of its range. This means that the maximum opening does not stay the same throughout all available focal lengths. It varies between f/2.8 at 18mm and f/4.0 at 55mm. For example, at 23mm, the maximum aperture of this lens is f/3.2, and it's f/3.6 at 35mm.

Since the maximum aperture of this lens is variable, the aperture ring does not display any f-stop markers.

R stands for ring, telling us that the lens features a dedicated aperture ring.

LM describes the linear motor of the AF drive and suggests that the autofocus of this lens operates particularly fast and almost silently.

OIS means optical image stabilization. According to Fuji sources, the OIS checks camera shake 8,000 times per second. Fuji also claims that the OIS can compensate for up to four f-stops of camera shake. This means that if you can achieve a crisp, steady shot at 55mm without using the OIS at 1/80 second, the same shot should (or at least could) be almost as crisp at 1/5 second with the OIS turned on. In my experience, this is a pretty realistic claim, but your results may vary.

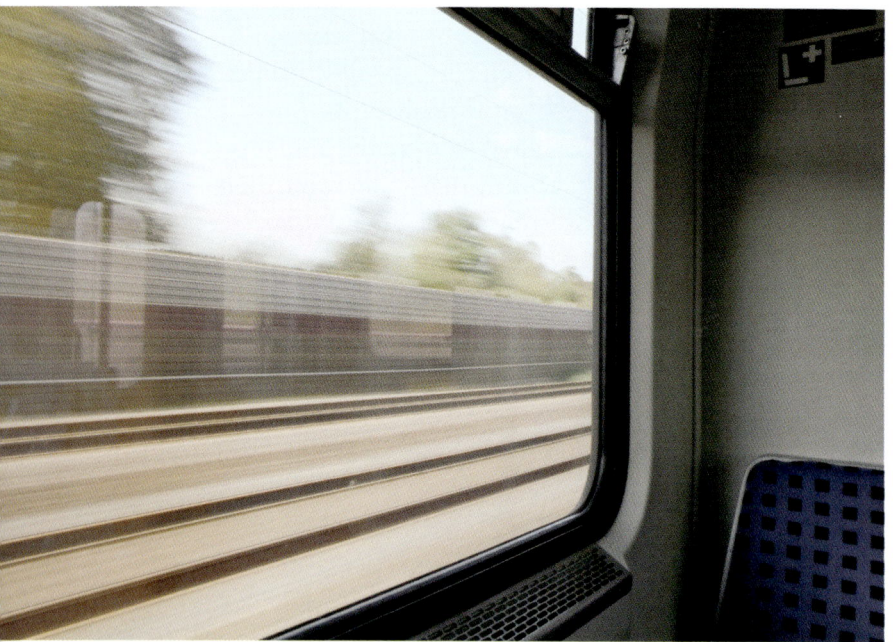

Figure 42: OIS at work: This was one of my first sample shots using an early prepro-duction sample of the XF18–55mmF2.8–4 R LM OIS. It was taken in a fast-moving commuter train at 1/10 second. The optical image stabilization kept the shot steady. That's how the train's interior appears crisp, while the exterior flies by in a blur.

Figure 43: Even renowned photographers like the British shooter ▶ Damien Lovegrove use X-mount cameras and the XF18–55mmF2.8–4 R LM OIS kit zoom lens for their professional work. I took this shot during one of Damien's inspirational workshops in Munich, where we were able to shoot in a state-of-the-art studio with the beautiful model Wlada Schüler. This high-key shot was lit with a single Profoto strobe and taken with an X-Pro1 at 55mm, set at f/4.5 and 1/125 sec-ond, at ISO 1600. The RAW file was developed in Apple Aperture 3.4.

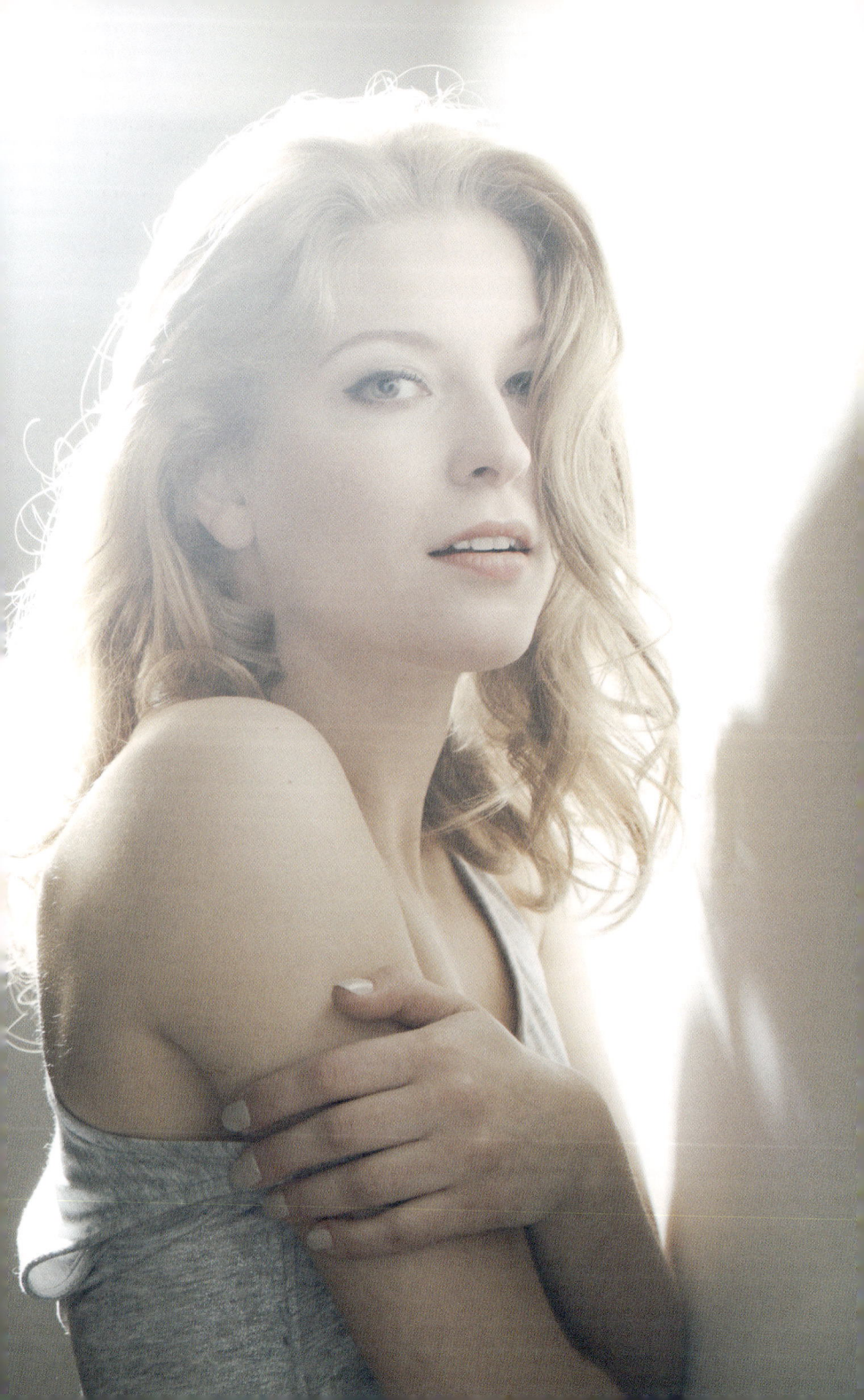

There are two different OIS modes, mode 1 (CONTINU-OUS) and mode 2 (SHOOTING ONLY), which you can select from in the shooting menu of your X-Pro1 or X-E1. Mode 1 steadies the lens at all times, while mode 2 only enables the OIS when you actually take the shot. However, the OIS motor is always operational, even when you turn the function off with the OIS ON/OFF switch on the lens barrel. This is not uncommon, by the way. Think of it as being like a hovercraft whose engine has to stay up and running to keep the vehicle afloat, even while it isn't going anywhere.

IMPORTANT

Remember to turn the OIS off on the lens when you operate the camera on a tripod, using long exposure times. Leaving it on could introduce unwanted camera shake to your shot. You should also disable the OIS for panning shots, and you don't need to use it with very fast shutter speeds that don't require image stabilization.

FUJINON XF55–200MMF3.5–4.8 R LM OIS

The XF55–200mmF3.5–4.8 R LM OIS is the kit zoom's big brother. It starts off where the other lens ends (at 55mm), and expands the X-mount system with telephoto capabilities.

Figure 44: Like its smaller kit zoom sibling, ▶ the XF55–200mmF3.5–4.8 R LM OIS telephoto zoom features an expedited autofocus with linear motors. This snapshot was taken with a prototype of the lens mounted on an X-E1. Exposure parameters: 172mm, f/4.8, 1/125 second, ISO 640. The RAW file was processed with Apple Aperture 3.4.

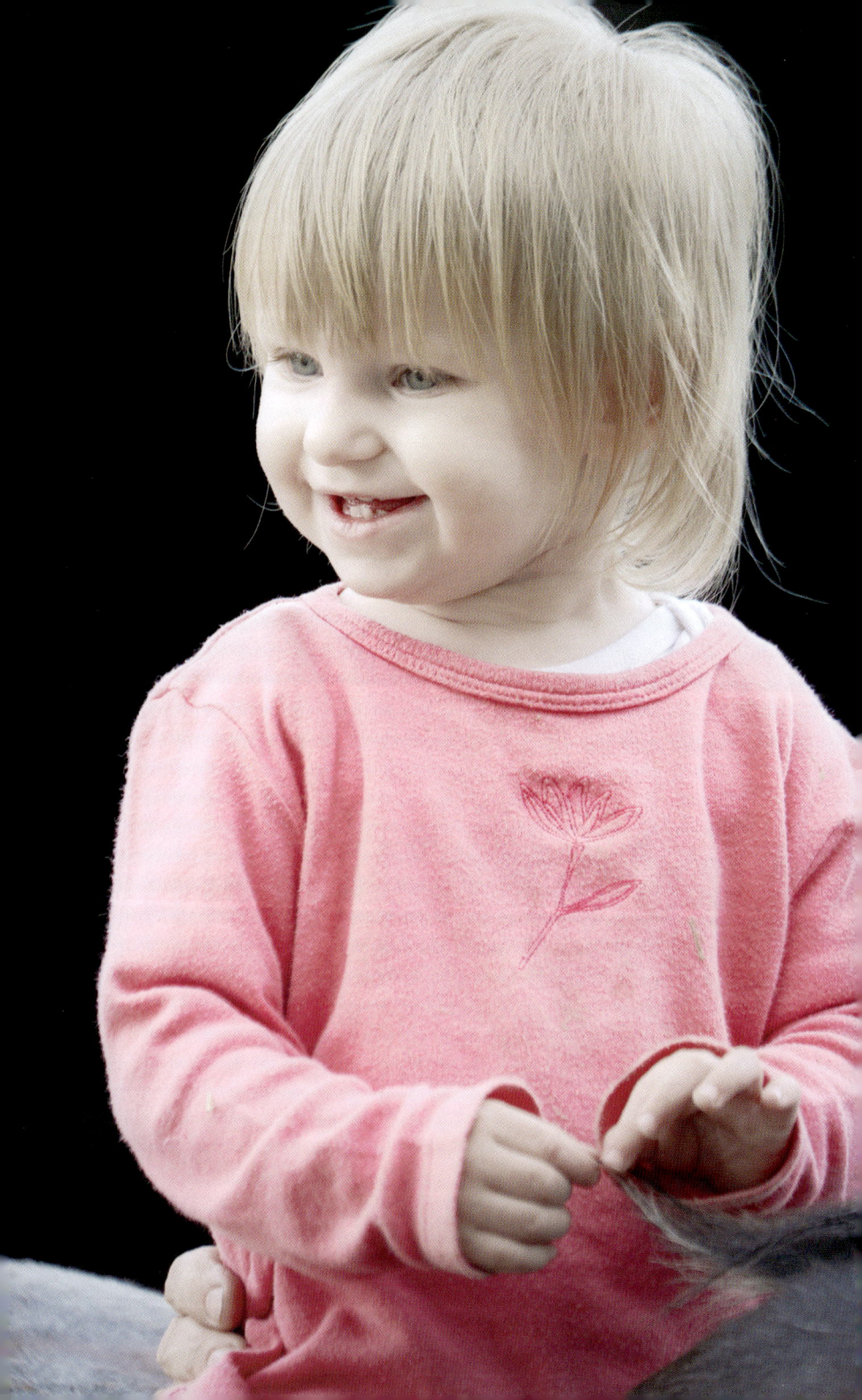

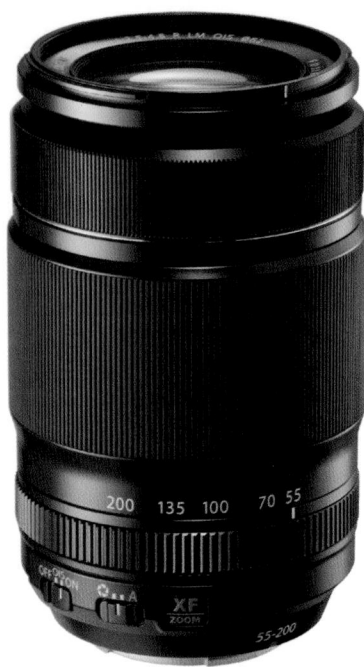

Figure 45: Like the XF18–55mmF2.8–4 R LM OIS, the **XF55–200mmF3.5–4.8 R LM OIS** telephoto zoom is quite affordable, yet delivers outstanding results.

Regarding operation and functionality, everything that has been discussed in the kit zoom section also applies to the telephoto zoom. Figure 44 shows a snapshot I took on April 14, 2013 with an early prototype of the XF55–200mmF3.5–4.8 R LM OIS lens. The resulting RAW file was processed with Aperture 3.4.

FUJINON XC16-50MMF3.5-5.6 OIS

The XC16-50mmF3.5-5.6 OIS is a lightweight, slower, and less expensive alternative to the XF18–55mmF2.8–4 R LM OIS kit zoom lens. The "C" in XC stands for "compact." The lens comes without an aperture ring (hence the missing "R" in its official name), and it has no external switch to turn the optical image stabilizer on or off.

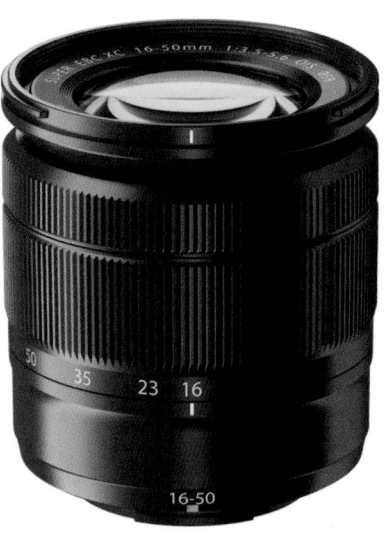

Figure 46: At only 195 grams (6.9 ounces), the **XC16-50mmF3.5-5.6 OIS** zoom is a light-weight and compact alternative to the standard XF18–55mmF2.8–4 R LM OIS kit zoom lens, which is not only larger and more expensive, but also more than 50% heavier.

This lens was specifically devised as a kit zoom lens for Fuji's new X-M1 and X-A1 mid-range and entry-level system cameras, but it can be used on any camera featuring an X-mount, including the X-Pro1 and X-E1.

While the exterior of the lens (including the mount) is made of plastic to reduce weight and costs, all optical elements are made of glass, resulting in above average optical performance. The wider field-of-view of the 16mm setting (which corresponds to 24mm in full-frame terms) may be particularly attractive to users shooting landscapes or working in cramped interiors.

With this lens, the aperture has to be set by turning the camera's command dial. Go to SHOOTING MENU > APERTURE SETTING (which is only available with lenses that do not feature an aperture ring) to configure this function. I recommend using the default setting of AUTO+MANUAL. This way, the command dial fully replaces the missing aperture dial, so you can either set the aperture manually or have the camera choose it automatically.

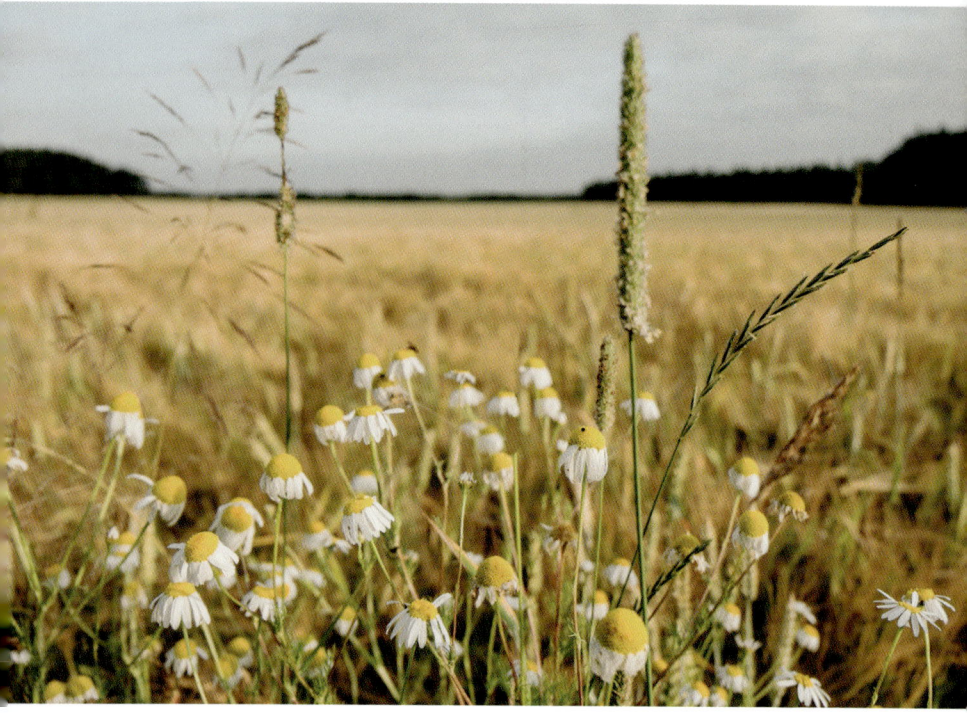

Figure 47: Even though the compact XC16-50mmF3.5-5.6 OIS zoom is slower than the heavier and more expensive XF18–55mmF2.8–4 R LM OIS lens, its rendering of out-of-focus areas (aka bokeh) is rather pleasing. This sample shot was taken with an X-E1 and processed in Adobe Lightroom 5 and Apple Aperture 3. Exposure parameters: 18mm, ISO 200, f/4, 1/600 second.

To configure the optical image stabilizer of this lens, go to SHOOTING MENU > IS MODE and select one of the two aforementioned OIS modes (CONTINUOUS or SHOOTING ONLY), or switch the OIS off altogether (OFF).

FUJINON XF27MMF2.8

The XF27mmF2.8 prime is a so-called "pancake" lens, alluding to its flat and lightweight build. Pancake lenses are popular with photographers who like to keep things small and simple, and who prefer an inconspicuous approach.

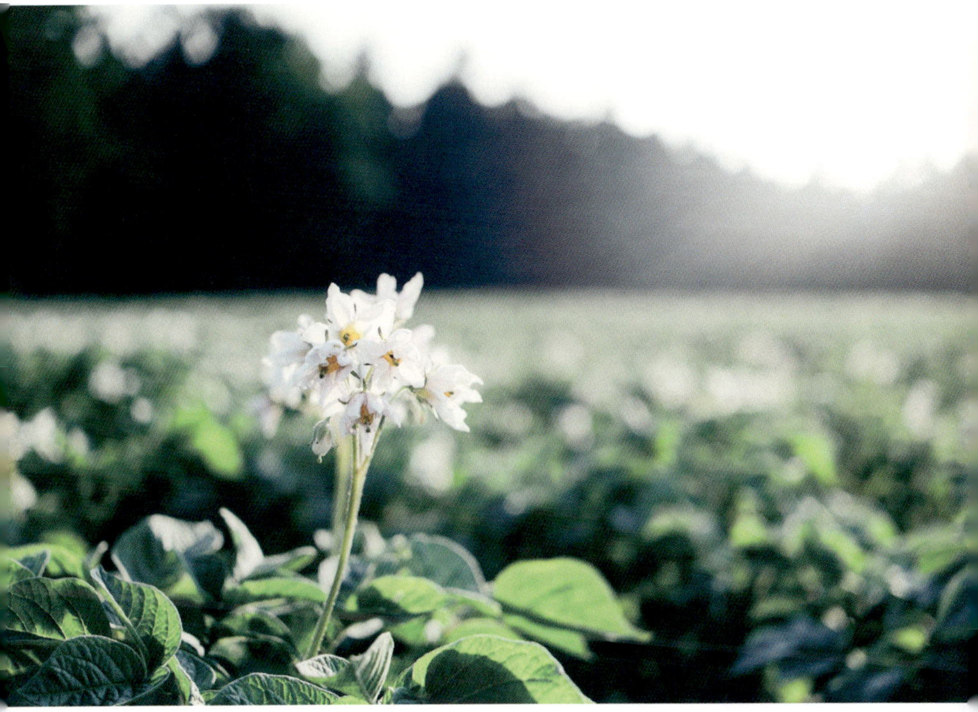

Figure 48: Fuji's XF27mmF2.8 pancake lens does not come with a lens hood or hood mount, but its improved wideband coating is rather effective. I shot this sample with a wide-open aperture against the morning sun and processed the RAW file in Lightroom 5 and Apple Aperture 3. Exposure parameters: X-E1, ISO 200, f/2.8, 1/1400 second.

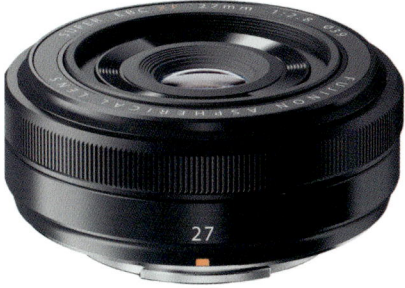

Figure 49: Size does matter: The **XF27mmF2.8** is a lightweight pancake prime for those who like to keep things small and simple without compromising optical quality.

The tiny XF27mmF2.8 lens weighs merely 78 grams and covers the field-of-view of a 41mm lens in full-frame terms. Despite its small size, the optical performance is top-notch. However, the very same size limitations resulted in the removal of an aperture ring, so once again, you'll have to use the camera's command dial to change the aperture.

You should avail yourself as much as possible of the lens hoods that come with the other Fujinon prime and zoom lenses. They not only shield your optics from unwanted stray light, but they also protect them from damage. The XF18–55mmF2.8–4 R LM OIS zoom and the XF14mmF2.8 R wide-angle prime lens conveniently share the same hood size, so you don't have to bring two lens hoods with you if you own both lenses.

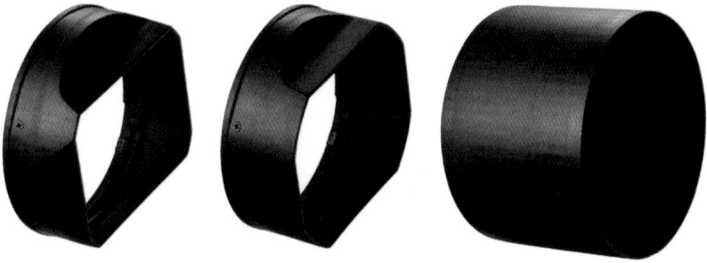

Figure 50: The included lens hoods belong on your lenses and not in a drawer.

You can also attach neutral filters to your lenses to protect them from damage. Fuji offers such filters for the different X-mount lens sizes. Such protective filters may be particularly useful in connection with the XF14mmF2.8 pancake lens, since this compact lens doesn't come with a lens hood or a lens hood mount.

Keep in mind, however, that every additional filter through which the camera captures an image has the potential of producing a negative effect on image quality. For this reason, you should only use a protective filter when you actually need it.

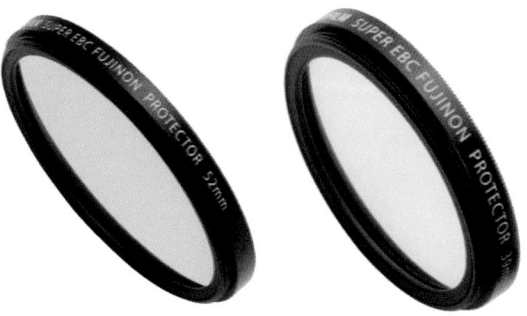

Figure 51: **Fujifilm protective filters** with 52mm and 39mm thread diameters. The 39mm small filter also lends itself well to functioning as a spacer ring for a 39-to-52mm step-up ring.

The cameras don't require any filters, such as the skylight or UV filters that may be familiar from the days of film photography.

ZEISS TOUIT X-MOUNT LENSES

In 2013, Zeiss started to offer a new line of APS-C autofocus lenses for mirrorless compact system cameras. While also available for X-mount, these so-called "Touit" lenses are mostly tailored to the Sony NEX camera series, filling open gaps in Sony's lens lineup.

The first two models are the Touit 1.8/32 standard lens and the Touit 2.8/12 wide-angle lens. The X-mount versions of these lenses feature aperture rings just like the Fuji's own Fujinon lenses. In fact, Fujinon itself is manufacturing these lenses under Zeiss contract, so full compatibility (regarding both hardware and firmware) should not be an issue now or in the future. This is a cooperative effort between Fujifilm and Zeiss.

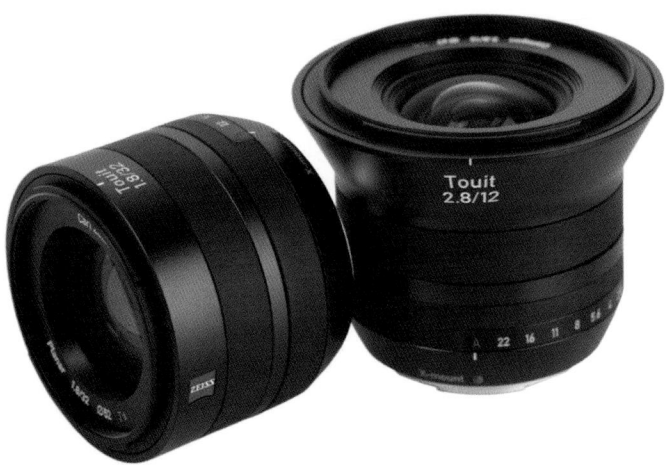

Figure 52: Zeiss Touit X-mount lenses are bulkier, heavier and more expensive than their Fujinon counterparts. On the other hand, the Zeiss brand traditionally bears the promise of distinctly superior image quality.

Many potential buyers ask themselves whether they should get a Touit 1.8/32 lens instead of Fuji's own XF35mmF1.4 R standard prime. After all, at 32mm vs. 35mm, the field-of-view of both lenses is very similar.

I am not able to tell you which is the overall better option. The Touit 1.8/32 offers superior sharpness at close range and wide-open aperture. On the other hand, the Zeiss lens is slower and its bokeh is harsher (which some people prefer, but most don't). The Touit 1.8/32 is also larger and more expensive than its Fujinon counterpart,

Figure 53: The Zeiss Touit 1.8/32 is an ▶ interesting alternative to Fuji's standard XF35mmF1.4 R prime lens. This sample portrait was taken almost wide open at f/2 and processed with Adobe Lightroom 5 and Apple Aperture. Exposure parameters: X-E1, ISO 200, f/2, 1/1400 second.

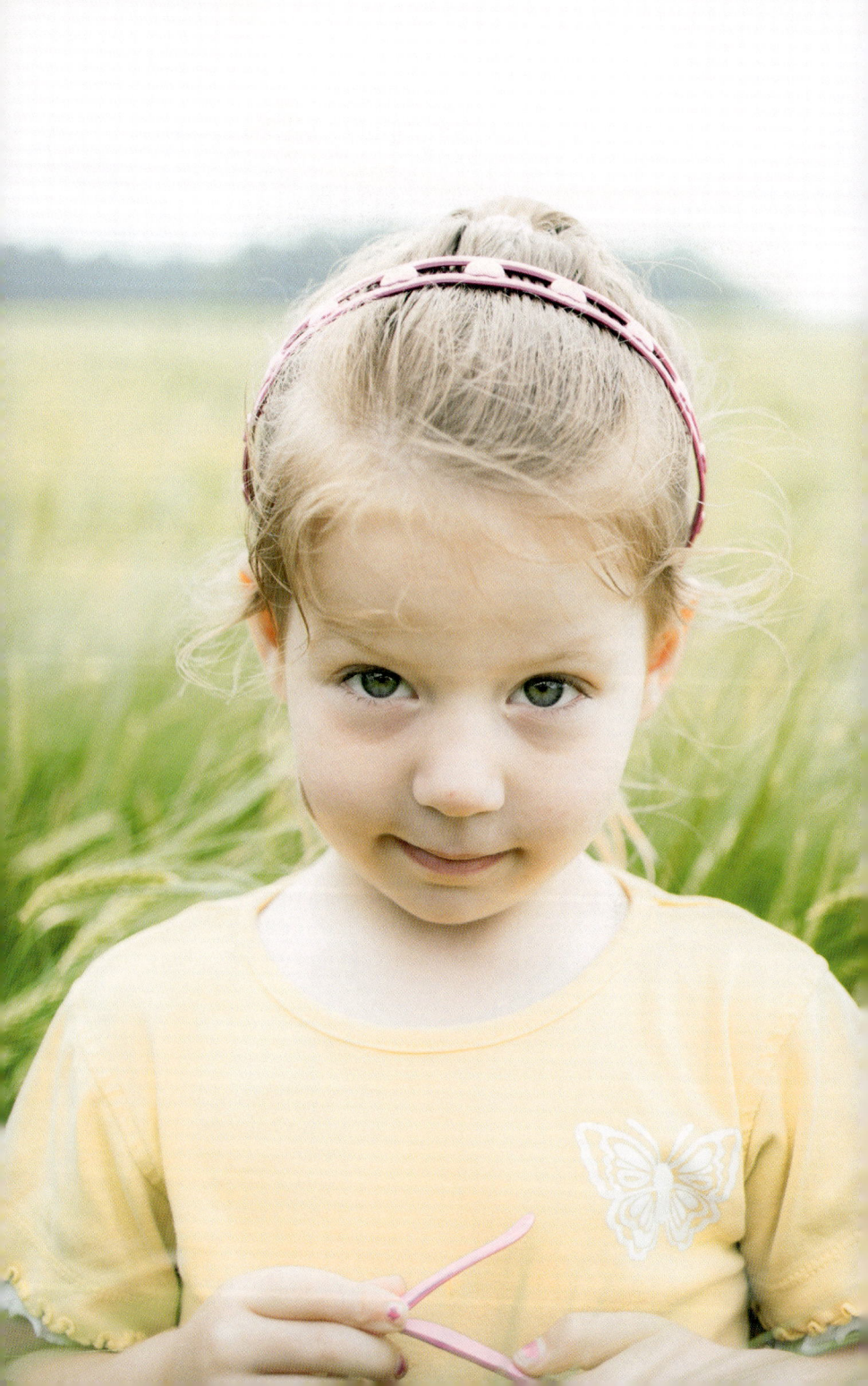

and attaching the rather bulky lens hood blocks a significant portion of the frame when using the optical viewfinder (OVF) of the X-Pro1.

In a similar fashion, wide-angle aficionados mull over getting either the Fujinon XF14mmF2.8 R lens or the Zeiss Touit 2.8/12. It's worth mentioning that the Touit's 12mm focal length is too wide for the optical viewfinder of the X-Pro1 (so you will have to use the electronic viewfinder or LCD), whereas the XF14mm lens enjoys at least partial OVF support. Unlike the XF14mm, the Touit 2.8/12 doesn't offer a custom manual focus mode with engraved focus and depth-of-field scales.

Regarding optical performance, it's hard to judge which lens is the better choice. Again, it will mostly come down to personal taste and brand preference.

One notable difference between the new Zeiss Touit lenses and their classic Fujinon counterparts is how they handle distortion correction: while both Touits employ digital correction at the RAW conversion stage, the XF35mm and XF14mm lenses are fully optically corrected.

For a more comprehensive comparison of the Zeiss Touit and Fujinon lens options, please read my practical X-Pert Corner review at

🌐 www.fujirumors.com/zeiss-touit-vs-fujinon-xf/

Figure 54: With a full-frame field-of- ▶ view equivalent of 18mm, the Zeiss Touit 2.8/12 is a true super wide-angle lens. The RAW file of this sample image (shot in the popular tourist town Rothenburg ob der Tauber) was processed in Capture One Pro 7 with disabled digital distortion correction. Exposure parameters: X-E1, ISO 200, f/8, 1/250 second.

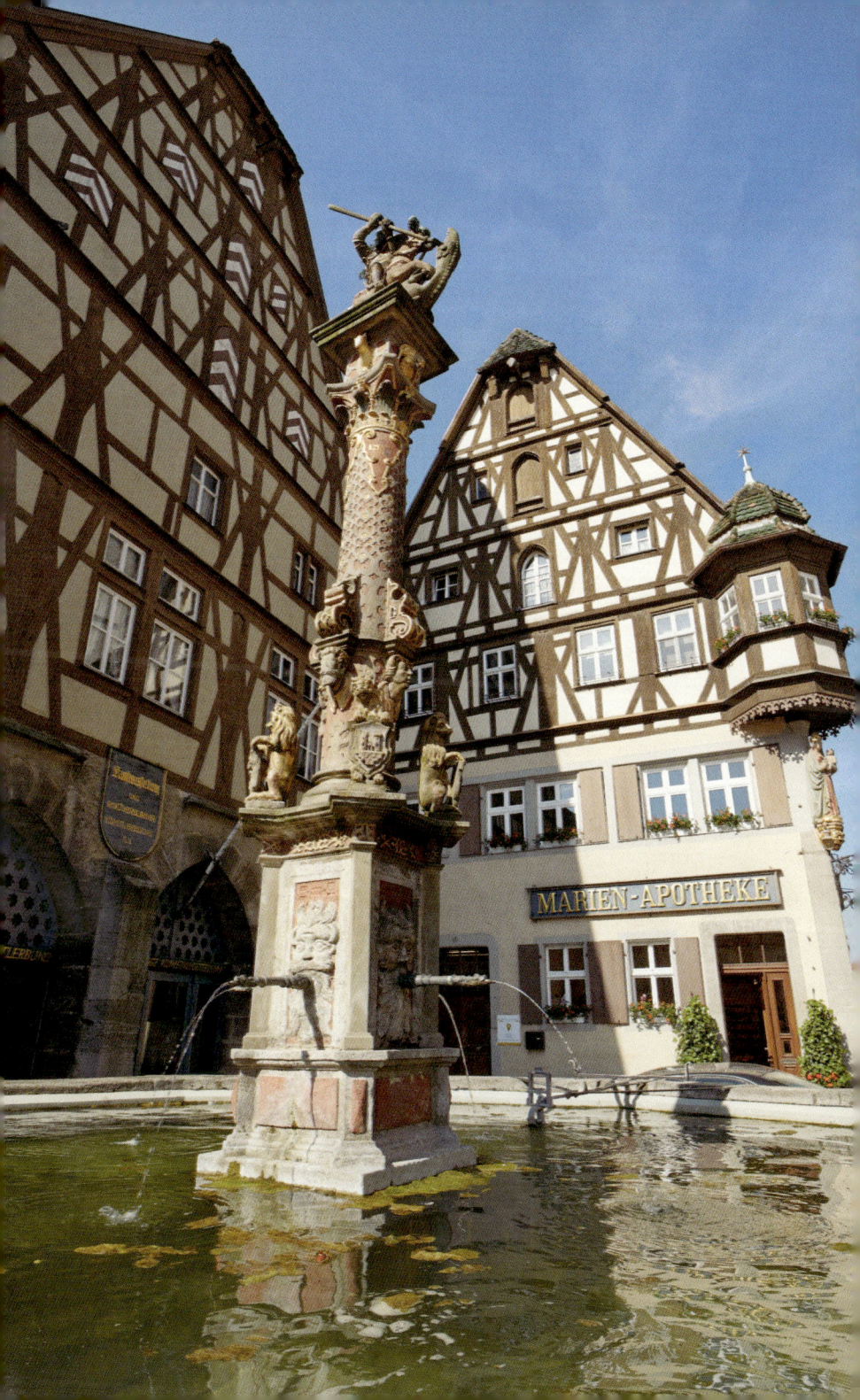

1.3 SYSTEM FLASH UNITS AND ACCESSORIES

In contrast to the X-E1 and all other current cameras available from Fujifilm, the X-Pro1 does not have an integrated flash. You can attach and use any flash unit available on the market to the hot shoe of both cameras or the X-Pro1's external flash connector, including studio flash units and remote triggers, but the automatic flash exposure metering and flash control features only work with TTL flash units from Fujifilm (TTL means that light is metered "through the lens").

Fuji offers three external units: the EF-42, EF-20, and EF-X20. The models EF-42 and EF-20 have been around for quite some time and were not specifically designed for use with the X-Pro1, X-E1, or other cameras in the X series. In fact, these two flash units weren't even developed by Fujifilm—they are essentially OEM versions of the models PZ-42X and RD2000 from the Japanese company Sunpak.

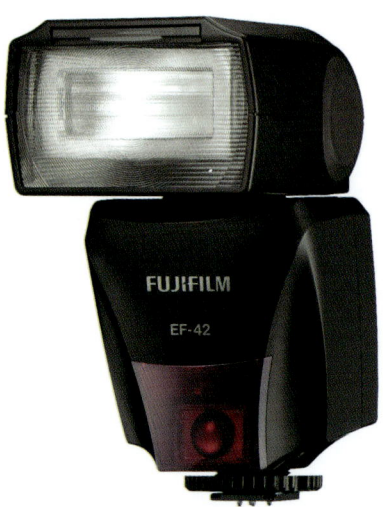

Figure 55: The **EF-42** is the most powerful and versatile flash in Fuji's offerings, but its ungainly dimensions and conventional shape don't fit the X-E1 or X-Pro1 particularly well.

The EF-42 design isn't ideal for the X-E1 and X-Pro1; it is better suited for bridge cameras like the X-S1 because of its size. Aside from its powerful performance (its output ranges from a guide number of 24 to 42 depending on focal length), its construction, which enables you to tilt and swivel the flash head, is a real advantage.

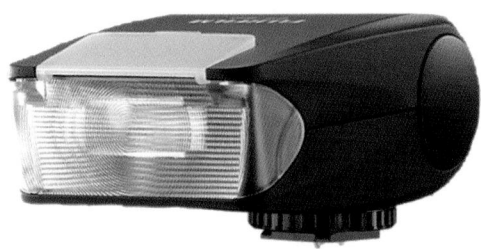

Figure 56: The relatively affordable **EF-20** is a well-liked and valued compromise of performance, size, and design. It is probably Fuji's most popular automatic flash.

The EF-20 is considerably handier than its bulky sibling, and its design fits much better with the X-Pro1 and X-E1. The flash head can be adjusted up and down but not from side to side. With a guide number of 20, this flash unit is well equipped to handle most everyday situations.

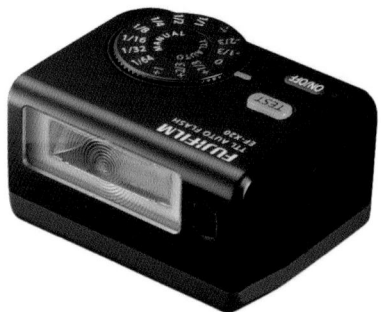

Figure 57: The compact **EF-X20** was specifically developed for the X-Pro1 (and successive X-series cameras) and is an ideal hot-shoe flash that can be mounted and removed in a matter of seconds thanks to its quick-release lock. Unfortunately, it is not cheap, and it can't be pivoted.

The EF-X20 was developed as a retro flash for the X-Pro1, but it also works very well with many other Fujifilm cameras, including the X-E1 and the remaining models of the X series. Its design brings to mind the TLA 200 flash for the Contax G2 film camera. The flash's head can neither be turned sideways nor pivoted up and down, which makes this compact shoe-mount flash around half as large as the EF-20 that features a comparable power output. The EF-X20 can also act as a wireless slave flash. When used in this manner, its output setting must be controlled manually—it is triggered optically by the camera's (or any other) flash. The slave flash also takes into account any camera preflash intended to reduce red-eye and ignores it.

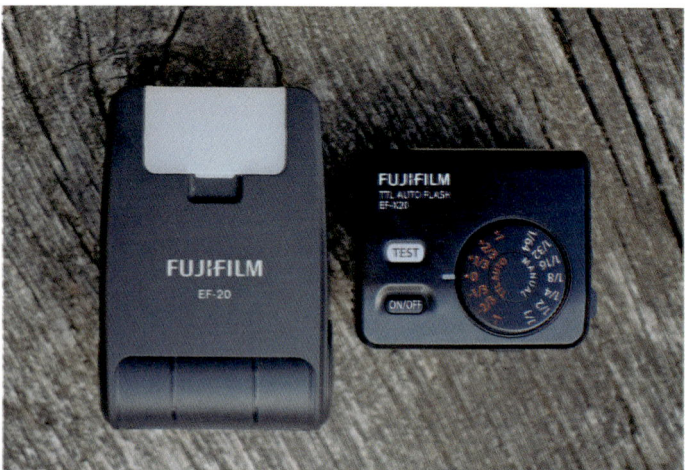

Figure 58: The EF-X20 and the EF-20 in a direct comparison of size.

All three TTL flash units offer built-in flash exposure compensation, and the EF-X20 and EF-42 also feature a manual mode.

REMOTE FLASH

All three of the Fujifilm flash units can be used remotely, but Fuji surprisingly doesn't offer an appropriate cable that would enable the automatic flash exposure metering and control to work with that setup. Canon offers calculated help here in the form of the relatively pricey OC-E3 flash cable, whose contacts are compatible with Fuji's system. Be careful: this doesn't mean that you can shoot in automatic mode using Canon flash units with the X-Pro1 or X-E1. Fuji and Canon use compatible hardware contacts but different software protocols.

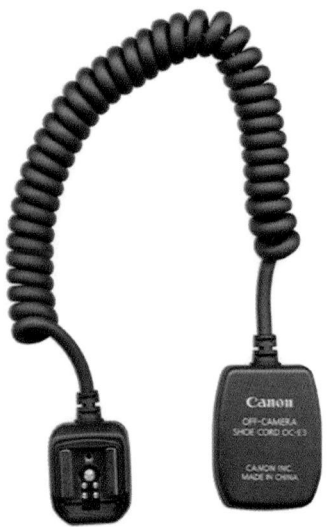

Figure 59: Canon's **OC-E3 TTL flash extension cord** with Fuji-compatible contacts.

If you don't want to spend the money on an original OC-E3 cable from Canon, you can use an inexpensive, compatible knockoff from China, which you should be able to find on the market. Exercise caution, however, and look for decent quality so you don't end up having problems with your contacts due to unregulated manufacturing tolerances.

I recommend using rechargeable Sanyo Eneloop NiMH batteries for your flash units. These are superior to conventional batteries because of their slow self-discharge, among other reasons.

ADDITIONAL HANDGRIP

The range of bags and cases, lens hoods, protective filters, thumb supports, shutter-release buttons, and various other toys for the X-Pro1 and X-E1 is extensive, but I would like to call your attention to the HG-XPro1 and HG-XE1 handgrips.

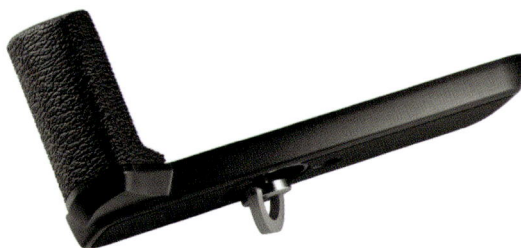

Figure 60: Many X-Pro1 and X-E1 users prefer to shoot with an optional handgrip.

Sure, they're not cheap, they make the camera somewhat larger, and they cover up the battery chamber and the memory card port, but these extra handgrips make the camera noticeably easier to handle for users with larger hands and those using heavier (adapted) lenses. They also shift the camera's tripod mount to be centered on the optical axis. Test one out at your retailer of choice!

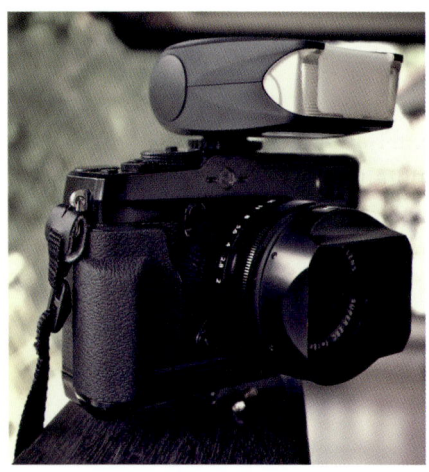

Figure 61: X-Pro1 with additional handgrip, EF-20 flash unit, and XF18mmF2 R lens.

1.4 REMOTE SHUTTER CONTROL

Releasing the shutter of your camera remotely can have several advantages. For one thing, not touching the camera reduces shake and vibrations, which is especially important at slow shutter speeds. Mounting the camera on a tripod is only half of the solution. Yes, you can use your camera's self-timer function for hands-free operation, but it's hard (if not impossible) to catch decisive moments with this method.

Other applications of remote shutter release devices include placing the camera at hard-to-reach locations and producing a series of well-timed shots for timelapse or HDR photography. Advanced timing solutions incorporate wireless operation (infrared, radio-controlled, Bluetooth, or WLAN), and they can be triggered by certain GPS coordinates or position changes (like taking a shot every 50 meters while moving in a car), by a person stepping in front of the camera (recognizing faces or movement), or by pretty exotic stuff like changes in the magnetic field.

Sadly, Fujifilm doesn't offer a common remote triggering interface for the X series; both the X-Pro1 and X-E1 offer classic threads for manual screw-in cable releases. The X-E1 also features an option to electronically release the shutter through the so-called RR-80 port (which hides in the Mini-USB port of this camera, using pins number 4 and 5). In addition, the X-E1 allows its microphone socket to moonlight as a remote trigger input that is compatible with a substantial range of camera makes and models, enabling a large number of remote triggering devices to be used with this camera.

MECHANICAL CABLE RELEASE

Cable releases can perform the same three basic functions as your camera's shutter button:

- Half-pressing the shutter to establish/lock focus and exposure

- Fully depressing the shutter to take the shot

- Keeping the shutter button depressed (and locked) for an extended period of time to take long exposures (bulb mode)

Cable releases come in several forms and usually don't cost much. There's no need to get a fancy model (unless you like fancy stuff); just make sure it operates smoothly.

RR-80 ELECTRONIC RELEASE (X-E1 ONLY)

Even though its interface is electronic, connecting an RR-80-based remote shutter release doesn't add any functionality beyond that of a mechanical cable release. There's no feature interaction between the camera and the remote. The remote isn't aware of any camera settings, and the camera isn't aware of what's set on the remote.

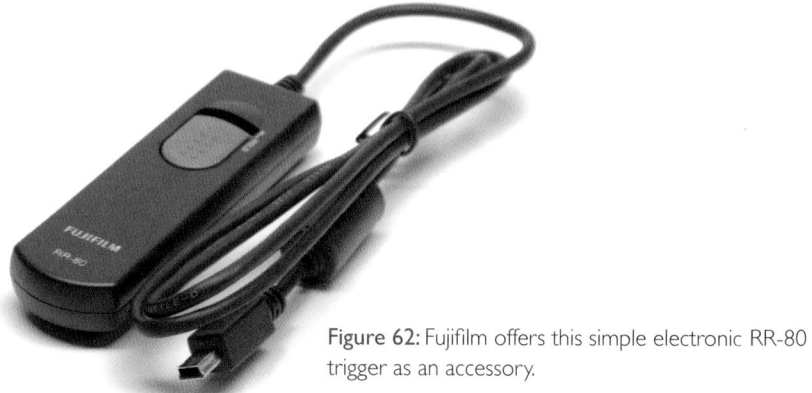

Figure 62: Fujifilm offers this simple electronic RR-80 trigger as an accessory.

There are also several RR-80-compatible "no-name" options available. Some of them offer wireless operation or sophisticated interval timers.

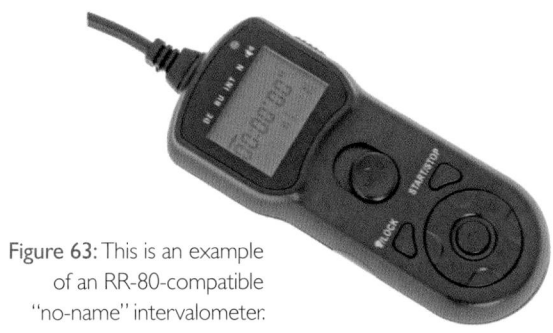

Figure 63: This is an example of an RR-80-compatible "no-name" intervalometer.

While an intervalometer is useful for time-lapse photography, a radio trigger will allow you to place the X-E1 at difficult-to-reach or dangerous locations, like on a car or on a pole.

MICROPHONE INPUT PORT TRIGGERING (X-E1 ONLY)

RR-80 is a rather Fujifilm-specific interface, but the internal microphone port trigger of the X-E1 is not. In fact, this port and its triggering protocol are compatible with a broad range of cameras, including the Canon EOS Digital Rebel, Canon EOS 1000D, Canon EOS 100D, Canon EOS 1100D, Canon EOS 300D, Canon EOS 350D, Canon EOS 400D, Canon EOS 450D, Canon EOS 500D, Canon EOS 550D, Canon EOS 600D, Canon EOS 60D, Canon EOS 60Da, Canon EOS 650D, Canon EOS 700D, Canon EOS Kiss Digital, Canon EOS Kiss F, Canon EOS Kiss Digital N, Canon EOS Kiss X2, Canon EOS Kiss X3, Canon EOS Kiss X4, Canon EOS Kiss X5, Canon EOS Kiss X50, Canon EOS Kiss X6i, Canon PowerShot G1 X, Canon PowerShot G10, Canon PowerShot G11, Canon PowerShot G12, Canon PowerShot G15, Canon PowerShot SX50 HS, Canon EOS Rebel SL1, Canon EOS Rebel T1i, Canon EOS Rebel

T2i, Canon EOS Rebel T3, Canon EOS Rebel T3i, Canon EOS Rebel T4i, Canon EOS Rebel XS, Canon EOS Rebel XSi, Canon EOS Rebel XT, Canon EOS Rebel XTi, Canon EOS Rebel T5i, Contax 645, Contax N, Contax N Digital, Contax N1, Contax NX, Hasselblad H1, Hasselblad H3D, Hasselblad H4D-200MS, Hasselblad H4D-31, Hasselblad H4D-40, Hasselblad H4D-50, Hasselblad H4D-50MS, Hasselblad H4D-60, Pentax 645D, Pentax *ist D, Pentax *ist DL, Pentax *ist DL2, Pentax *ist DS, Pentax *ist DS2, Pentax K-30, Pentax K-5, Pentax K-7, Pentax K-m, Pentax K10 Grand Prix, Pentax K100D, Pentax K100D Super, Pentax K10D, Pentax K110D, Pentax K200D, Pentax K20D, Pentax MZ-6, Pentax MZ-L, Pentax ZX-L, Samsung GX-1L, Samsung GX-1S, Samsung GX-20, Samsung NX10, Samsung NX100, Samsung NX11, Samsung NX5, Sigma SD1, Sigma SD1 Merrill, and Sigma SD15.

Whoa!

This means that a triggering device that is compatible with any of these cameras is also supposed to trigger your X-E1. You can choose from a large number of triggering options, one of them being the ingenious Triggertrap software for iOS and Android devices. In connection with a suitable hardware dongle and cable kit, Triggertrap will trigger your X-E1 electronically via the camera's external microphone input, which is located at the left side of the chassis.

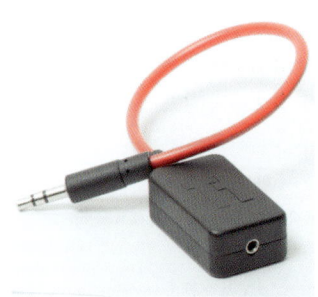
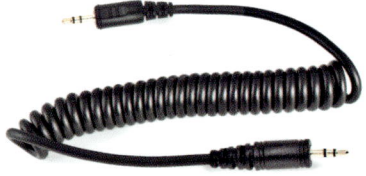

Figure 64: In order to use your smartphone as a remote shutter release, you need a suitable Triggertrap dongle and a CL-E3 connection cable.

Triggertrap offers an impressive number of triggering modes and functions, such as:

- Timelapse mode
- TimeWarp mode
- Bang (sound sensor) mode
- Seismic (shock and vibration sensor) mode
- Tesla (metal and magnetism sensor) mode
- Peekaboo (facial recognition) mode
- Long Exposure HDR mode
- Long Exposure HDR Timelapse mode
- DistanceLapse mode
- Motion (motion detection) mode
- Cable Release mode
- Star Trail mode
- Bramping (bulb ramping timelapse) mode
- Wi-Fi Slave mode
- Wi-Fi Master mode (trigger other devices running Triggertrap Mobile)
- Sunset and sunrise calculator
- Lag-o-Meter

If you want to learn more about these modes and how they work, I recommend reading the help displays in the free Triggertrap app or having a look at the online PDF manual on www.triggertrap.com.

Make no mistake: as sophisticated as it looks, the interface between Triggertrap and the camera is still as simple as any mechanical cable release or an RR-80 trigger. There's no digital communication between the camera and Triggertrap, so Triggertrap doesn't know about any camera settings (and can't change them), and the camera doesn't know about Triggertrap. This means Triggertrap can merely release the shutter and perform these three familiar functions:

- Half-pressing the shutter button to establish/lock focus and exposure

- Fully depressing the shutter button to take the shot

- Keeping the shutter button depressed (and locked) for an extended period of time to take long exposures (bulb mode)

However, Triggertrap offers plenty of options to control when, where, why, and how often to release (and hold) the shutter button, and it features wireless operation via a Bluetooth device or via a second iOS device (iPhone or iPad, for example) and Wi-Fi. The sheer number of options may be overkill for many users, but who says you have to use them all?

2 SHOOTING WITH THE X-E1 AND X-PRO1

2.1 HERE WE GO!

Are you ready to get started with the X-E1 or X-Pro1 system? Here are a few tips for an all-purpose configuration and for handling your camera:

- Set the camera to auto ISO (SHOOTING MENU > ISO > AUTO [6400]) and auto DR (SHOOTING MENU > DYNAMIC RANGE > AUTO). This set-up gives the camera the maximum amount of flexibility and will immediately provide you with high-quality JPEG results. Don't worry about high ISO values! The X-Pro1 and X-E1 produce great images all the way up to ISO 6400. The ISO values that are increased by one or two exposure values when the dynamic range function is activated do not actually mean a true increase in ISO sensitivity (even in bright light, the camera's automatic ISO may opt to shoot with ISO 400 or 800). Many other cameras use these methods too (such as those from Nikon, Canon, and Sony), but they are not always as honest with their ISO values as the X-E1 and X-Pro1 (section 2.6).

- It's best to use the RAW+JPEG mode (SHOOTING MENU > IMAGE QUALITY > FINE+RAW). This will allow you to delay making decisions about various image settings such as film simulation, sharpness, contrast, color, noise reduction, white balance, etc., and to concentrate on photographing your subject. You can take some time to consider various settings and compare their results either by availing yourself of the camera's internal RAW converter (PLAYBACK MENU > RAW

CONVERSION) or by using a software program on your computer (see "Internal vs. External RAW Conversion" in section 2.7).

• The optical viewfinder (OVF) of your X-Pro1 will never delineate the exact same image frame that the camera will actually capture. This parallax effect is physically unavoidable and also influences the accuracy of the autofocus, especially with subjects that are somewhat close to the camera. You can partly compensate for this fact by navigating to SHOOTING MENU and then activating the CORRECTED AF FRAME function (see section 2.2).

• The X-Pro1 features a hybrid viewfinder, which can show either an optical or an electronic image, according to your preference. This doesn't mean that you need to settle on one or the other display option. Quite the opposite, actually: you can use both options in parallel and use the viewfinder selector on the front of the camera as often as you like to switch between the OVF and the electronic viewfinder (EVF). The EVF lends itself to precise focusing, while the OVF provides an actual realtime image of the scene (see section 2.2).

• With both cameras, you'll normally want to use Area AF for your autofocus mode (SHOOTING MENU > AF MODE > AREA). This mode gives you the highest degree of flexibility and focus precision by allowing you to choose the position and size of the autofocus field freely, especially when using the EVF (see section 2.4).

• The standard shooting setting for most situations will be single autofocus (AF-S—position the focus mode selector on the front of the camera so it's pointing toward S) and single-frame exposure (DRIVE button > STILL IMAGE) (see section 2.4).

- The X-E1 and X-Pro1 are mirrorless system cameras, not reflex cameras. Don't expect your camera to operate like a DSLR or you'll be setting yourself up for bitter disappointment. Photographers who are upgrading from the X100 or X100S will have a good foundational knowledge, but those who are switching from DSLR cameras will need to reorient themselves. But don't worry—this book will help with just that!

- Unlike DSLR cameras, the X-E1 and X-Pro1 use contrast detection autofocus (CDAF) as their method of focusing. This method is fundamentally different from phase detection autofocus (PDAF), which is common in reflex cameras. Object edges shouldn't be the target of contrast detection autofocus; you should instead attempt to focus on surfaces, ideally ones exhibiting stark contrast. In addition, make sure that no objects within the autofocus frame are positioned at different distances from the camera. A good rule of thumb for quick and precise focusing is to make the selected AF frame as small as possible and as large as necessary (see section 2.4).

- The operation of the X-Pro1 and X-E1 features various shortcuts that you can use to make your everyday shooting easier:

  – Hold the Q button for a few seconds to go directly to the menu for custom shooting profiles (section 2.7).

  – Press and hold the MENU/OK button to lock or unlock the arrow keys of the selector.

  – Press and hold the Fn button (or arrow down button) to bring up its respective configuration menu, where you can assign one of any number of functions.

  – Press the DISP/BACK button for a couple seconds to activate (or deactivate) the camera's silent mode. When this mode is turned on, the camera functions quietly and inconspicuously. It won't make any artificial noises and it abstains from using both the flash and the AF-assist lamp. The latter, however, you should definitely otherwise use, because it will improve the effectiveness of the autofocus in poor lighting conditions (SHOOTING MENU > AF ILLUMINATOR > ON).

– Switch into and out of the macro mode quickly by pressing the MACRO button twice in quick succession (see "Closeups" in section 2.4).

– When using the camera's playback mode, press the command dial (yes, in addition to turning this dial, you can press it) to enlarge the current image as much as possible and inspect its sharpness. In contrast, pressing the command dial while in shooting mode and using the manual focus magnifies the image in the electronic viewfinder to help you focus. Turn the dial to cycle between the two magnification levels (see "Image Playback" in section 2.2). Press and hold the command dial to cycle through the MF assist (focus meapking) options.

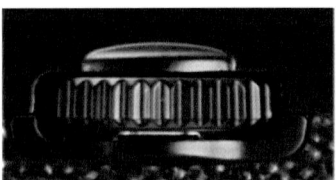

Figure 65: In addition to turning the command dial, you can also press it.

– On the X-Pro1, press and hold the viewfinder selector to switch manually between the two magnification levels of the OVF that are normally automatically determined. This is especially handy when you're using the XF18–55mmF2.8–4 R LM OIS zoom lens

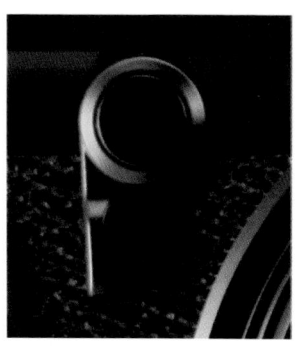

Figure 66: The viewfinder selector
on the front of the X-Pro1.

– Rather than selecting a function in the shooting
menu by pressing the OK button, press the shutter
button halfway down (to the first stopping point).
Pressing the shutter button halfway down while in
playback mode switches the camera directly into
shooting mode.

– Wake the camera up from its sleep mode (SET-UP
> AUTO POWER OFF) by pressing and holding the
shutter button halfway down as well (See "Batteries
and Chargers" in section 1.1).

• Make things as easy as possible for yourself and your
camera: activate the quick start mode (SET-UP >
QUICK START MODE > ON), avoid using the energy
save mode (SET-UP > POWER SAVE MODE > OFF),
and instead bring along one or more fully charged replacement batteries. Also, use the fastest memory card
you can find (see "SD Memory Cards" in section 1.1).

• If you need to be able to take multiple exposures in
quick succession, it may make sense to disable the
automatic image preview (SET-UP > IMAGE DISP. >
OFF). This will allow you to keep your sights on your
subject without interruption.

• Whenever possible, press the shutter button halfway
down in anticipation of the decisive moment when you

will release the shutter and capture your subject. When the shutter button is depressed halfway, the camera—unless configured otherwise—takes and saves various measurements related to focus and exposure and sets the desired aperture. Doing so will minimize the delay that occurs when you actually snap your shot. This tip also applies to situations in which you manually expose and focus your shot or use an adapted lens. The one exception is the so-called autofocus trick for moving subjects (see "Focusing on Fast-Moving Subjects" in section 2.4).

- Clean the image sensor regularly by navigating to SET-UP > SENSOR CLEANING and by using a cleaning bellows designed for the purpose (see "Cleaning the Sensor" in section 1.1).

- Before you leave home with your camera equipment, insert an SD card, double-check that your batteries are charged and inserted correctly into your camera, and check your flash units by turning them on briefly. You wouldn't be the first person to leave his or her batteries at home in the charger or to have inserted them incorrectly.

RAW OR JPEG?

If you spend time in online photography forums, you'll discover that there's hardly a debate that generates more controversy and discussion than the question of whether it's better to shoot in RAW or JPEG format. Since this back-and-forth has been raging for years already, you can assume that there's no right answer.

For this reason, I don't have any intention of trying to resolve the question, but I would like to address it specifically as it relates to the X-Pro1 and X-E1 and reassert my earlier recommendation that you can have your cake and eat it too by shooting with both formats: RAW+JPEG (SHOOTING MENU > IMAGE QUALITY > FINE+RAW).

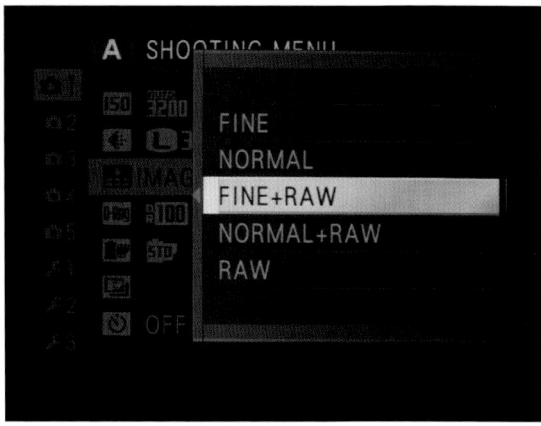

Figure 67: **Image quality:** You can opt to shoot in JPEG (FINE or NORMAL), RAW, or both formats simultaneously. Your camera offers the greatest degree of flexibility and quality with the FINE+RAW setting.

Since this ongoing issue is always complicated by misunderstandings, I'd like to clear up a few things at the outset:

In the days of film photography, there was a negative and there were prints made from that negative. Some photographers developed their own prints, but most amateurs brought their negatives to a photo lab that would produce prints of the desired size (for cost reasons, this process was mostly automatic). This unfortunately meant that it was common for different photo labs to produce prints from the same negative that looked different, and the discrepancy between them was often enormous. While most specialist labs would produce good prints, drugstore labs would often disappoint with bland, unattractive, or arbitrary color results.

Today the RAW file is the digital equivalent of the negative, and a JPEG file is the digital counterpart of a photographic print. This means that there are many different possibilities for interpreting a RAW file and "developing" a JPEG from it. Each and every RAW file can be interpreted in various ways, thus producing any number of JPEGs, some with better results than others. Cameras are accordingly evaluated in part based on how well they can convert RAW files into JPEGs—and many photographers who use the X-E1 and X-Pro1 sing the praises of Fuji's "legendary colors."

By opting not to save RAW files—the digital negatives—you're reducing your X-E1 or X-Pro1 to a sort of instant camera: after you press the shutter button, the camera displays one JPEG, which you can accept or delete. Take it or leave it.

Why should you be content with this very first result from your camera's internal processing lab? And why would you want to rack your brain trying to figure out how to program your camera to interpret a specific RAW file in the best way possible? Wouldn't it be more pleasant to allow yourself to concentrate on your subject and the focus and exposure settings of your shot? Wouldn't you rather leave all of the digital post-processing (white balance, push/pull, film simulation, sharpness, color, contrast, noise reduction, dynamic range extension, color space, etc.) for later when you have time to sit in front of a larger monitor to evaluate your images?

Basically, the X-Pro1 and X-E1 offer two ways of interpreting your saved RAW files and developing them into attractive JPEGs:

• Using the camera's integrated RAW converter (PLAY-BACK MENU > RAW CONVERSION). This is more or less the quick and simple counterpart of the conventional, partially automated photo lab.

• Using external software on a personal computer (such as Adobe Lightroom, Apple Aperture, Capture One, or Silkypix). These programs are more complicated and better approximate the process of developing photos by hand in a specialized lab. A free, but somewhat older version of Silkypix called RAW FILE CONVERTER EX comes with your camera on an included CD-ROM.

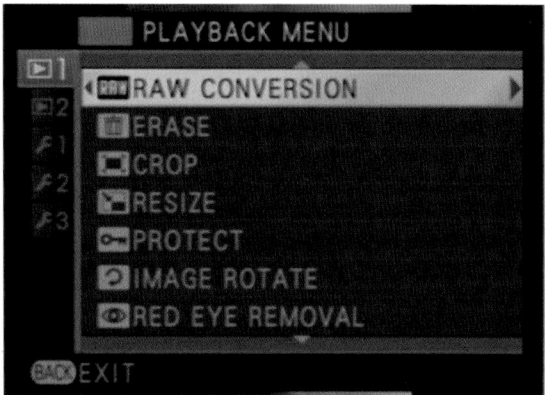

Figure 68: Your camera features an internal RAW converter that allows you to develop your digital negatives (RAW files) into attractive JPEGs. You can customize various settings, including white balance, color, sharpness, film simulation, noise reduction, and dynamic range, even after you have snapped an exposure.

Let's continue our comparison of film and digital technology:

As is the case with film negatives, RAW files contain much more information than a finished print or JPEG file. A RAW file includes all of the raw data that the sensor records during an image exposure (which explains the file's name). The X-Pro1 and X-E1 write RAW files with a color depth of 12 bits per RGB channel, which amounts to 4,096 brightness values. JPEGs conversely contain only 8 bits per channel, which amounts to only 256 brightness values. This difference means that you can get a lot more out of a RAW file when working with it on your computer than you can out of a JPEG.

If this is all true, why would you want to shoot in the RAW+JPEG mode instead of only saving RAW files? Not saving JPEGs saves memory space and allows the camera to operate faster!

There's a good reason to opt for RAW+JPEG: you can only preview exposures on your camera in JPEG format. This means that your camera has to produce a JPEG out of every RAW file it creates (even in the "RAW only" mode) to provide you with a preview file to examine in playback mode.

The preview JPEG that the camera produces when you choose to exclusively save RAW files has a low resolution— often so low that it's impossible to tell whether or not the image is in focus. Shooting in FINE+RAW mode solves this problem by saving a high-resolution JPEG "print" in addition to the RAW "negative." You can use this JPEG to check your focus immediately after you snap it by pressing the command dial to zoom in. (To enable maximum zoom, you need to navigate to SHOOTING MENU > IMAGE SIZE and select one of the size options with a capital L for large.) Moreover, the high-res JPEG file is a good point of reference for developing the RAW file later with the hope of achieving better results.

You could also opt to shoot in NORMAL+RAW mode instead of FINE+RAW, which doesn't actually affect the resolution of the JPEG. This setting does, however, produce a file with greater compression and the attendant compromises in image quality. Dedicated RAW shooters should also pay attention to this fact, because the camera only saves JPEGs (without any RAW files) in modes such as motion panorama, ISO bracketing, film simulation bracketing, and dynamic range bracketing. In those modes, the camera silently switches the image quality setting from NORMAL+RAW to NORMAL, which means the only image it writes to the memory card is a quality-reduced JPEG. And what X-Pro1 or X-E1 user likes to skimp on quality?

When you create a JPEG using the internal RAW converter (PLAYBACK MENU > RAW CONVERSION), the camera automatically uses the highest quality setting. In other words, it always produces a JPEG with maximum resolution and size, regardless of the camera's image size, format, and quality settings when the exposure was captured.

> **TIP**
>
> Even if you intend to shoot only in JPEGs and don't plan to use any external software to develop RAW files, it still makes sense to shoot in the RAW+JPEG mode (with an image quality setting of FINE+RAW). The internal RAW converter of the camera offers the opportunity to develop alternate JPEG "prints" of your RAW file even after exposure by adjusting various settings.
>
> In addition, if shooting exclusively in RAWs to develop them later with external computer software is your aim, you should still opt for the image quality setting FINE+RAW. The high-res JPEG file that is saved separately will act as a point of reference that you can use to develop your own images from the raw image data. It also allows you much better control over critical image focus.

You can read more about internal and external RAW conversion under "Internal vs. External RAW Conversion" in section 2.7.

SETTING THE IMAGE SIZE AND FORMAT

In addition to the image quality, you can also set the image size in the shooting menu. This setting applies to the JPEG file that the camera creates and not to the RAW file, which always comprises the sensor's full resolution.

By navigating to SHOOTING MENU > IMAGE SIZE you can select from three resolutions (Large, Medium, and Small) as well as three aspect ratios (3:2, 16:9, and 1:1). To the right of the various size and aspect ratio options, you will find a number that indicates the capacity for the remaining exposures you can save to the SD card with each of those size settings. The respective number of pixels of your current settings is displayed below.

Once again for good measure: however you customize your settings here, they will only affect the JPEG files that the camera produces immediately after you press the shutter button. If you work with a RAW file later—either by using the internal RAW converter or by using an external program—it will exhibit the maximum camera resolution as well as the sensor's full aspect ratio of 3:2.

If that's the case, what's the point of setting the image size at all? There are several reasons to do it:

To begin with, the camera's light metering is influenced by the current JPEG format settings. If you want to shoot images with an aspect ratio of 16:9 or 1:1, the light metering works more effectively when the image format is set accordingly. Parts of the image that are superfluous (because they will be automatically cropped out) won't affect the metering. In other words, the camera will meter only those parts of the image that appear in the cropped (16:9 or 1:1) live view image, and ignore the rest.

Furthermore, it's easier to compose your desired image area when the image in the camera's viewfinder matches up with the appropriate frame for your image format.

Finally, the camera adjusts the size and shape of the autofocus field according to your selected image format. This means that you can continue to use all of the camera's AF fields even when you are shooting in the exotic 1:1 format.

SUMMARY

The RAW data that the camera saves always contains color versions of your exposures with the highest possible resolution at the aspect ratio of 3:2. You can, however, adjust the size and shape of the JPEG files that the camera creates immediately after snapping an image. You can set the quality (compression) of these JPEGs by going to the IMAGE QUALITY submenu and selecting NORMAL or FINE. I recommend using the setting FINE+RAW. You can define the settings for resolution (the number of pixels) in your JPEG files by going to the IMAGE SIZE submenu and selecting a size of L, M, or S as well as an aspect ratio of 3:2, 16:9, or 1:1. I recommend using the L size in all cases. Last but not least, if you convert the RAW data of an already exposed shot by using the internal RAW converter, you will always create a JPEG file that is of the best possible quality (FINE), has the highest possible resolution (L), and is in the standard aspect ratio 3:2.

2.2 VIEWFINDER AND MONITOR

The X-Pro1's novel hybrid viewfinder was probably one of the reasons that led you to choose this camera. The combination of the OVF, the EVF, and the LCD monitor makes the X-Pro1 a truly flexible recording device. While the X-E1 lacks this novelty and features a more conventional electronic viewfinder, this omission is offset by the EVF's higher resolution.

Press the VIEW MODE button to switch between the main LCD and the viewfinder. This cycles through the following options:

- Activate LCD monitor

- Activate viewfinder

- Activate eye sensor, which automatically determines whether the display should be shown on the LCD monitor or in the viewfinder

The eye sensor is located directly to the right of the viewfinder and switches the display over to the viewfinder as soon as the photographer's face (or some other object) covers it up.

When the viewfinder of your X-Pro1 is activated (and you are in shooting mode), you can switch between the optical and the electronic viewfinder displays using the viewfinder selector on the front of the camera. A diopter adjustment with an appropriate lens may be necessary to make this fully functional for your personal vision (see "Diopter Correction Lenses" in section 1.1).

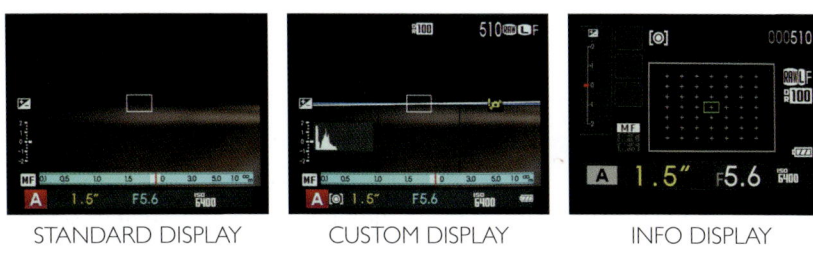

STANDARD DISPLAY   CUSTOM DISPLAY   INFO DISPLAY

Figure 69: **Different displays:** You can use the DISP/BACK button to cycle through three displays for the LCD monitor and two for the viewfinder. When using the viewfinder, you can choose between a standard display and a custom display. The extra display on the LCD monitor is the info display, which contains yet more information about the camera's current operating settings.

All viewing options (LCD, EVF, and the X-Pro1's OVF) offer the choice of a standard or custom display. The LCD monitor has the additional option of providing an info display with additional information about the current settings of the camera. Since the info display doesn't include a live image, you will want to use it with the eye sensor activated (VIEW MODE button).

The DISP/BACK button allows you to cycle through the two—or three on the LCD monitor—displays in whichever view is currently active. Note to X-Pro1 users: to change the display of the OVF, the optical viewfinder needs to be currently active when you press the DISP/BACK button. This makes it possible, for example, to have the custom display in the electronic viewfinder, the standard display in the optical viewfinder, and the info display on the LCD monitor all at the same time.

You can program which information you'd like to appear in the custom display by navigating to SHOOTING MENU > DISP. CUSTOM SETTINGS.

SUMMARY

The VIEW MODE button allows you to switch the display between the viewfinder and the LCD monitor and to activate the eye sensor. The viewfinder selector, on the front of the X-Pro1, controls whether the OVF or the EVF is active. The DISP/BACK button on both cameras enables you to choose which display you'd like to see in the currently active view mode. Finally, you can program which details you would like to be shown in the custom display by opening up SHOOTING MENU > DISP. CUSTOM SETTINGS.

Let's now take a closer look at the X-Pro1's optical view-finder.

X-PRO1 ONLY: THE OPTICAL VIEWFINDER (OVF)

The OVF offers a distortion-free view of the real world. When you program and activate the custom display, the OVF can also relay many useful details about your exposure with the help of digital indicators.

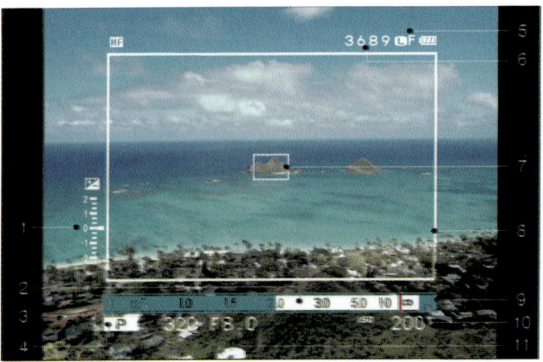

Figure 70: A look through the optical viewfinder (simulated): (1) exposure compensation/exposure indicator, (2) depth of field bar, (3) shutter speed, (4) shooting mode, (5) image size and quality, (6) capacity for remaining exposures on the memory card, (7) AF/magnified viewfinder frame, (8) image bright frame, (9) distance scale, (10) ISO setting, (11) aperture

One highlight of the optical viewfinder is that it has two different magnification levels, which allow it to work with focal lengths between 18mm and 60mm.

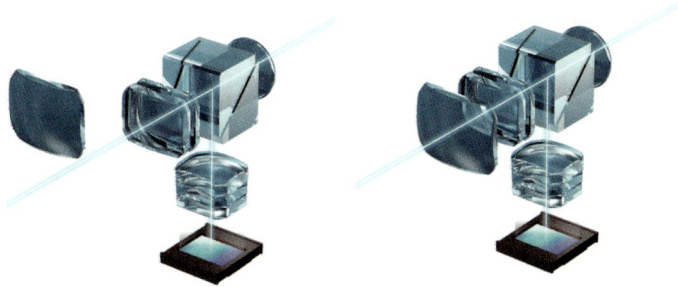

Figure 71: The X-Pro I's optical viewfinder offers two different magnification levels. Level I (left) is optimal for wide-angle lenses starting at 18mm. Level 2 (right) is designed for normal lenses with a focal length of 35mm and up. When switching from level I to level 2, the camera slides a magnification lens into the optical axis of the viewfinder.

When shooting with an X-mount lens, the camera automatically detects its focal length and sets the OVF to the appropriate magnification level by adding a magnification lens to the optical axis of the viewfinder or removing it. The two magnification levels are optimized for focal lengths of 18mm and 35mm. If you use a different focal length, the superimposed frame for the image outline updates accordingly.

IMPORTANT

With Fujinon zoom lenses, you have to manually switch to the desired magnification level by pressing and holding the viewfinder selector lever on the front of the X-Pro I.

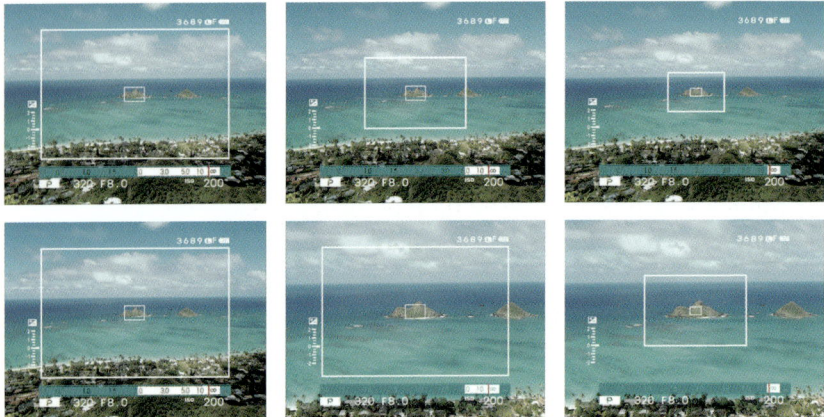

Figure 72: **Conventional viewfinder** (top row) and multiview viewfinder (bottom row): Without any additional magnification, the X-Pro1's OVF is optimized for a focal length of 18mm (left). If you attach a lens with a focal length of 35mm (middle) or 60mm (right), the superimposed bright frame adjusts to the actual image frame by becoming smaller—at a focal length of 60mm the display is hardly usable.

The multiview capability of the viewfinder solves this problem (bottom row). For lenses that have a focal length of at least 35mm, the OVF automatically switches to a higher magnification level, enlarging the entire viewfinder image instead of shrinking the frame. The rectangular indicator for the image frame of a 35mm lens (middle) fills up the viewfinder, and the bright frame for the 60mm lens (right) also appears noticeably larger.

You can manually switch between the two magnification levels by holding the viewfinder selector for a couple of seconds while the OVF is activated.

The optical viewfinder offers an instantaneous view of reality and helps you to decide when to pull the trigger in the critical moment. The fact that the viewfinder typically offers a field of view that is larger than the actual image area is also very helpful—the OVF window area is larger than the digital frame. This allows you to discern and react to moving subjects that appear in your viewfinder before they enter the actual image frame. And you can always frame a scene through the optical viewfinder, even when a strong neutral density filter on the lens blocks out a substantial amount of light (e.g., for long exposure shots).

The optical viewfinder also has the disadvantage of not "seeing" the exact image that the camera does. This is because it lies on a different optical axis from the lens, creating a parallax error that all non-TTL optical viewfinder cameras exhibit.

Human vision is also based on input from sensors on two different optical axes: our left and right eyes. This trait allows us to demonstrate the parallax effect with a small experiment. Hold your pointed index finger at a short distance from your nose. Now view it alternately with your left and then your right eye and you will see how your finger appears to jump from one side to the other. Next, move your finger farther away from your face and repeat this test. The difference between the appearance of your finger as seen with your left and right eye should be much smaller now.

The X-Pro1 is also subject to this effect, since the lens and the optical viewfinder are on different optical axes. This characteristic gives rise to two undesirable phenomena:

- The white image frame that you see in the optical viewfinder doesn't correspond exactly to the image frame that the camera exposes, which encompasses a slightly larger area. The camera errs on the side of caution and frames something like 85% of the actual exposure area.

- The measuring field for the autofocus shifts in the same way that the image frame itself shifts as a result of parallax error. This creates the possibility that you will target a specific (usually small) object in the OVF, only to have the camera focus beyond the object by a hair's breadth.

Just as was the case with our small experiment, both effects are more pronounced when the subject is closer to the camera. The greater the distance between the lens and the subject, the less significant the problem becomes and the more you can forget about it.

In contrast to other (often more expensive) non-TTL viewfinder cameras, the X-Pro1 benefits from Fuji's attempt to mitigate the problem of viewfinder parallax. After you successfully measure the distance for a shot by pressing the shutter button halfway and allowing the autofocus to settle on a distance, the rectangle indicating the image frame shifts and adjusts in size accordingly.

The camera also attempts to adjust the AF detection areas to balance out any undesirable effects stemming from parallax. To enable this feature, you must go to SHOOTING MENU > CORRECTED AF FRAME and select ON.

Two white autofocus fields will now appear in the OVF (only in AF-S mode): one will be delineated by a solid border and the other, which will be slightly below and to the right of the first one, will be indicated by a dashed line. The solid border indicates the field for objects that are far away, and the dashed border marks the field for objects at the OVF's minimum focus distance for your lens and focal length—if the subject were any closer, the camera would have to switch into macro mode and switch from the OVF to the EVF.

After you successfully focus your shot (by pressing the shutter button halfway), a third frame with a green border will appear in between the two white AF fields. This is the location on which the camera is actually focusing. If this green rectangle doesn't target the subject you'd like to focus on, adjust your camera so that it exactly covers your object. Then refocus the camera by letting go of the shutter button and pressing it again to the halfway point.

You can, as an alternative, use the EVF, which will always show exactly the same image frame that the camera actually "sees."

Because of viewfinder parallax, the OVF cannot be used in macro mode. When the power save mode is active, the OVF display doesn't include a live histogram. This is one of the reasons why I recommend that you don't use this energy saving mode.

X-E1 AND X-PRO1: THE ELECTRONIC VIEWFINDER (EVF)

Welcome back, X-E1 users! The EVF displays the exact image that the camera "sees." In other words, it will look similar to the result of your exposure. There are no optical shifts and no parallax problems. The EVF and the LCD screen on the camera's back reproduce the image that the camera sensor captures through the lens.

This is what makes the EVF so valuable. While the scene that you see through the optical viewfinder will always be sharp and well exposed, you will be able to detect any major problems with the exposure or focus in the EVF display before you actually release the shutter. Even the best cameras, including yours, have a much smaller dynamic range than human sight.

While our eye can register extreme contrast in a scene (such as dark shadows at the same time as white clouds), the camera will show either blocked-up shadows or blown-out highlights in the EVF, depending on the exposure settings. This gives you the opportunity to react to the problem and adjust the exposure parameters accordingly (see section 2.3).

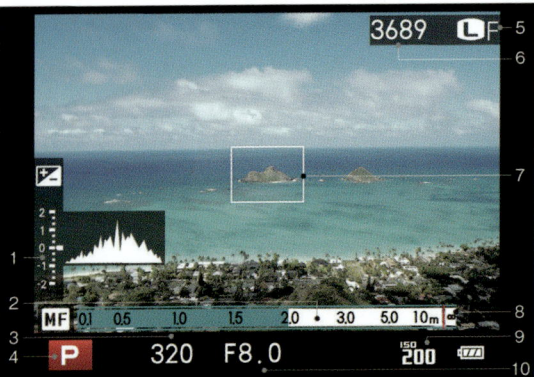

Figure 73: A look through the electronic viewfinder (simulated): (1) exposure compensation/exposure indicator, (2) depth of field bar, (3) shutter speed, (4) shooting mode, (5) image size and quality, (6) capacity of remaining exposures on the memory card, (7) AF/magnified viewfinder frame, (8) distance scale, (9) ISO setting, (10) aperture

The EVF has much more utility than just this, however, since it also displays the camera's current JPEG settings (see section 2.7). These settings include the film simulation (Provia, Velvia, Astia, Sepia, etc.), the color saturation, and the contrast settings for highlights and shadows. This means that the EVF allows you to preview the results of the various settings you have programmed on your camera.

The EVF and LCD monitor are not without shortcomings, however. Aside from their limited resolution, the largest drawback to using these view modes is a certain lag between reality and what appears on the digital displays. In combination with the slight shutter lag, this delay can mean that the decisive moment in critical situations can pass you by.

X-E1 AND X-PRO1: THE LCD MONITOR
The LCD monitor functions just like the EVF and accordingly shares its advantages and disadvantages. Bright lighting conditions can limit its utility, but it enables you

to move the camera away from your face, which attracts less attention. You can also shoot from unconventional perspectives (such as above your head or from your hip), but the monitor doesn't fold out and you can't swivel it, so this advantage has its limitations. The monitor is especially practical when shooting from a tripod.

The info display, which I've already discussed in this chapter, lends itself nicely to being used in combination with the eye sensor for the view mode. With this setup, the LCD monitor will display the camera's current settings, while you can determine the image frame with the viewfinder. Switching between the two displays will be automatic.

LCD/EVF BRIGHTNESS

You can adjust the brightness of the LCD monitor and the electronic viewfinder by navigating to SET-UP > EVF/LCD BRIGHTNESS, but the more convenient method is to use the Quick Menu (Q button). As usual, the setting will apply to whichever view (EVF or LCD) is currently active based on the VIEW MODE button settings or input from the eye sensor.

The camera automatically adjusts the brightness of the digital indicators in the optical viewfinder based on the ambient light.

IMAGE PLAYBACK

Press the playback button on the back of the camera to examine your exposures. When doing this, you again have the option of using the EVF or the LCD monitor to view them. You can use the VIEW MODE button to control where the images are displayed, or activate the eye sensor to let the camera automatically determine which screen to use.

The camera remembers your preferred view settings for both shooting and playback mode. You could, for example, set the camera to use the LCD monitor for taking pictures (shooting mode) and to use the viewfinder for viewing them (playback mode)—or the other way around. With my cameras, I prefer to use the eye sensor while both shooting and reviewing my images. That way the image or information is always right in front of me. I only turn off the eye sensor and use the VIEW MODE button to set these options manually in situations where other objects or unfavorable light conditions might accidently activate the eye sensor.

TIP

There are two ways to switch back to the shooting mode while in the playback mode. You can either press the playback button again, or you can simply press the shutter button down halfway.

The camera also offers various display options for the playback mode, which you can select with the DISP/BACK button. In contrast to shooting mode, the LCD monitor and EVF will always display the same information.

In the exposure display (INFORMATION ON), you will see the picture with various indicators displayed over it that reveal information about the settings used when the image was snapped. The full image display (INFORMA-TION OFF) shows just the picture without any informa-tion. The favorites display (FAVORITES) allows you to rate your images with one to five stars by using the up and down selector keys. You can use these ratings to help you sort and select your images later. The detailed display (DETAIL INFORMATION) relays extensive infor-mation and displays a histogram. It also indicates overex-posed (blown-out) highlights with a flashing black/white exposure warning ("blinkies").

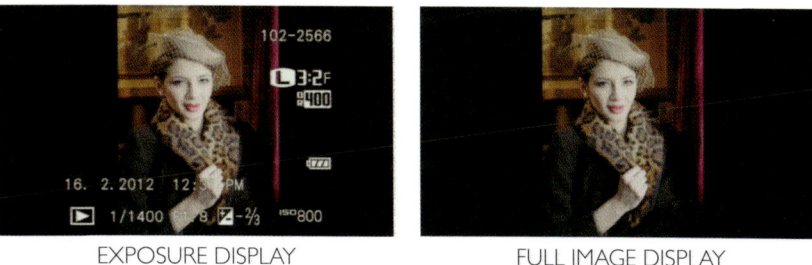

EXPOSURE DISPLAY   FULL IMAGE DISPLAY

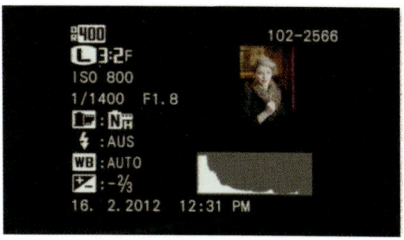

FAVORITES DISPLAY   DETAILED DISPLAY

Figure 74: **Displays in playback mode:** Press the DISP/BACK button to cycle through the four playback displays.

Unless you're viewing the favorites display, you can use the up and down selector keys to reveal even more information. There are an additional two screens of exposure information as well as a screen featuring the full image with a green cross indicating the autofocus target. Keep in mind that this cross marks the position of the AF point in the exposure after you focused the image (but before you made any final reframing adjustments to the image).

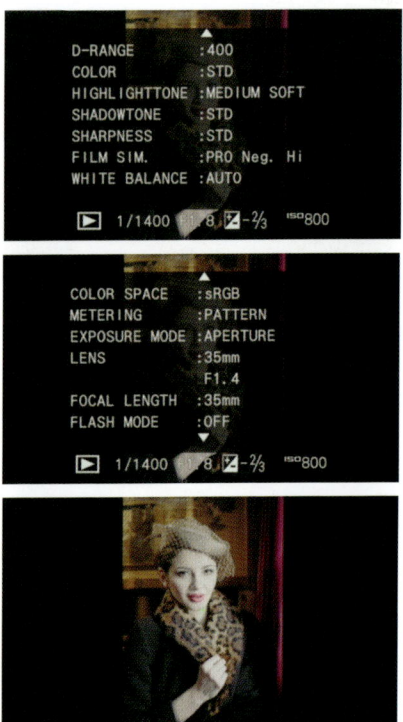

Figure 75: While in playback mode, use the selector keys (up and down) to access further information about an exposure. There are two additional screens of information as well as a full reproduction of the image with a green cross to indicate the point of focus. These additional pages are not accessible from the favorites display.

You can either use the left and right selector keys to flip through the exposures you've already taken, or you can use the command dial.

The magnifying buttons (the secondary functions of the DRIVE and AE buttons) zoom in and out gradually on the exposure. When in playback mode, you can press the zoom-in button to enlarge the image. You can also press the command dial to automatically enlarge the image to the maximum magnification level, which is my preferred method. This shortcut zooms in directly on the area that the AF selected as the focus point of the exposure.

The selector keys allow you to examine the various details of your image while the image is enlarged. Pressing the command dial a second time will bring you immediately back to the full frame of the image.

Figure 76: There are two ways to enlarge images while in playback mode: you can either press the zoom-in button or you can press the command dial. Doing so will allow you to be in a better position to judge the quality of your exposure. Once the image is enlarged, use the selector keys to navigate around the picture. The indicator on the left shows the current level of magnification, and the small window over the full image will help you orient yourself as you scan the different image areas.

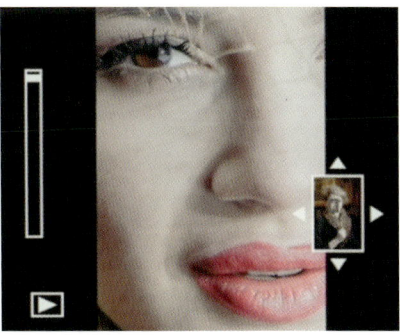

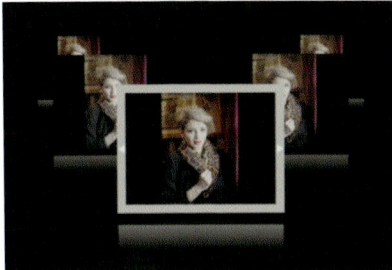
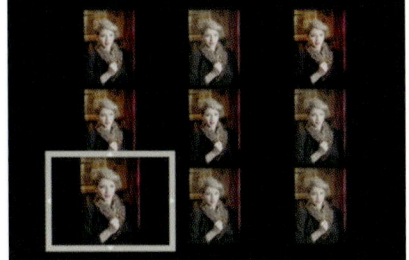

Figure 77: Pressing the zoom-out key several times will allow you to view multiple images at the same time in a gallery format. You can view up to 100 images simultaneously. You can navigate through this overview of your exposures by using the left and right selector keys or by turning the command dial. Press the zoom-in button to gradually reset the view to looking at one single image or press the command dial to immediately jump back. The illustration shows two of the four available gallery views.

To delete an image, press the delete key (AF button) while in playback mode and confirm the command by pressing the OK button. If you want to delete more than one image at a time, navigate to PLAYBACK MENU > ERASE > SELECTED FRAMES and mark the images you wish to remove with the OK button. After you have finished marking your selection, press the DISP/BACK button and select OK to confirm.

2.3 EXPOSURE AND METERING

A well-exposed image ultimately and always depends on the selection of an appropriate combination of aperture and shutter speed.

The lens's internal aperture regulates the amount of incident light: the more impeding the aperture (i.e., the higher the f-stop setting), the less light will shine through the lens and onto the sensor. A high f-stop also deepens the camera's depth of field, which is the range of distances from the camera in which objects will appear in focus.

The shutter speed controls how quickly the camera's focal plane shutter opens and closes, or, in other words, the length of time that the quantity of light determined by the aperture is able to reach the sensor. Shorter durations permit less light to reach the sensor (you can think of each pixel as a mini reservoir for photons); longer durations allow more. Short exposure times (like 1/2000 second) capture the action of a specific moment and freeze it in place, while longer times (e.g., one second) often lead to motion blur and other intentional effects.

If the quantity of captured light overwhelms the capacity of the light reservoirs (i.e., the pixels) on the sensor, the final image will exhibit a phenomenon called blooming, which is an intense overexposure that causes a loss of detail and texture. Conversely, if too little light is captured, the affected dark areas of the image literally disappear beneath the image noise. The captured signal, in other words, is too weak for the sensor to distinguish between the details of the image and the background noise.

For these reasons, correctly exposing photos with digital cameras is of great importance. Photographers must attempt to expose their images so that the important details of their subjects are neither blown out by blooming nor engulfed by image noise. This is unfortunately easier said than done; the dynamic range of everyday scenes (the range between their brightest and darkest areas) constantly overpowers the capabilities of digital camera sensors. We will concern ourselves with the question of correct exposure several times in the remainder of this book when considering topics such as ISO settings (section 2.5), extending the dynamic range (section 2.6), JPEG settings (section 2.7), and RAW conversion (section 2.7).

In this section, I'd like to lay the groundwork for these discussions by going over the camera's four exposure modes and three methods of metering, as well as an indispensable option for ambitious photographers: the ability to correct the camera-determined exposure manually.

2.3.1 EXPOSURE CONTROL

The X-Pro1 and X-E1 offer the four typical exposure modes, which you're probably familiar with from working with other cameras:

- **Program automatic** **P** : The camera will automatically choose an effective combination for the aperture and shutter speed.

- **Aperture-priority with automatic shutter speed** **A** : You set the aperture manually, and the camera selects an appropriate shutter speed.

- **Shutter-priority with automatic aperture** **S** : You set the shutter speed, and the camera determines the aperture.

- **Manual exposure** **M** : You determine both the aperture and the shutter speed and are therefore entirely responsible for correctly exposing your shot.

Let's take a closer look at these different settings.

PROGRAM AUTOMATIC P

To configure your camera to be in the program automat-ic exposure mode, adjust both your lens aperture ring (or, on a zoom lens, the aperture mode switch) and your shutter-speed dial to the A position, for automatic. The camera will then automatically select a combination of aperture and shutter speed (i.e., exposure time) based on the lighting conditions of your shot. When your camera is configured for this exposure mode, a P will be displayed on the LCD monitor and in the viewfinder, which indicates that the program automatic mode is active.

If you don't like the combination of aperture and shut-ter speed that the camera automatically selects, you can use the program shift feature by pressing the left and right selector keys on the back of the camera. The left key will make the aperture smaller while increasing the exposure time. The right key will conversely open up the aperture while decreasing the exposure time. When you shift the shutter speed and aperture settings in this way, the camera will display these settings in yellow instead of the usual white, indicating that you're not using the camera's automatically determined selections.

You can only use the program shift feature under specific circumstances:

• The auto ISO must be disabled (section 2.5).

• The auto DR must be disabled (section 2.6).

• No flash unit with an active automatic TTL exposure mode can be in use (section 2.9).

If your camera fails to react when you press the left or right selector key while in the program automatic exposure mode, there's a good chance that one of these requirements has not been met.

Despite these limitations, the program automatic mode outperforms its reputation. It can detect information about the optical characteristics of the lens that's currently attached, including its set focal length and OIS status, and use this information to determine the best combination of aperture and shutter speed for specific lighting conditions. This mode is ideal for spontaneous snapshots when you don't have enough time to manually select the aperture or shutter speed, and for occasions when you need to hand your camera to someone who isn't familiar with it (or with photography at all).

> **HINT**
>
> When using the program automatic exposure mode, the camera will never choose an exposure window that is longer than 1/4 second.

APERTURE-PRIORITY WITH AUTOMATIC SHUTTER SPEED A

In aperture-priority mode, you set an aperture and the camera selects a shutter speed that complements your aperture selection. To program your camera for this mode, turn the shutter-speed dial on top of the camera to the A setting and select your desired aperture by simply adjusting the lens aperture ring. To enable the aperture ring with zoom lenses, you have to set the aperture mode switch to the aperture symbol. If your lens doesn't offer an aperture ring, you can change the aperture by turning the command dial.

The camera conveniently offers intermediate steps of 1/3 aperture stops or exposure values (EV). The active view—either the main monitor or the viewfinder—will indicate that you are in this mode with an A for aperture-priority.

As previously indicated, a large f-stop number (i.e., a small aperture) will produce a large depth of field (which can be ideal for landscape shots, for example), and a small f-stop (i.e., a large aperture) will produce a shallow depth of field ideal for isolating subjects in front of out-of-focus backgrounds (which can work well for portraiture). The concrete measure of the depth of field for a shot depends on focal length and the distance of the subject (and the background) from the camera. (More on the camera's autofocus below.)

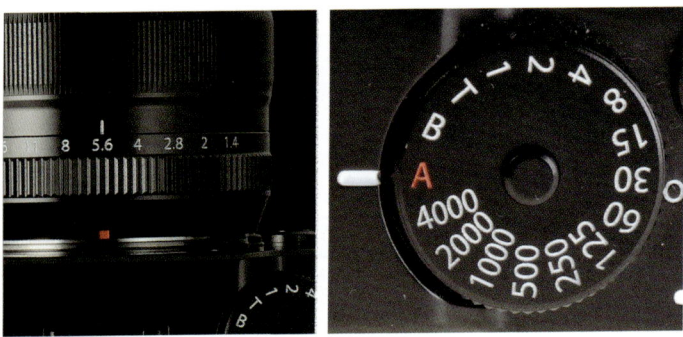

Figure 78: Selecting the aperture-priority exposure mode: Set the lens aperture to your desired value and adjust the shutter-speed dial to A for automatic. You can also configure your camera for the other three exposure modes by making similar adjustments.

The aperture not only influences the depth of field; it also affects the imaging performance of the lens. As a rule, the lenses on APS-C sensors achieve their best performance with apertures between f/5.6 and f/11. A wide-open aperture has a tendency to lead to blurring and vignetting around the edges of an image. On the other end of the spectrum, the smallest apertures can produce diffraction blur. These effects are measurable and can be assessed with tests; in practice, however, they play a smaller role than many pixel peepers would like to admit.

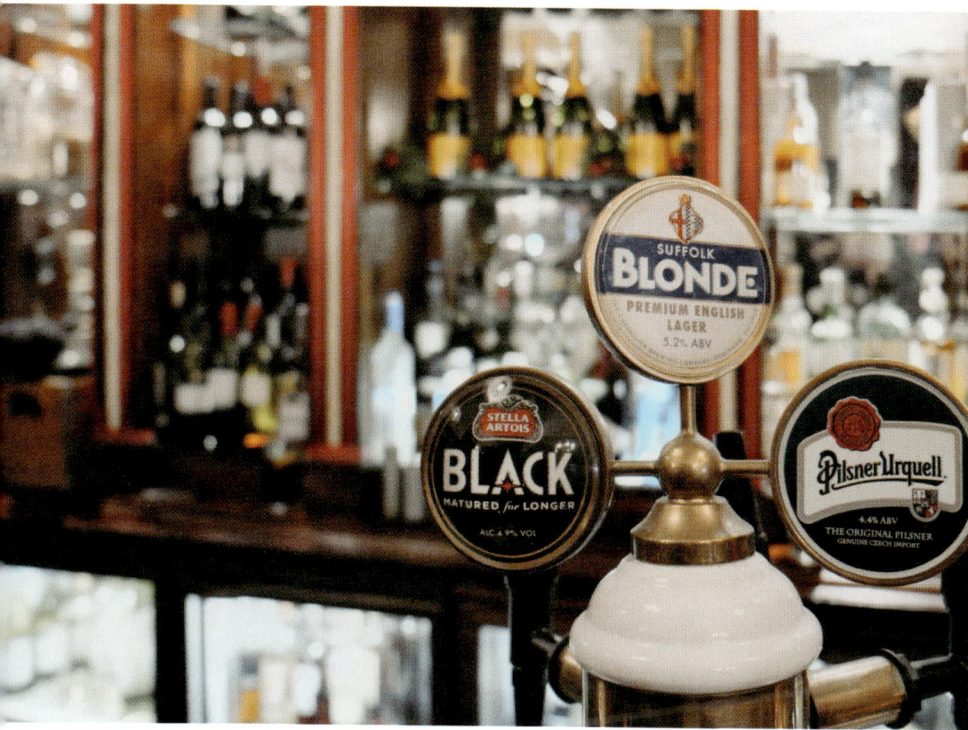

Figure 79: **Aperture and depth of field** (1): This image was shot with the 18–55mm kit zoom lens at 18mm and fully open aperture (f/2.8) with the conveniently shallow depth of field.

For example, it's not prudent to choose your exposure settings based on your lens's optimal range for diffraction blur if that means you have to forfeit shooting with a depth of field that would improve your image.

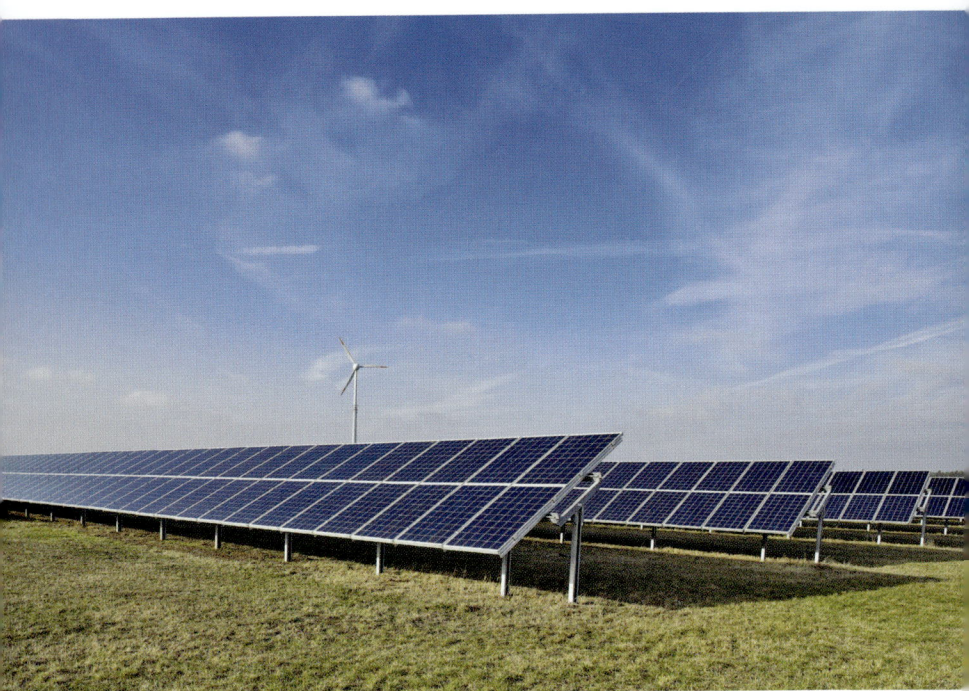

Figure 80: **Aperture and depth of field** (2): This image was shot with the 14mm f/2.8 lens and a small aperture (f/8), producing a large depth of field and an image that is sharp in the foreground as well as the background.

HINT

In aperture-priority mode, the camera won't ever select an exposure time of longer than 30 seconds.

SHUTTER-PRIORITY WITH AUTOMATIC APERTURE **S**

The shutter-priority setting is analogous to aperture-priority: here, you choose the desired shutter speed and the camera automatically selects an appropriate aperture. For this, you'll want to bring the lens aperture ring (or the aperture mode switch of your lens) to the **A** setting for automatic. You'll see an **S** in the viewfinder and on the monitor for shutter-priority.

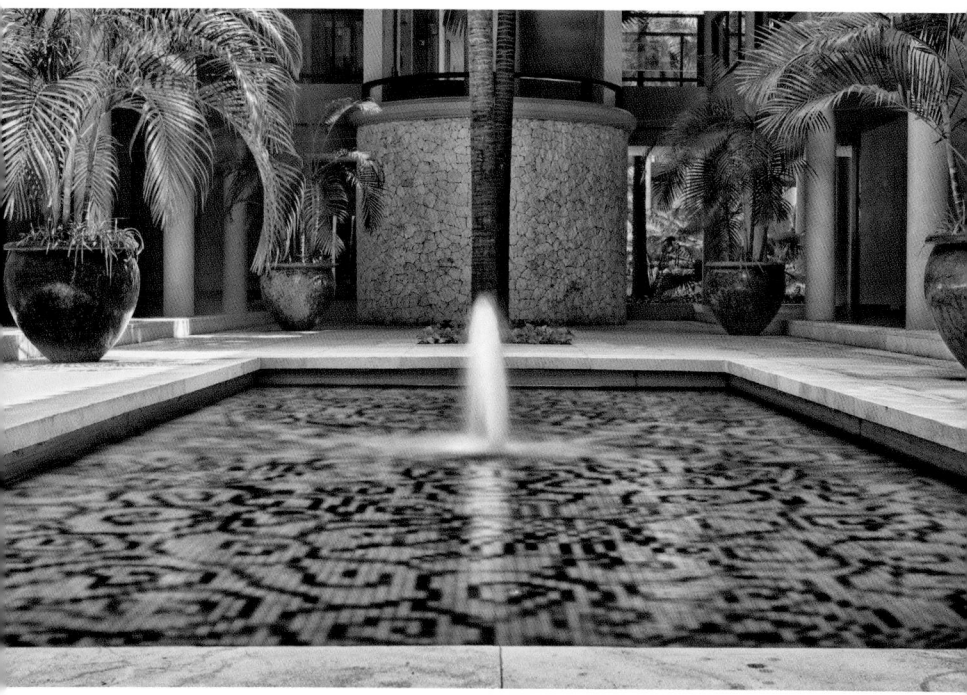

Figure 81: **Exposure time** (1): Long exposure times allow you to blur movements and smooth out surfaces of water. This image was shot with the 35mm f/1.4 lens. I used a software program called Nik HDR Efex Pro to compose it out of three different brightly exposed images to circumvent the sensor's limited dynamic range. Each individual image was taken with an exposure window of several seconds. Not only is the surface of the water soft and smooth, but the fountain is also a haze thanks to the motion blur induced by the slow shutter speed. The aperture setting (f/11) created an appropriate depth of field for the scene. Exposures such as these require the use of a tripod, or at least something stable to rest your camera on, and possibly a neutral density gray filter.

In shutter-priority mode, you can set the shutter speed dial to your desired value, choosing exposure times that range from 1/4000 second to one second, with each step on the dial twice as fast (or slow) than the step before it. You can also opt for intermediate steps by using the left and right selector keys. For example, if you turn the shutter speed dial to 250 for 1/250 second, you can then use the left and right selector keys to choose the values 1/200

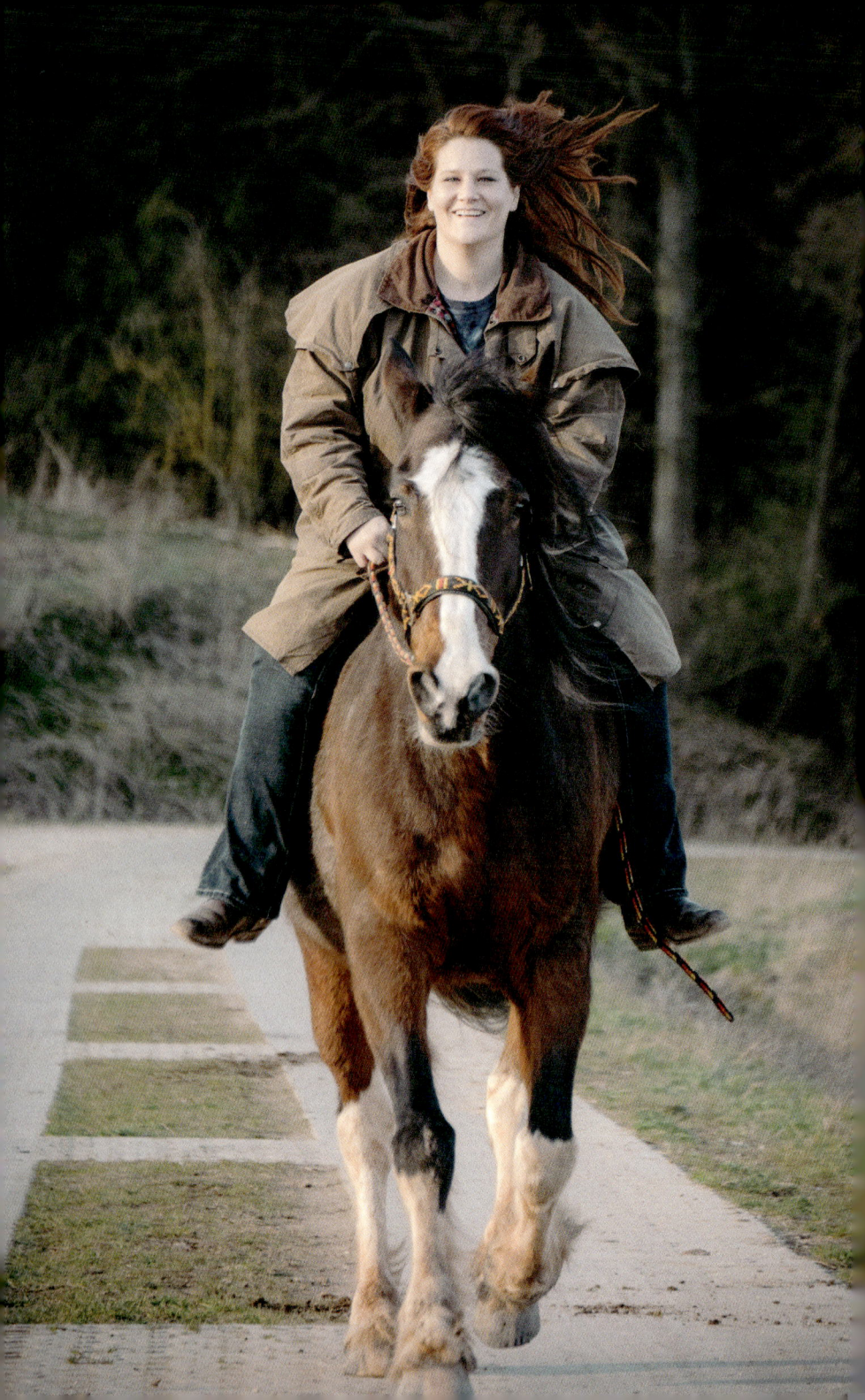

◀ Figure 82: **Exposure time** (2): Short exposure windows allow you to freeze action shots. This image was shot with an X-E1 and a prototype of the 55–200mm zoom lens at 128mm with an aperture of f/4.5. The 1/800-second exposure time succeeded in making time appear to stand still.

and 1/160 as well as 1/320 and 1/400 second. Whichever value you select will be displayed on the monitor or in your viewfinder.

To use exposure times of longer than 1.5 seconds, turn the shutter-speed dial to the T setting and use the selector keys to choose an exposure window up to 30 seconds long.

TIP

Go to SHOOTING MENU > LONG EXPOSURE NR to turn on a setting that will reduce noise and improve image quality in long-exposure shots. This doubles the effective time that the camera needs to work on an image, however.

MANUAL EXPOSURE M

In manual mode, you select both the aperture and the shutter speed. Neither the lens aperture ring (or aperture mode switch) nor the shutter-speed dial should be set to A, and you will see an M for manual mode indicated on the active camera display.

IMPORTANT

You can't rely on the live histogram when setting the aperture and shutter speed in manual mode. Instead, you need to pay attention to the exposure indicator on the left side of the monitor.

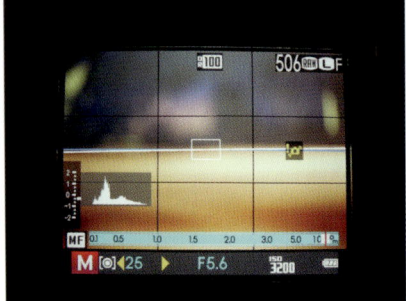 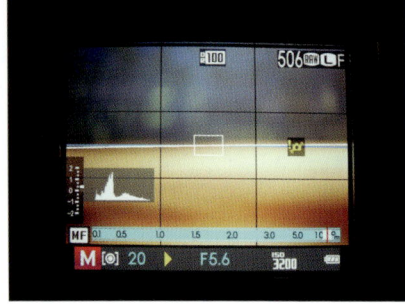

Figure 83: When the camera is in manual mode, the live histogram doesn't show the distribution of tonal values for the image that is actually captured. You should thus ignore it and instead heed the digital exposure indicator on the left side of the display to figure out whether your aperture and shutter speed settings will under- or overexpose the image (in relation to the exposure measured by the camera). In this example, the scale for the image on the left shows a slight underexposure (when using an exposure time of 1/25 second), and the scale for the image on the right reveals a slight overexposure (when using an exposure time of 1/20 second). To take a picture in manual exposure mode that is optimally exposed from the perspective of your camera, you need to adjust the aperture and shutter speed so that the marker in the exposure indicator is located at 0. In the other exposure modes, this scale functions as an indicator for the exposure compensation (see section 2.3.2).

As with shutter-priority mode, you can also work with longer exposure times in the manual mode by setting the shutter-speed dial to T. The upper limit here is also 30 seconds.

You can use even longer exposure times when working in the manual exposure mode by setting the shutter-speed dial to B, for bulb. With this setting, the shutter will stay open for as long as your finger holds the shutter button down. Since using your finger is cumbersome and can easily lead to images ruined by camera shake even when using a tripod, it's much better to use a commercially available, lockable cable release that you can screw into the camera's shutter button. In addition to that, the X-E1 also allows for several electronic shutter remote control options (see section 1.4).

The maximum exposure window when using the bulb setting is 60 minutes. Again, going to SHOOTING MENU > LONG EXPOSURE NR and turning this feature on will deliver long-exposure images with less noise and fewer problems (for example, hot pixels will be eliminated). As mentioned previously, however, this feature will double the processing time for each exposure, because after each capture, the camera requires the same amount of time again to run the so-called dark-frame subtraction process.

COLOR CODES AND EXPOSURE CONTROL

Everything is so colorful! The camera displays the values for aperture and shutter speed on the monitor or in the viewfinder in white, blue, yellow, or red. What do all these colors mean? Let's quickly go through each exposure control mode:

Program Automatic

Aperture and shutter speed ▸	Camera-determined settings; exposure is okay.
Aperture and shutter speed ▸	The user has altered the camera-determined settings by using program shift; exposure is okay.
Aperture and shutter speed red ▸	The exposure is either under- or over-exposed; exposure is not okay.

In program automatic mode the values for aperture and shutter speed will appear in red when an image is still overexposed, despite using an exposure time of 1/4000 second and the smallest possible aperture, or when an image is still underexposed, despite using an exposure time of 1/4 second and the maximum aperture. When this situation arises, you'll need to use a different ISO setting (section 2.5).

Aperture-Priority A

The camera displays your manually selected aperture in `blue` in this setting.

Shutter speed `white`   ▶   Exposure time is less than 1 second; exposure is okay.

Shutter speed `yellow`   ▶   Exposure time is between 1 second and 30 seconds; exposure is okay

Shutter speed `red`   ▶   The maximum exposure time of 30 seconds is not sufficient; exposure is not okay (underexposure), or the minimum exposure time of 1/4000 second is insufficient; exposure is not okay (overexposure).

Red shutter speed values indicate that you should use a different aperture so the camera can select a shutter speed that will lead to a properly exposed image.

Shutter-Priority S

The camera displays your manually selected shutter speed in `blue` in this setting.

Aperture `white`   ▶   Camera-determined aperture based on the shutter speed; exposure is okay.

Aperture `red`   ▶   The camera can't select an aperture that works with the selected shutter speed; exposure is not okay (either under- or overexposure).

When you receive a red aperture value, you should choose a different shutter speed so your camera can select an appropriate aperture.

Manual Exposure

Aperture and shutter speed `blue`

▶ User-determined settings; the exposure status is indicated in the exposure scale.

Shutter speed `yellow`

▶ Exposure time is between 1 second and 30 seconds; the exposure status is indicated in the exposure scale.

When an exposure time is longer than the inverse of the selected focal length (based on a conversion to the classical 35mm format), the camera provides a shake warning in the viewfinder or on the monitor in the form of a small yellow camera symbol. When you're using the 60mm f/2.4 lens, for example, this warning will appear with an exposure time of longer than 1/90 second. When you're using the 35mm f/1.4 lens, it will appear with times longer than 1/50 second.

To counteract camera shake you can employ a tripod or stable base, steady yourself against something, or opt for a shorter exposure time—or, if available, switch on the optical image stabilizer (OIS) of your lens. There's no universal rule because some photographers have hands that are shakier than others.

2.3.2 METERING

This much you already know: your camera features a manual exposure mode as well as three additional exposure control options that enable it to determine an appropriate aperture and/or shutter speed automatically. But how does the camera "know" which exposure settings will work? And how do photographers know if the camera is right or if they need to intervene to correct the exposure settings?

I will forestall any potential illusions you may develop right at the start: the camera doesn't know what the correct exposure for a scene is. The best it can do is to guess, which is why you and your camera have three methods of metering light: multi metering, average metering, and spot metering. Don't expect miracles from these sophisticated (in some ways) methods, though.

With all three metering methods, the camera portrays uniform black or white subjects as almost equal middle gray areas.

But don't take your camera back to the store out of frustration. There's nothing amiss here; all cameras function this way. In practice you will need to correct the camera's exposure settings now and then—for example, when you'd like to photograph a white field of snow or a pitch black wall. And if you happen to be shooting a black wall in the middle of a white field of snow, then your manual adjustments will be especially critical. Later in the book, you'll learn how to handle situations like these, but first let's discuss how the camera's three metering methods work.

MULTI METERING

Multi metering, which is also often called matrix metering, is the camera's most sophisticated light metering method—and the most popular. The camera divides the image into many small fields (a matrix) and analyzes the composition, color, and brightness of each area. This information is then compared with saved templates of common subjects (such as a backlit face or a snow-covered winter landscape) to determine the correct exposure. Multi metering usually produces good results and is the best choice when you need to work quickly or don't want to devote a lot of thought to your exposure settings.

AVERAGE METERING

Average metering is in some ways the brainless op-posite of multi metering: it generates a mean exposure value for the entire frame area. This method lends itself particularly well to landscape photography and tends to produce images that are conservatively exposed. Average metering only rarely produces overexposed pictures, so it can be helpful when shooting a sky with bright clouds, for example. On the other hand, you will often need to brighten up dark and middle tones afterward when edit-ing your images. We'll touch on this topic again later.

SPOT METERING

Spot metering only factors in information from a small point in the middle of the image, which amounts to ap-proximately 2% of the entire image frame. Due to view-finder parallax, you should avoid using this method in combination with the optical viewfinder of the X-Pro1 when shooting subjects that are relatively close to your camera. Spot metering determines the exposure of the measured area of your image as though it were a gray card with 18% reflectance. The camera assigns a medium brightness to the metered area (middle gray) that corre-sponds to Zone 5 in the Zone System, developed by Ansel Adams for balanced exposure.

In scenes with difficult lighting conditions, such as a backlit portrait, spot metering can help you portray a part of your picture in the best light. If the area of the scene in question is not located at the center of your shot, first me-ter it with the center of the frame (by pressing the shutter button halfway), then turn the camera to your final desired position while keeping the shutter button halfway down.

Spot metering can be a powerful tool, but it can also lead you astray. This is a mode best used when you have time to set it up for a specific subject, not when you need to point and shoot quickly.

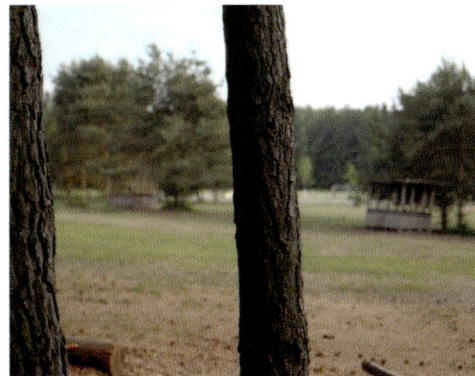

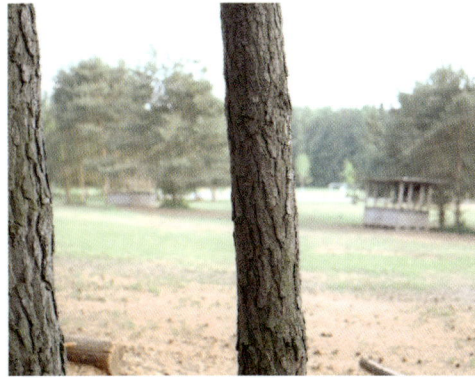

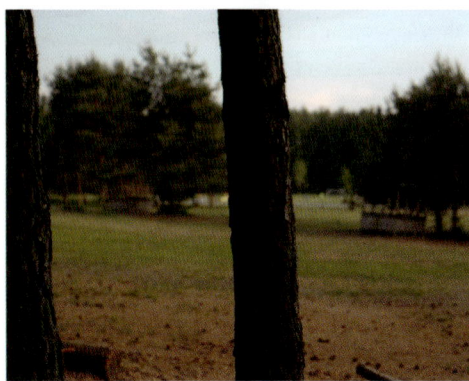

Figure 84: Light metering methods: This example illustrates how the camera's three different light metering methods work. This high-contrast test scene features a foreground with a dark tree trunk, a much brighter empty field, and a sky with very bright clouds. When using multi metering (top), the camera analyzed the contents of the image frame and decided on a (somewhat lazy) compromise: the tree trunk still shows some detail, the field is properly exposed, and the sky is overexposed, appearing white and devoid of almost any detail.

Spot metering (middle) homed in directly on the dark tree trunk and assigned it a middle gray value. This resulted in a tree trunk that is (artificially) light while the remaining elements in the image are even brighter. This method resulted in several areas for which the sensor couldn't capture any detail at all.

Average metering (bottom) assigned greater value to the large bright areas of the image than to the dark tree trunk. The result is a much more conservative exposure and a darker image. Here we see detail in the sky for the first time, but the tree trunk now appears underexposed.

At first glance you might not agree, but the average metering produced the best results in this instance, despite the underexposed areas. While blown-out highlights are impossible to fix, blocked-up shadows can be rescued with image-editing software. More on this in the following pages.

Which light metering method is best? In our example (figure 84, which was admittedly and intentionally difficult), none of the methods produced particularly compelling results. In the end, the metering performance has less to do with the method than the photographer—his or her abilities, habits, and needs.

I personally use multi metering predominantly and switch over to the spot and average methods in specific situations that play to their strengths, such as landscape shots for average metering and difficult light situations that require additional attention for spot metering.

What it comes down to is finding the appropriate correction for the camera's metered exposure. The camera's live histogram is a useful tool here. More on that in a moment; next I would like to describe how you program the camera's light metering methods.

SELECTING A METERING METHOD

Press the AE button on the left side of the camera's back and choose multi, spot, or average metering with the left and right selector keys. Confirm your choice by pressing the OK button, by pressing the shutter button halfway, or by pressing the AE button again. You will see a symbol in the viewfinder or on the monitor that indicates the metering method that is currently active.

EXPOSURE COMPENSATION

You can surmise the importance of exposure compensation just by observing that Fuji endowed the X-Pro1 and X-E1 with a mechanical dial solely for this purpose in immediate range of the right thumb on top of the camera. This exposure compensation dial allows you to adjust the camera's metered and suggested exposure up or down by two exposure values (EV) in increments of 1/3 EV. The camera displays the level of compensation on the exposure scale found near the left edge of the viewfinder or monitor display.

Unfortunately, the digital indicator for the compensation correction is not particularly conspicuous, which means that often you will inadvertently forget to change the correction setting from one shot to the next. Make a habit of checking the indicator in the viewfinder or the actual compensation dial before snapping each new exposure— it may happen that the compensation dial was accidentally shifted in your equipment bag or when you were changing out a lens.

EXPOSING CORRECTLY WITH THE LIVE HISTOGRAM AND EXPOSURE COMPENSATION

As we've already seen, the "correct" exposure isn't always the best one—as is the case when photographing a white wall. In reality, we often have to improve on the camera's best effort. To some degree, this is a question of experience: veteran photographers instinctively know how the camera will behave in certain circumstances and make appropriate adjustments. Others play it safe and make use of the automatic exposure bracketing (DRIVE button > AE BKT). The most common tool for mirrorless system cameras such as the X-Pro1 and X-E1, however, is the live histogram, which delivers useful guidance in every exposure mode except manual.

The live histogram is available to you in the custom viewfinder or monitor display. If needed, press the DISP/BACK button to navigate to this viewfinder display from your current one. Make sure that you have the histogram activated by going to SHOOTING MENU > DISP. CUSTOM SETTINGS and that the X-Pro1's energy saving mode (SET-UP) is turned off.

The live histogram reveals the approximate distribution and frequency of tone values in an image before the sensor captures it. The left side of the histogram shows the black and dark tonal values, and the right side shows the white and bright ones. The spaces in between correspond to the various intermediate values. The higher the levels for each area of the graph (i.e., the taller the peak), the more frequent those particular brightness values occur within the image frame.

Remember that the live histogram doesn't work properly in the manual exposure mode (**M**). In this mode, you'll need to rely on the exposure scale and your own experience. The histogram also does not produce reliable results with very dark subjects in the three other exposure modes (**P**, **A**, and **S**).

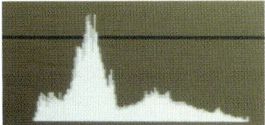 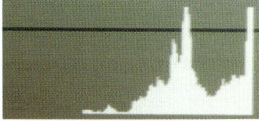 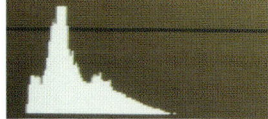

Figure 85: By using the live histogram, you can identify over- and underexposed areas of an image—and make the corresponding compensation adjustments—before you press the shutter button. The example on the left shows a well-balanced exposure: the tonal values are evenly distributed and they don't extend beyond the left (dark) or the right (bright) sides of the diagram. The example in the middle is another story: here the peaks pile up on the right side of the histogram. This is an indication of overexposure, as is the clear gap on the left side of the graph (where the shadows are indicated). In cases like this, it's necessary to reach for the exposure compensation dial to move those peaks from the right. The example on the right corresponds to a conservatively exposed image. In this case, you need to ask yourself whether this effect is intentional (as it might be, for example, if you're shooting a dark subject that shouldn't look artificially bright). If it's not, then you can correct the exposure using the steps described above to balance the distribution of tonal values. In particular, photographers who work with external RAW development software can counteract these exposure conditions with the compensation dial. This practice is sometimes called ETTR, for expose to the right, which you can read more about in section 2.7.

The live histogram reveals the brightness distribution for your subject. You can examine this distribution more closely by taking a test shot and having a look at the result in the detailed display of the playback mode (press the DISP/BACK button). Let's look closely at the three images I shot using the different metering methods, giving particular attention to their respective playback histograms.

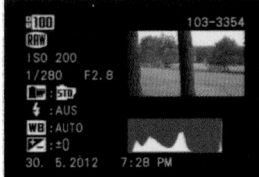 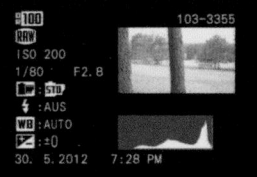 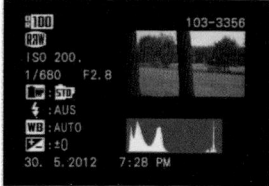

Figure 86: **Comparing the histograms of the three metering modes:** In the example on the left, which was the multi metering method, the camera attempted a balancing act. About two-thirds of the histogram represent the landscape, then there is a gap, and on the right edge you can see the values for the sky pile up, signaling overexposure. Though you can't see it in this still shot, the camera also indicates this overexposure with a blinking warning on the areas of sky shown on the monitor.

The example in the middle demonstrates the result from spot metering. The obviously overexposed sky is now indicated on the histogram with an even thinner white stripe at its right border. On the monitor, the camera shows an exposure alert with a blinking warning over the entire area of sky. The dark tree trunk, which the camera used for metering the shot, is represented by the hill in the middle of the histogram (and is exposed with a brightness equivalent to middle gray).

On the right is the image created with average metering. Here you can see the values for the sky in the histogram, indicating that these areas aren't overexposed. There is accordingly no blinking warning on the camera monitor. You can tell, however, that the remaining areas of the image—the trees and the field—are somewhat crunched on the left side, while there is a large empty space on the right side of the graph. You can also see a bit of room to the right of the values for the sky, which means a brightness compensation of +1/3 EV can optimize this image and shift the sky values just over to the edge of the histogram's range.

How can we create a correctly exposed and attractive photo out of this high-contrast example? It's easy: by using a combination of the best possible exposure and the appropriate processing of the captured RAW file.

We can optimize the exposure by using average metering and setting the compensation dial to +1/3 EV. Doing so shifts the brightness values for the sky, which are critical to the image, to the right edge of the histogram. That means the sky is still within the sensor's functional range. The other tonal values that are located on the left side of the histogram will get a bit more air and be exposed more brightly.

Since we're shooting on the FINE+RAW setting, we have the additional choice of processing the image with the internal RAW converter or using an external one.

Opting for the internal RAW converter (PLAYBACK MENU > RAW CONVERSION), we use the following settings to adjust the standard JPEG parameters: film simulation Astia, highlight tone medium soft, shadow tone soft. These settings reduce the contrast and boost the dark areas particularly well. More information about JPEG settings can be found in section 2.7.

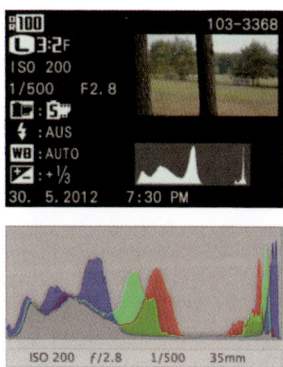
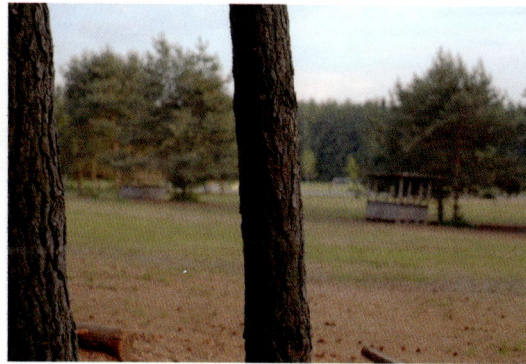

Figure 87: We can bring the contrast of our test image under control by using the average metering method, adjusting the default JPEG parameters (film simulation Astia, highlight tone medium soft, and shadow tone soft), and applying an exposure compensation of +1/3 EV. The dark and bright areas of the image have kept their detail and the gap that existed between the main subject and the sky in the histogram is much smaller now. Next to the screenshot of the camera's playback display, I've included an illustration of the RGB histogram produced by the image-editing software Apple Aperture 3, which shows more detailed information on the JPEG file that I transferred to my computer. You can further optimize the image with this editing software, or—as I discuss in section 2.6—by extending the dynamic range of the exposure.

Using an external RAW converter, you can manipulate the tonal values stored in an exposure almost at will. The example in figure 88 was created in Adobe Lightroom 4, a program that's very popular with photographers.

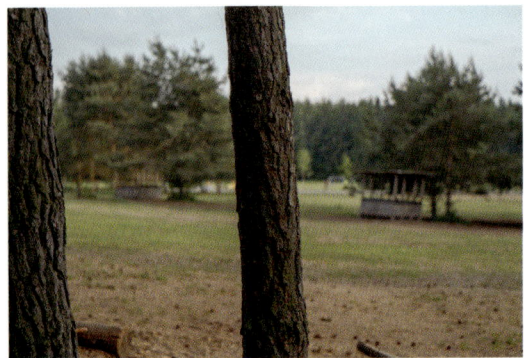
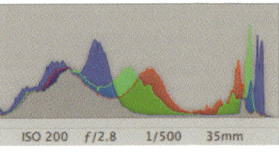

ISO 200   f/2.8   1/500   35mm

Figure 88: You can use Adobe Lightroom (or any other compatible RAW converter) to manage difficult lighting situations. In this case I was even able to fill in all the gaps in the histogram and create a seamless gradation of tonal values between the main subject and the sky. It's worth mentioning that this is only possible when the necessary image information is present in the RAW file, especially in the highlights. If the image data for the highlights is lost (as a result of overexposure), the best RAW converter in the world won't be able to bring it back.

AUTOMATIC EXPOSURE BRACKETING

When you're not certain about how to expose an image or how much to compensate the exposure for a specific situation, you can use the automatic exposure bracketing feature. The camera will then take three exposures with different exposure settings in short succession. You can decide which image turned out best when you examine the results in playback mode (detailed display) or on your computer.

Press the DRIVE button and select AE BKT to use this feature. Here you will need to select one of three available options: ±1, ±2/3, or ±1/3. Confirm your selection by pressing the OK button, tapping the DRIVE button again, or pressing the shutter button halfway. Now your camera will take not just one image, but three: one with normal exposure (based on your current settings) as well as one corrected up and another corrected down by 1/3, 2/3, or 1 EV.

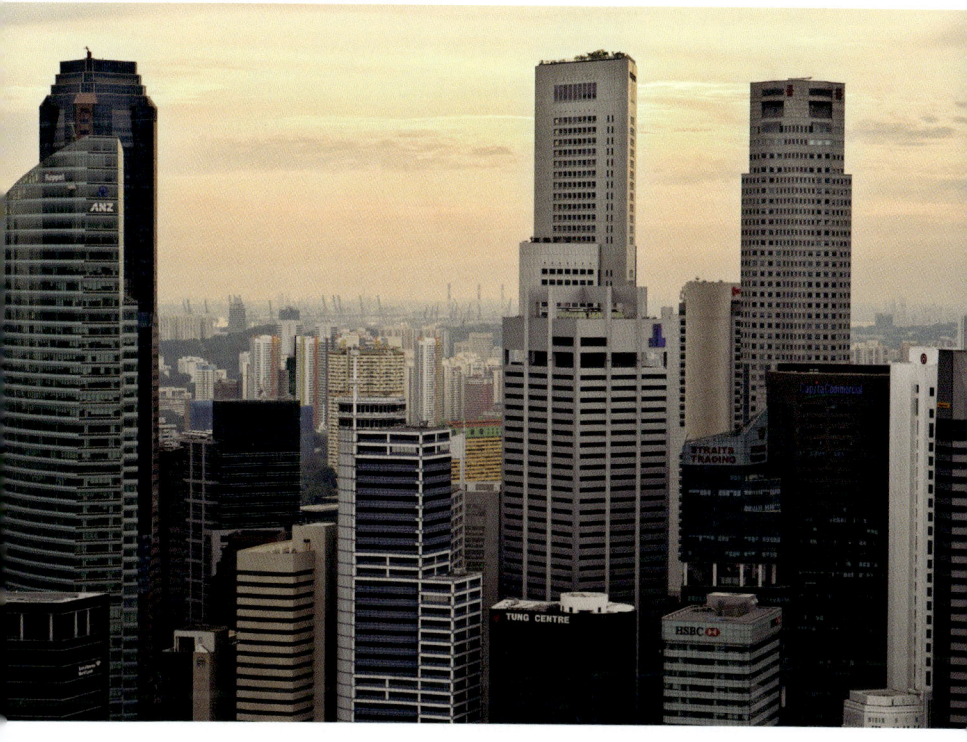

Figure 89: **Playing it safe with automatic exposure bracketing:** Determining the optimal exposure for a subject right off the bat can be more difficult than it sounds. Using the automatic exposure bracketing feature, you can snap three images in rapid succession so that each exhibits different exposure characteristics. Then you can examine the results and decide which is the best exposed. This function lends itself best to static subjects that won't run away from you and situations that don't require you to release the shutter at a precise moment. I shot this high-contrast image with a preproduction camera and preproduction 60mm f/2.4 lens at ISO 200 and ended up selecting the version that was compensated −1/3 EV as the best.

This feature also has one quirk: after you press the shutter button, the camera locks up until all three exposures of the bracketing are completely saved to the SD memory card. If you are using the image quality settings I recommend—FINE+RAW—this process can take several seconds. This is another reason why I recommend using the fastest memory card on the market.

HDR EXPOSURES

High dynamic range (HDR) pictures are a common use for images resulting from automatic exposure bracketing. HDR images are made up of several individual shots that were each exposed differently and composited to create a final picture with a large dynamic range. Photographers usually achieve this by using HDR software such as Photomatix Pro from HDRsoft or HDR Efex Pro from the plug-in provider Nik Software (now a part of Google).

The automatic exposure bracketing feature of the X-Pro1 and X-E1 is not ideal for HDR images, because it only produces three individual shots with a maximum exposure variance of ±1 EV. This wouldn't suffice for many serious HDR applications because many subjects exhibit a wider contrast or a larger dynamic range than you can capture with just three images. Those who excel at HDR photography often use up to seven exposures exhibiting an additional exposure variance of ±3 EV in 1 EV increments.

You can produce this kind of range on the X-Pro1 and X-E1 by using the automatic exposure bracketing feature in combination with the exposure compensation dial. You'll need to use a tripod, or at least a very stable base for your camera, and you shouldn't adjust your image frame until the process is complete.

For example, complete the following steps to create a series of seven shots with exposures of −3, −2, −1, 0, +1, +2, and +3 EV in relation to the camera's automatic metering.

- Press the DRIVE button and select AE BKT with the option ±1.

- Take the first three exposures of your subject.

- Now set the exposure compensation dial to +2 EV.

- Take the next three exposures of your subject.

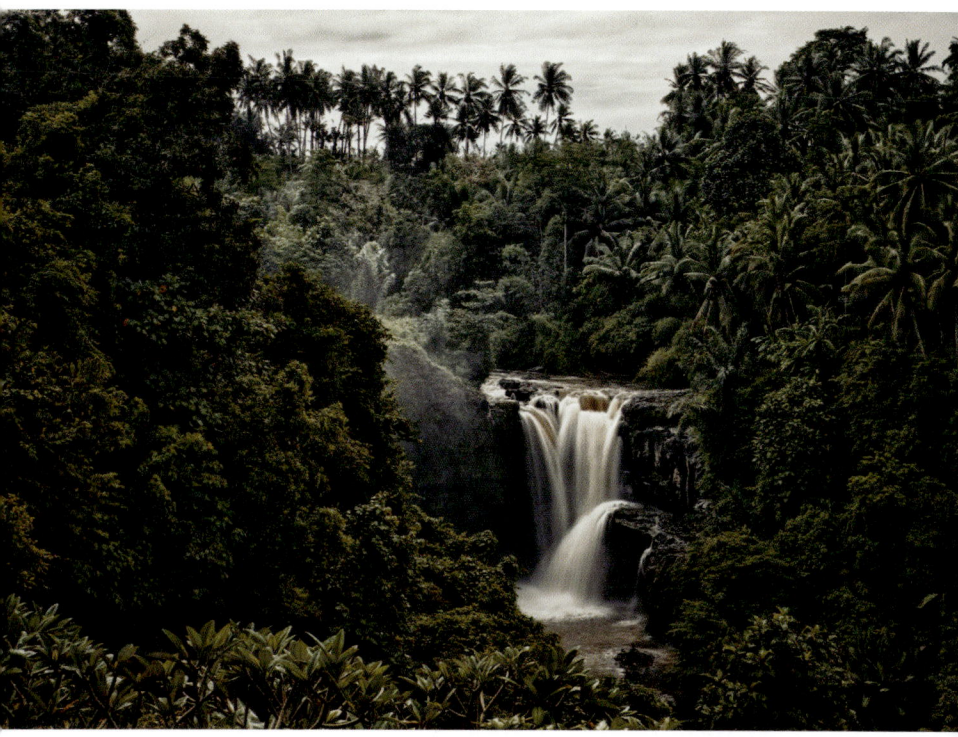

Figure 90: Automatic exposure bracketing combined with the compensation dial: To photograph this rain forest idyll, I mounted my X-Pro1 on a small table tripod. In order to slow down the shutter speed, I attached an ND1.8 neutral density filter to the 35mm f/1.4 lens, which effectively allowed me to slow the shutter by a factor of 64 by blocking six stops. I snapped seven exposures with a preset aperture of f/8 (in aperture-priority mode and with multi metering), exhibiting exposure compensation levels of –3, –2, –1, 0, +1, +2, and +3 EV. Then I transferred these JPEGs to my computer and used HDR Efex Pro to assemble an HDR image with a significantly increased dynamic range and added some final touches with Apple Aperture 3.

- Now set the exposure compensation dial to –2 EV.

- Take the last three exposures of your subject.

You now have nine frames stored away at seven different levels of exposure. The images that were corrected by –1 EV and +1 EV were snapped twice, so you can select whichever version turned out better. When you're not sure, opt for the exposures from the initial three-shot burst, since they were snapped in shorter succession and have less potential to exhibit ghosting. Ghosting is the result of objects or people that have moved between the individual exposures. When the individual images are composited, anything that has moved will appear as a translucent "ghost" in multiple locations.

HINT

When combining multiple automatic exposure brackets, your camera may automatically adjust the white balance for each series of shots. If you plan to use an external RAW converter to develop your pictures later, this isn't a problem, because you can bring the white balance settings back in line later. But if you plan to transfer the finished JPEGs from the camera directly to an HDR imaging program, it's wise to lock the white balance before getting started. You can learn more about the topic of white balance in section 2.7.

2.4 FOCUSING WITH THE X-E1 AND X-PRO1

Like most compact and system cameras, the X-Pro1 and X-E1 rely on contrast detection autofocus (CDAF) technology. This focusing method has several advantages over the phase detection autofocus (PDAF) method used by single-lens reflex cameras:

- CDAF systems are very accurate and require no adjustment. There are no front- or back-focus issues (in contrast to DSLR cameras).

- In principle, with CDAF the entire area of the image sensor is available for AF metering, even near the edges.

- AF frames can be defined in almost any number, shape, size, and position. This allows you to focus directly on your desired target without needing to reframe the shot.

CDAF also has significant drawbacks in comparison to PDAF technology:

- CDAF systems like the one in your camera work more slowly than PDAF systems. They're also not able to track subjects that move toward the camera or away from it. In other words, the camera can't predict where a fast-moving subject will be at the moment of exposure.

- CDAF systems focus best on high-contrast surfaces while PDAF systems focus best on edges. Photographers who are used to shooting with DSLRs will need to reorient themselves and shouldn't expect the autofocus to behave similarly to the AF system in a single-lens reflex camera.

The X-Pro1 and X-E1 offer two autofocus modes: AF Single (AF-S) and AF Continuous (AF-C). These two modes are only modestly different from auch other because the camera's AF system is not capable of tracking objects in anticipation of where they're going to be. The most commonly used mode is AF-S because it offers the most flexibility. There is also the option to focus manually (MF). You can tell the camera which mode to use by adjusting the focus mode selector on the front of the camera to the desired setting: S, C, or M.

FUNCTIONALITY
It's helpful to understand how the camera's CDAF works so you can use it effectively. The principle is straightforward, and hinges on one idea: from the camera's perspective, an object is optimally in focus when its contrast is greatest.

Imagine you're standing in front of a wall that's been painted with the black-and-white pattern of a chessboard. If the wall is not in focus, you won't see clearly defined squares of black and white; you'll see blurry gray areas—some lighter and some darker. The more clearly you focus on the wall, the sharper the edges of the squares will become; the contrast will increase. At the point of optimal focus, the edges will finally be sharp as a knife and exhibit maximum contrast.

CDAF works very similarly: it focuses until the object in the current AF frame exhibits the greatest degree of contrast. The camera doesn't know which direction to focus, so it just guesses. If the contrast increases, the focusing mechanism continues in that direction. If the contrast decreases, it tries the other direction and continues until it has passed its goal and the contrast begins to diminish again. Then it changes its direction again, iteratively back and forth until it settles on the optimal (i.e., highest-contrast) position.

This process takes time (and energy), which is why the
CDAF method is somewhat slower than the efficient
PDAF method used in single-lens reflex cameras. It is,
however, more precise.

PRACTICAL AUTOFOCUS TIPS

Here are some practical tips based on the functionality of
CDAF and the construction of your camera:

- Contrast-detection technology works best and quickest
  when the AF frame is aimed at a high-contrast subject.
  Whenever possible, avoid focusing on low-contrast,
  monotone subjects in low-light circumstances and opt
  instead to target high-contrast objects.

- Don't focus on the edges of objects. Instead try to fill
  up the AF frame completely with your targeted object.

- When shooting a low-contrast subject in dim lighting,
  use the camera's built-in AF-assist lamp. Turn this
  on by navigating to SHOOTING MENU > AF ILLUMI-
  NATOR. With this option activated, the camera will
  automatically shine the assist light in poor lighting
  conditions, which will lead to noticeably better AF performance with subjects that aren't too far away from
  the camera. Do note, however, that this lamp won't
  turn on when silent mode is activated. To turn silent
  mode on and off, hold down the DISP/BACK button for
  a few seconds.

- As an alternative to the AF-assist lamp, you can use a
  flashlight or any other light source to briefly illuminate
  your subject while focusing and then save the focus
  setting by pressing the AE-L/AF-L button.

- Make sure that there aren't any objects in the AF
  frame that are positioned at different distances from
  the camera. Otherwise, there is a risk that the camera

will settle on the wrong object or even fail to find a satisfactory point of focus (after searching for a while). In the latter case, the AF frame border will turn red instead of its usual green to indicate an AF warning.

- When in the AF-S mode, you have the choice of two submodes: Multi and Area, which you can select by going to SHOOTING MENU > AF MODE. As a general rule, you'll probably want to use Area AF since this is the only mode that allows you to define the size and location of the AF frame manually. You can also quickly switch back and forth between the Multi and Area AF submodes in the Quick Menu (Q button) or define an Fn button accordingly. To reassign the function of an Fn button, hold it down for a few seconds.

- A general rule when using the AF-S mode: make the AF frame as small as possible and as large as necessary. The camera allows you to use five different-sized AF frames when shooting in Area AF and when using the EVF or the LCD monitor. To change the size of the AF frame, press the AF button when in shooting mode and turn the command dial. To revert the AF frame back to its standard size, press the command dial. After you've determined which size you would like to use, confirm your choice by pressing the AF button again or pressing the shutter button halfway. To repeat: circumstances permitting, use the smallest possible AF frame; only choose a larger one when the targeted area is too low-contrast for a smaller one. To enable one-handed operation, it's possible to assign the function of the AF button to one of the camera's two Fn buttons.

- Another tip for working with the single autofocus (AF-S): when shooting with the Area submode, take advantage of the opportunity to define the location of the AF frame manually. Press the AF button (or a reassigned

Fn button) and then use the four selector keys to
pick one of the EVF or LCD monitor's 49 available AF
frames. Make your selection based on where the target
area of focus will be in your image. This will save you
from needing to retarget the camera after focusing and
prevent the uncertainties attendant with this method.
Post-focus pivoting ("focus and reframe") is popular
with DSLR photographers but can lead to focus errors
because of the resulting shift in the focus plane (especially with subjects that are relatively near the camera),
short focal lengths, and an open aperture. To jump
directly back to the central AF frame, you can simply
press the OK button instead of using the selector keys.

• When it comes to focusing on small or critical objects,
keep in mind that you should work with either the EVF
or the LCD monitor. The OVF in the X-Pro1, as already
discussed, is affected by parallax and subsequently
has only 25 AF frames available, and their size can't be
changed. My earlier advice to turn on the corrected AF
frame by going to SHOOTING MENU > CORRECTED
AF FRAME is helpful here; it should always be activated, but you'll only be able to focus with true accuracy
by using the EVF or the LCD monitor. Make use of the
viewfinder selector to switch between the OVF and the
EVF when focusing. It's often safer to focus precisely
on a specific detail with the EVF, then lock the focus
setting with the help of the AE-L/AF-L button, and
finally switch to the optical viewfinder to snap the image. Of course, users of the X-E1 don't have to worry
about this.

• The most precise method of focusing is the MF mode.
Even here, you can press the AF button to define a
desired part of the frame for the focus and then use the
AE-L/AF-L button to bring that area into focus automatically. The camera will indicate successful focusing

with a beep. Then activate the magnified viewfinder by pressing the command dial, and use the focus ring on the lens to fine-tune the focus manually. Turn the command dial to cycle between two different magnification levels.

Now let's take a closer look at the individual focus modes.

SINGLE AUTOFOCUS (AF-S)

The single autofocus (AF-S) is the most commonly used method for focusing automatically with the X-Pro1 and X-E1. To set the camera to operate in this mode, move the focus mode selector on the front of the camera to S.

The single autofocus has two submodes: Multi and Area AF. You can switch between these two options by opening up SHOOTING MENU > AF MODE. As an alternative, you can use the Quick Menu (Q button) or assign the AF submode selection to one of the Fn buttons by holding it down for a few seconds.

The AF-S mode with the Multi option activated is more or less a fully automatic method for focusing. The camera determines by itself which of the 49 AF frames should be used. As soon as you press the shutter button halfway, the camera analyzes the current contents of the image frame and chooses a particularly high-contrast area that it attempts to bring into focus. If the camera executes this process successfully, a green AF frame will appear and a short beep will sound. If it is unsuccessful, the AF frame will turn red and you will see "AF!" in the viewfinder as a warning. The focus setting will remain stored (along with the exposure settings) as long as you keep the shutter button partly depressed.

One advantage of the Multi method is that it's relatively quick and reliable even in bad light and with low-contrast subjects. Another is that it's completely automatic; you don't need to think about it at all and you can literally shoot from the hip.

The decisive disadvantage of using the Multi submode is the fact that you don't know if the object that the camera focuses on is actually the part of your picture that you'd like to have in focus. This is a problem especially for subjects with different levels (foreground, middle ground, and background). This focus setting lends itself to shots in which the elements are all more or less the same distance from the camera, such as a group of people in front of a wall or a landscape panorama. It also can be useful in situations that don't allow you enough time to define the frame for the autofocus manually.

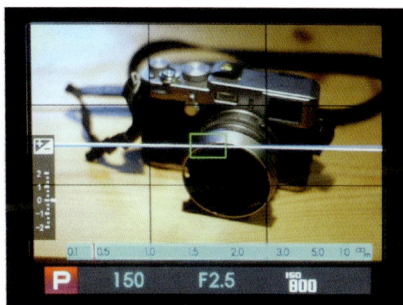 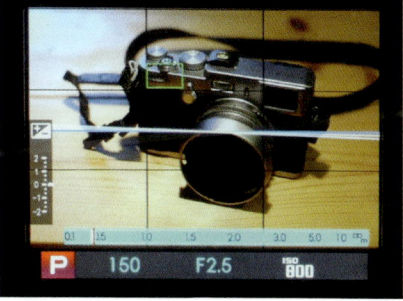

Figure 91: **Single autofocus (AF-S) and multi:** When programmed in this way, the camera will automatically pick an AF frame. The disadvantage: you don't decide which part of your image should be in focus—the camera does. In this example, the camera could decide to focus either on the lens or on the body of this X100.

The second submode of the AF-S, Area AF, requires that you (not the camera) select one of the 49 AF frames (in the X-Pro1's OVF only 25 are available). When you press the shutter button halfway, the autofocus will bring the area you have identified into focus. Everything else functions exactly like in the Multi submode (green or red AF frame, confirmation beep, AF warning, focus lock, etc.). Press the AF button to define your desired AF frame in the AF-S Area submode, and then use the left, right, up, and down selector keys to choose from the 49 (or 25 in the OVF) AF frames. If you're shooting with the LCD monitor or EVF, you can also adjust the size of the AF frame by turning the command dial. There are a total of five different sizes available. Pressing the command dial resets the AF frame back to its original size, and pressing the OK button returns the frame back to the center. To confirm your settings for the location and size of the AF frame, press the AF button again or press the shutter button halfway (a quick tap will do). A white border will now indicate the AF frame in your desired location and at your desired size when you look through the viewfinder or at the LCD monitor.

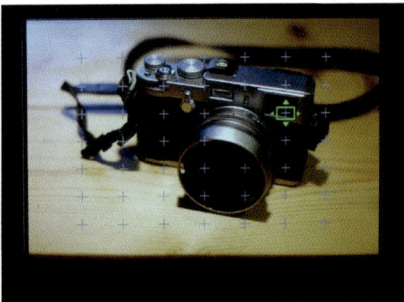 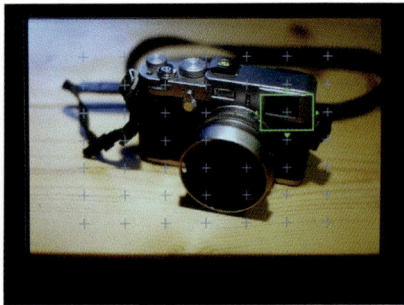

Figure 92: **Single autofocus (AF-S) and area:** With this setting you must program the size and position of the AF field yourself. Press the AF button and use the selector keys to adjust the location of the AF frame and the command dial to adjust its size.

My recommendation, again, is to make the AF frame as small as possible and as large as necessary. The reason for this is fairly obvious: the smaller the AF frame, the more precise the AF system can be in targeting the object within the frame. Don't aim at edges—try instead to direct the autofocus to an object that fills the entire area of the AF frame. If there is more than one high-contrast object in the selected AF frame, the camera won't know which it should bring into focus.

This method will only work when the surface pattern of the object framed by the smallest-possible AF field size provides enough contrast and detail for the camera to run its focusing system successfully. If this isn't the case, it's advisable to increase the size of the AF field and give the camera more to work with. The X-Pro1 and X-E1 allow you to pick from five different AF frame sizes for good reason. Make use of them!

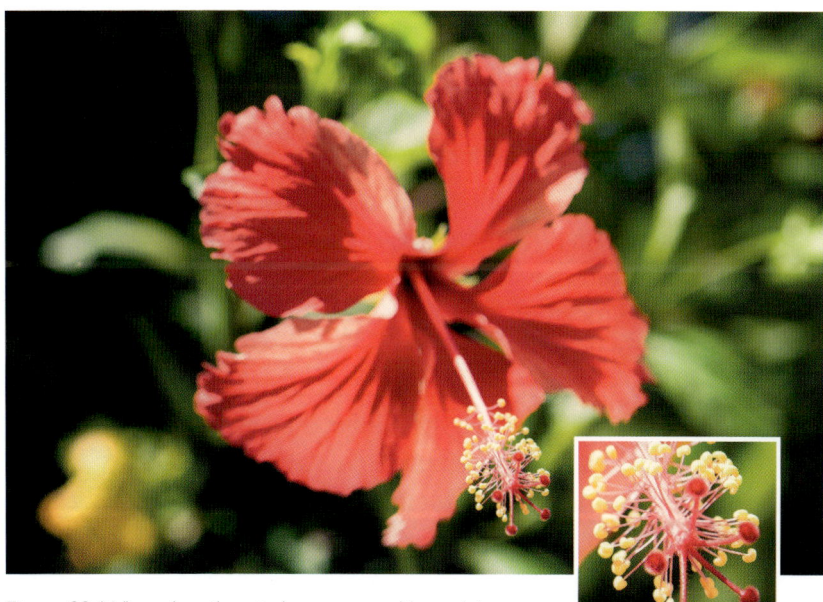

Figure 93: When shooting at close range with a minimum depth of field, it's especially important to use the smallest AF frame possible and to direct the autofocus to the exact area of the image that you would like to have in focus. Doing so will mean you can avoid needing to reframe after focusing, which will increase your chances of attaining a razor-sharp result. I shot this example image with the XF60mmF2.4 R Macro lens and an aperture of f/4 while holding the camera. I then developed the RAW data using Adobe Lightroom 4 and Apple Aperture 3.

X-Pro1 users should use the EVF or the LCD monitor when precise focusing is paramount. Because of the unavoidable parallax effect, the optical viewfinder is too inaccurate for critical work. For less critical subjects (e.g., large, distant objects or landscapes), the 25 autofocus frames in the OVF are perfectly sufficient.

In any case, X-Pro1 users should turn on the corrected autofocus frame for the OVF by going to SHOOTING MENU > CORRECTED AF FRAME and selecting ON. With this option activated, the camera will display two borders for every AF measuring frame—one solid and one made of dashes. The solid border indicates the position of the AF frame for objects that are far away (at infinity); the dashed border that is somewhat below and to the right corresponds to the focus region for objects nearby. After you successfully focus on an object by pressing the shutter button halfway, a third, green AF measuring frame that is adjusted for parallax will appear between the other two—this green border indicates the actual position of the AF frame based on the detected distance of the target. If the green frame surrounds the area or object that you want to be in focus, then you're all set. If it doesn't, then abort the shot and try again with an adjusted image frame.

The distance indicator in the viewfinder display can be another clue as to whether or not the camera focused correctly. For example, if you've targeted an object that is less than two yards away, but the camera's distance scale indicates five yards, then something has obviously gone awry.

When the camera starts to focus on an object in AF-S mode, it always makes its first attempt at the last used or found distance setting. For instance, if the last object you focused on was two yards away, then the camera starts its next focusing effort with that exact distance setting. You can thus improve the performance and speed of your autofocus by presetting the AF before an all-important moment. To do this, locate a subject that is at about the same distance as your eventual target and start the focusing mechanism by pressing the shutter button halfway. When your actual subject appears in the scene (e.g., a playing child), the autofocus will have less work to do and will therefore be able to find its target faster and more reliably.

CONTINUOUS AUTOFOCUS (AF-C)

With continuous autofocus (AF-C), the camera constantly works to focus on the central area of the image frame marked with a crosshair—even when you don't have the shutter button halfway depressed. All you need to do is point your camera at any target.

This function is often misunderstood. Photographers switching from DSLRs often confuse it with predictive object tracking, which the contrast detection autofocus in your camera is not capable of performing. AF-C actually performs more like the method that I described in the previous tip: it attempts to focus constantly on the approximate distance of whatever object is targeted in the crosshair. This method enables the camera to focus quickly and reliably when needed because the autofocus usually only has to make a small adjustment to get from the preset focus to the actual current one.

This mode also has some disadvantages: it requires lots of energy (the AF is constantly in action, after all), and only the central AF field is available for use—the size and position of which can't be adjusted. Furthermore, you can only speculate about the actual size of the AF frame in this mode based on the ambiguous crosshair (the actual size may be variable and expand as the camera sees fit).

That said, AF-C is able to perform faster and more reliably than AF-S in certain critical situations (poor lighting, low-contrast subjects, shots in close proximity). For subjects that prove challenging for the AF-S, it certainly can't hurt to switch over to the continuous autofocus and test it out.

THE AE-L/AF-L BUTTON

When you press the shutter button of the camera halfway, it meters the light and activates the autofocus based on the subject currently in the image frame. Both values—exposure and the distance determined by the autofocus—stay saved as long as you keep the shutter button pressed halfway down.

In practice, though, many photographers prefer to execute and save each of the two values independently. The X-Pro1 and X-E1 (like many other cameras) offer the AE-L/AF-L button for just this reason: with its help, you can determine and save the exposure and/or focus settings without needing to hold your finger on the shutter button.

AF-L stands for autofocus lock, AE-L for auto exposure lock. By using this button, you can easily apply the same focus and/or exposure settings to more than one shot.

You can program the exact functionality of the AE-L/AF-L button yourself in the shooting menu. Go to SHOOTING MENU > AE/AF-LOCK BUTTON to program the button to meter and save only the exposure, AE LOCK ONLY; to apply only to the focus setting, AF LOCK ONLY; or to save both values, AE/AF LOCK. In the SHOOTING MENU > AE/AF LOCK MODE submenu, you can decide how you want the camera to save these values. One option is to have it save them only for as long as the AE-L/AF-L button is pressed (AE&AF ON WHEN PRESSING); the other option is to have the button function as a switch (AE&AF ON/OFF SWITCH). If you select the latter option, the camera will save the exposure and/or autofocus settings when you first press the button and they will stay saved until you press the button another time.

It's your choice how to program this button to suit your habits, preferences, and assignments—that's the reason these options exist. In practice and often when I'm shooting, the following option presents itself as a logical setting: AF LOCK ONLY and AE&AF ON/OFF SWITCH. The reason? It's often desirable to separate the focus setting from the automatic exposure. While the circumstances affecting exposure constantly change (your image frame shifts a tiny bit or a cloud wanders in front of the sun), it's often desirable to use an optimal focus setting for several exposures of the same subject without needing to start the focusing process from the beginning for each image in the series. A green AF frame will appear in the viewfinder or on the LCD monitor if the autofocus is locked.

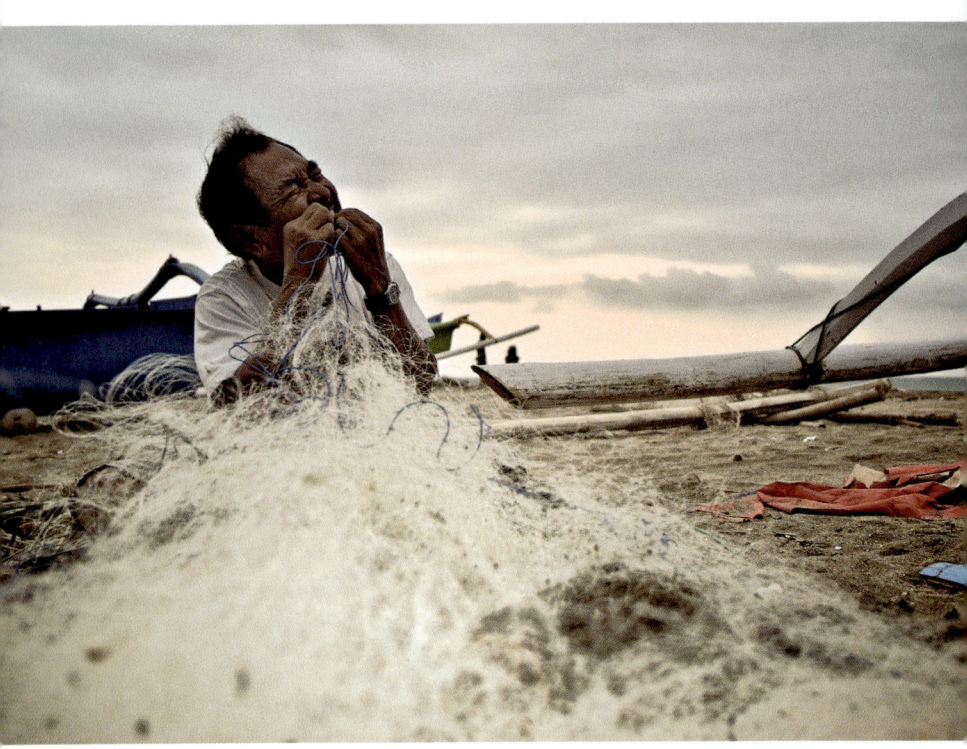

Figure 94: An example of a practical use for the AF-Lock function: The charm of this image depends in part on snapping the exposure at just the right moment. To achieve this with the camera's relatively sluggish CDAF system it is often best to establish and save the autofocus setting for the subject in advance of the actual exposure(s). In this instance, I programmed my camera for AF LOCK ONLY and AE&AF ON/OFF SWITCH following the logic I just described. Next I set an appropriate size and location for the AF frame and pressed the shutter button halfway to focus on the fisherman's head. When the camera had brought the frame into focus, I pressed the AE-L/AF-L button to lock the focus setting. Now I was free to shoot an entire series of exposures that show the fisherman in various moments. Keeping the shutter button halfway depressed now was only for the purpose of saving the exposure settings—the focus settings remained constant. If the fisherman had changed his position, I would have expunged the saved focus settings by pressing the AE-L/AF-L button again, focused the camera on his new position, and then saved the updated focus settings with another press of the AE-L/AF-L button. With practice, this process will become second nature and you will only need to run the camera's precise but time-consuming autofocus when you actually need to. If you use this method, you'll be able to capture critical moments with success more often and you'll be able to apply an optimal focus setting to more than one image in a series.

The AE-L/AF-L has its pitfalls too: if the button is activated, it will lock up any changes to the exposure settings even when used in the way I've recommended, with
AF LOCK ONLY selected. Any adjustments made to the
lens's aperture ring or the exposure compensation dial
have no immediate effect. You can still adjust these rings
and dials mechanically with the AF lock active, but the
adjusted settings won't become active until the moment
you release the AF lock. To get around this firmware
quirk, you need to quickly turn the AF lock off and then
on again. This will cause your new exposure settings to
become effective.

Don't worry, though: as long as you don't press the
shutter button halfway down, the current focus settings will
stay saved, even if you temporarily disable the AF lock.

IMPORTANT

In AF-S or AF-C mode, the camera does not establish and
save a new focus setting each time you turn on the AF lock
by pressing the AE-L/AF-L button. It instead saves and locks
whatever the current focus parameters are (i.e., the last-
used focus setting). However, in the button's other function
as AE lock (i.e., storing the exposure metering), it does take
and save a new light measurement as soon as the AE lock is
turned on with a press of the AE-L/AF-L button.

FOCUSING IN THE DARK

Low-light conditions make contrast less detectable—a
fact that can naturally pose some problems for a CDAF
system. The quick fix for this is to increase the contrast
for the subject you intend to photograph with artificial
light. The camera offers an AF-assist lamp for just this
purpose, which you can activate by going to SHOOT-
ING MENU > AF ILLUMINATOR and then selecting ON.
Since this light shines mostly on the center of the image

area, it's best to position the AF frame in a central location when using it. Do note, however, that the AF illuminator doesn't function in silent mode, which you can turn on and off by pressing the DISP/BACK button and holding it for several seconds. When silent mode is active, the camera doesn't make noise, and also disables the flash and any auxiliary lights.

An alternative to using the AF illuminator is to use temporary lighting such as a flashlight or switching on the light in a room. Then the autofocus can establish the correct reading and you can save it by using the AF lock before turning off your temporary light. Make sure that you have the AE-L/AF-L button programmed to lock only the focus settings (AF LOCK ONLY); otherwise the camera may (incorrectly!) use an exposure setting based on the temporarily brightened conditions.

If the subject you intend to capture is so far away that the AF-assist lamp or another temporary light source wouldn't help improve its contrast, you can try to focus on another object that is about the same distance from you but exhibits a stronger contrast. Set the focus based on this object and save it with the AF lock. This also works for situations in which you don't want to call attention to yourself with the AF-assist lamp, in which case it's wise to turn on the silent mode just to be safe. You can also give the AF-C mode a try if the AF-S is unable to attain sharp focus on a stubborn subject.

The manual focus mode (MF) is a last resort for photographing difficult subjects.

MANUAL FOCUS (MF)
Turn the focus mode selector on the front of the camera to M if you wish to shoot in the manual focus mode. When you're shooting in MF mode, the autofocus is not entirely inactive. Quite the opposite: pressing the AE-L/

AF-L button initiates the autofocus search. If the camera successfully establishes a focus reading, it will sound a brief tone, and you can then use the automatically determined focus as a starting point and make small adjustments using the lens's focus ring. The magnified EVF (or LCD display) can be a big help when you're focusing manually, since it shows an enlarged portion of the image frame. To toggle the magnified viewfinder on and off, press the command dial when in MF mode. To cycle between the two magnification levels, turn the command dial left or right.

To select the part of your image frame that you would like the camera to bring into focus, and to enlarge it when you use the magnified viewfinder, proceed in the same way that you would in the Area AF-S mode. First press the AF button; then use the four selector keys to select your area of choice. The OK button automatically relocates the highlighted area back to the central frame position in this mode as well.

Using the focus ring and establishing a focus reading with the help of the AE-L/AF-L button both function the same way, whether the viewfinder image is magnified or not. The order in which you use these three tools—AE-L/AF-L button, focus ring, and magnified viewfinder—and how often you use them is entirely up to you. You should, however, select an area of the frame to be brought into focus or magnified as soon as you start trying to focus manually for an exposure. Once again, this allows you to avoid ruining your focus by reframing the shot after fine-tuning the focus.

IMPORTANT

The magnified viewfinder won't be accessible immediately after shooting until your exposures are completely saved to the SD memory card. Since it's a good idea after taking a few shots to examine the last focus setting and do some fine-tuning, this limitation is rather unpleasant (and another reason to use the fastest memory card available).

By the way, the method for manual focusing described here also works when you use the optical viewfinder of the X-Pro1. If you're using the OVF, the camera automatically switches to the EVF when you activate the magnified viewfinder display.

The focus ring of Fujinon X-mount lenses is electronic. Employing this focus-by-wire technology means the focus mechanism won't have the immediate response that you're probably used to from working with mechanical lenses. After you turn the focus ring there is an ever-so-slight delay before the camera reacts. It therefore makes sense to use the AE-L/AF-L button as an aid when focusing manually and to rely on the focus ring principally for fine-tuning.

FOCUS PEAKING

Focus peaking can assist your manual focus efforts by highlighting the edges of those parts of a scene that are currently in focus. You can enable focus peaking by choosing SHOOTING MENU > MF ASSIST > FOCUS PEAK HIGHLIGHT, then selecting one of two different strength levels. Focus peaking is available in both standard and magnified views.

Alternatively, you can turn focus peaking quickly on and off by pressing and holding the command dial for a few seconds while the camera is in manual focus (MF) mode.

DISTANCE AND DEPTH OF FIELD INDICATORS

The distance scale displayed in the viewfinder and on the monitor features a small red stripe to indicate the (approximate) distance at which the focus is set. A white bar on this scale gives information about the depth of field (DOF) for the current exposure; it displays the range of distances from the camera in which objects will appear sharp in the final image.

When you're using an autofocus mode—AF-S or AF-C—this indicator is only available if the shutter button is pressed halfway. In the MF mode, conversely, the display is always available, but depth of field bar isn't meaningful until you press the shutter button halfway. This is because the camera, when in the exposure modes P (program automatic) and S (shutter-priority), only measures the final exposure value once the shutter button is partly depressed. This is when the camera chooses which aperture to use and consequently calculates the actual depth of field.

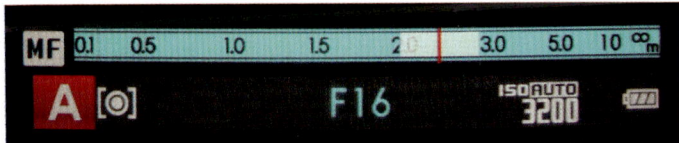

Figure 95: **Distance and depth of field indicator:** This scale is available in all exposure and focus modes. It conveys information about the focus setting (vertical red line) and the depth of field (white bar) based on the aperture in use. The depth of field indicator is very conservative and only marks the range in which objects retain the maximum focus in the final image, even when zoomed to 100%.

The focus distance indicator (vertical red stripe) is also helpful when you're using the OVF of the X-Pro1, because you can easily tell if the camera has focused incorrectly with just a quick look. If you're trying to shoot a portrait of a person who is two yards removed from your camera but the distance indicator displays that the focus is set at eleven yards, then something has obviously gone wrong.

There's some debate about the usefulness of the depth of field scale (i.e., the white bar in front of and behind the focus distance indicator). The reason? Fuji is particularly conservative with its methods and calculates the depth of field based on a circle of confusion with a diameter of just 0.005mm. More traditional depth of field measurements use the much larger basis of 0.02mm. Objects that fall within the depth of field that the camera indicates appear completely sharp even when enlarged to the pixel level (at the 100% zoom view). Please note that the XF14mmF2.8 R wide-angle prime lens features its own less conservative DOF scale, as described in section 1.2.

To get a real sense for the practical depth of field, you can assign an Fn button to preview it by pressing and holding the button for a second and then choosing PREVIEW DEPTH OF FIELD from the menu. Then, when you press the Fn button in the aperture-priority (**A**) and manual (**M**) exposure modes, the camera will stop down to the preset aperture and you can observe the depth of field in the EVF. When in MF mode, you also have the benefit of being able to use the magnified viewfinder display by pressing the command dial.

CLOSEUPS (MACRO MODE)

As you know by now, the X-Pro1's optical viewfinder (OVF) is affected by a parallax error that becomes more significant as the distance between the camera and your subject becomes shorter. At close distances, the auto-focus shuts down in the OVF. To continue using the AF,

Figure 96: **Balinese woman in temple:** ▶
Exposure parameters: X-Pro1, XF60mmF2.4 R Macro, f/3.6, 1/150 second, ISO 200. Developed from the RAW file with a beta version of RPP and polished off with Aperture 3.

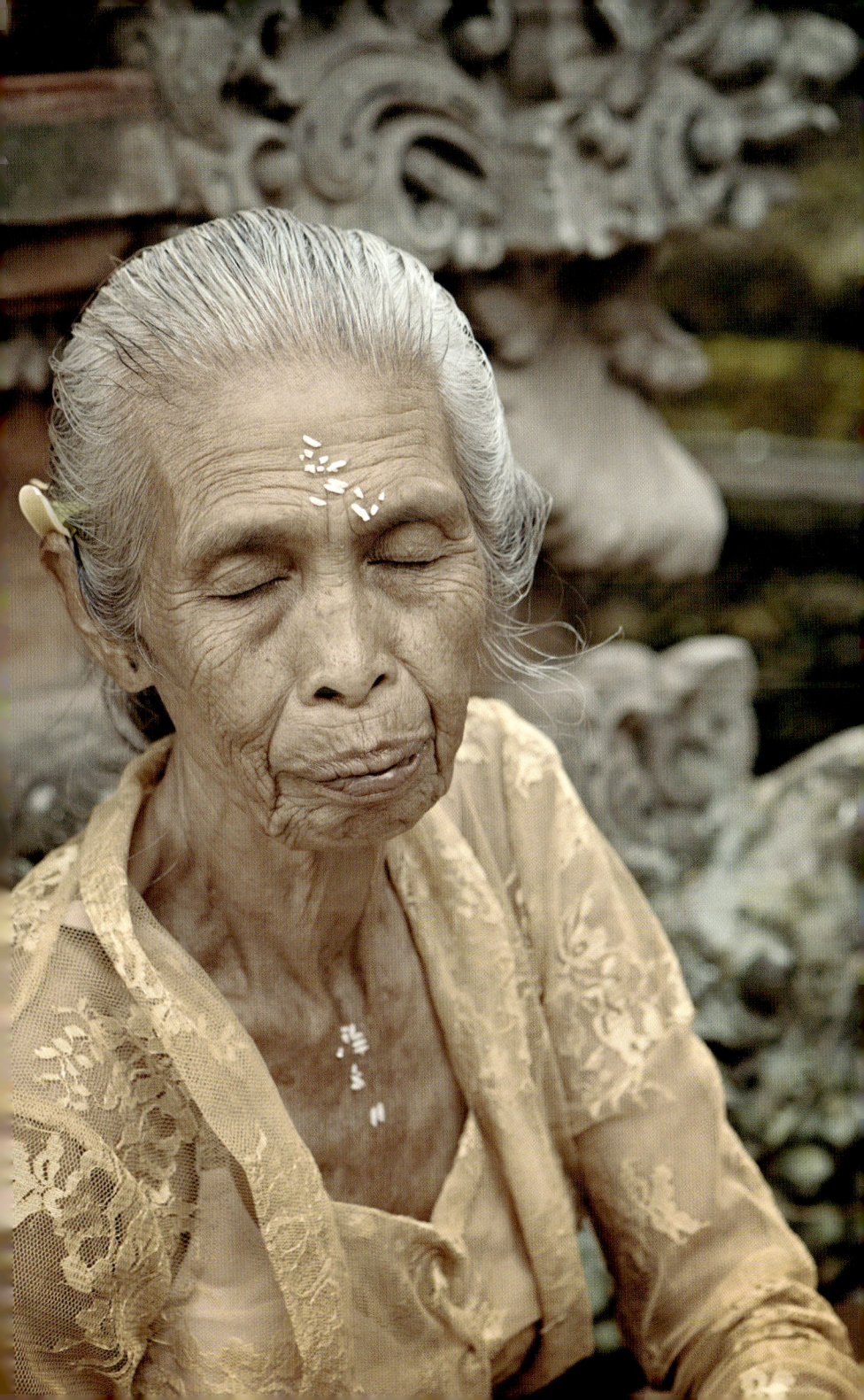

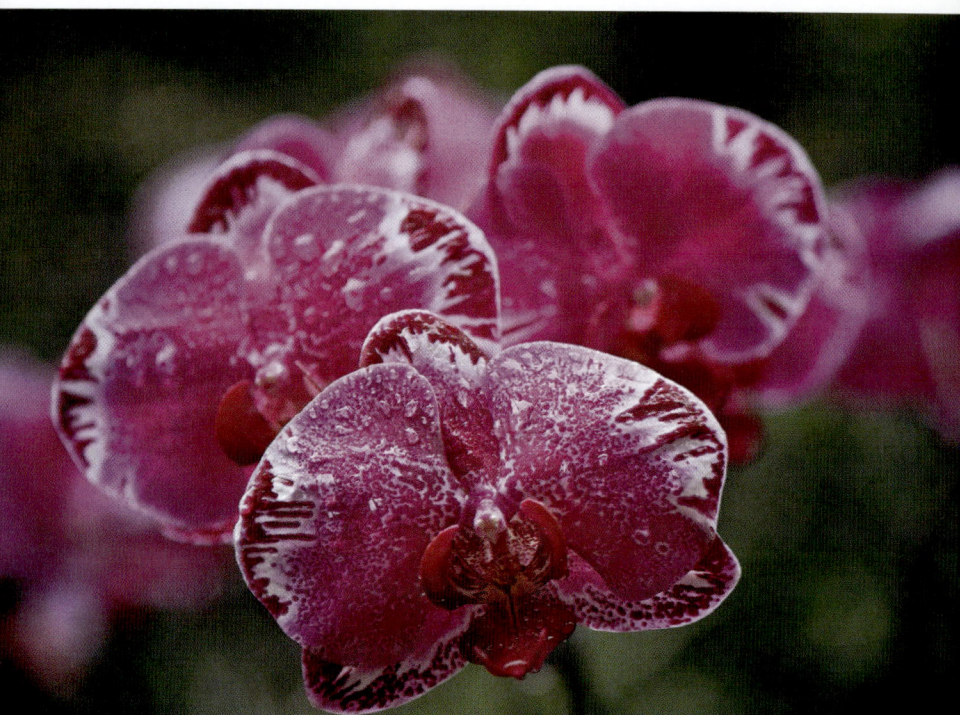

Figure 97: Precise focusing is paramount for macro exposures because of the shallow depth of field, as you can see in this image taken at the botanical gardens in Singapore. It's best to use a tripod (a piece of advice I follow all too infrequently). Use the AF button and the four selector keys to position the smallest possible AF frame directly over the portion of the image that you want to be in focus. Avoid needing to pivot the camera after establishing the focus to select a different image frame. Exposure parameters: X-Pro1, XF60mmF2.4 R Macro, f/2.4 (maximum aperture), 1/90 second, ISO 320.

you need to activate the macro mode for closeup exposures. The same is true when you go below the normal minimum focus distance of the EVF/LCD of your camera (X-Pro1 or X-E1) and lens.

While in shooting mode, you can turn the macro mode on by pressing the MACRO button on the back of the camera—a flower symbol will appear in the viewfinder and on the LCD monitor when it's turned on. As a shortcut, you can turn the macro mode on and off by tapping the MACRO button twice quickly and waiting for two seconds or pressing the OK button immediately (pressing the shutter button halfway works, too). The X-Pro1 automatically switches from the OVF to the EVF when you activate the macro mode.

When in the manual focus mode, you don't necessarily need to turn on the macro mode to shoot closeup subjects—the focus search that starts when you press the AE-L/AF-L button searches over the camera's entire focal range. In macro mode, however, both the X-Pro1 and X-E1 use a focusing method that is optimized for subjects in close proximity. So don't forget to turn off macro mode when you've finished capturing closeups.

FOCUSING ON FAST-MOVING SUBJECTS

How to focus on fast-moving subjects is a hot-button issue that tends to spark intense debate on the Internet. Disappointed expectations tend to fuel the issue—usually from photographers switching over from DSLRs, who demand that a CDAF camera behave in the same way as a PDAF single-lens reflex camera. The X-Pro1 and X-E1 can't live up to those expectations any better than any mirrorless system camera with a large sensor and CDAF. The oft-made assertion that the X-Pro1 and X-E1 are unsuited for action shots, however, is mistaken. Taking this type of exposure just puts an added bit of responsibility on the photographer.

Option 1: The Autofocus Trick

One way to capture fast-moving subjects with the X-E1 and X-Pro1 is to use the so-called autofocus trick. It's best to set the camera to AF-S for this method, which takes advantage of one of the camera's special features: if you press the shutter button all the way down in one motion—without stopping at the halfway point—the camera prioritizes the focus above anything else. In other words, if you "mash" the shutter button in one quick motion, the camera captures the exposure immediately after the autofocus settles on its target (or abandons its search).

Follow these steps:

1. Set the camera's focus mode to Area AF-S and switch to the EVF or LCD monitor.

2. Select an appropriate AF frame that you can use to follow the subject in your viewfinder.

3. Now track the subject in your viewfinder (and don't press the shutter button halfway). Make sure that the selected AF frame stays over the portion of your image frame that you ultimately want to be in focus.

4. Press the shutter button completely and hold it down as you continue to track your subject in the viewfinder and as you keep the AF frame located on the area you want to be in focus.

5. The camera will now focus on this portion of the subject and, as soon as the focus locks, expose the image. It snaps a shot, however, even if the autofocus search fails to settle definitively on anything. In this case, your result will likely be unusable.

This autofocus trick has an obvious disadvantage: the camera ultimately decides when the image is captured,

Figure 98: **Shooting with the autofocus trick:** This horse ▶ was trotting at the camera at a rate of around 12 mph. To capture it with the X-Pro1's CDAF, I set the camera to AF-S and then tracked the horse's head with my AF frame for 1 to 2 seconds while I held the shutter button completely down and waited until the camera locked its focus and exposed the image automatically.

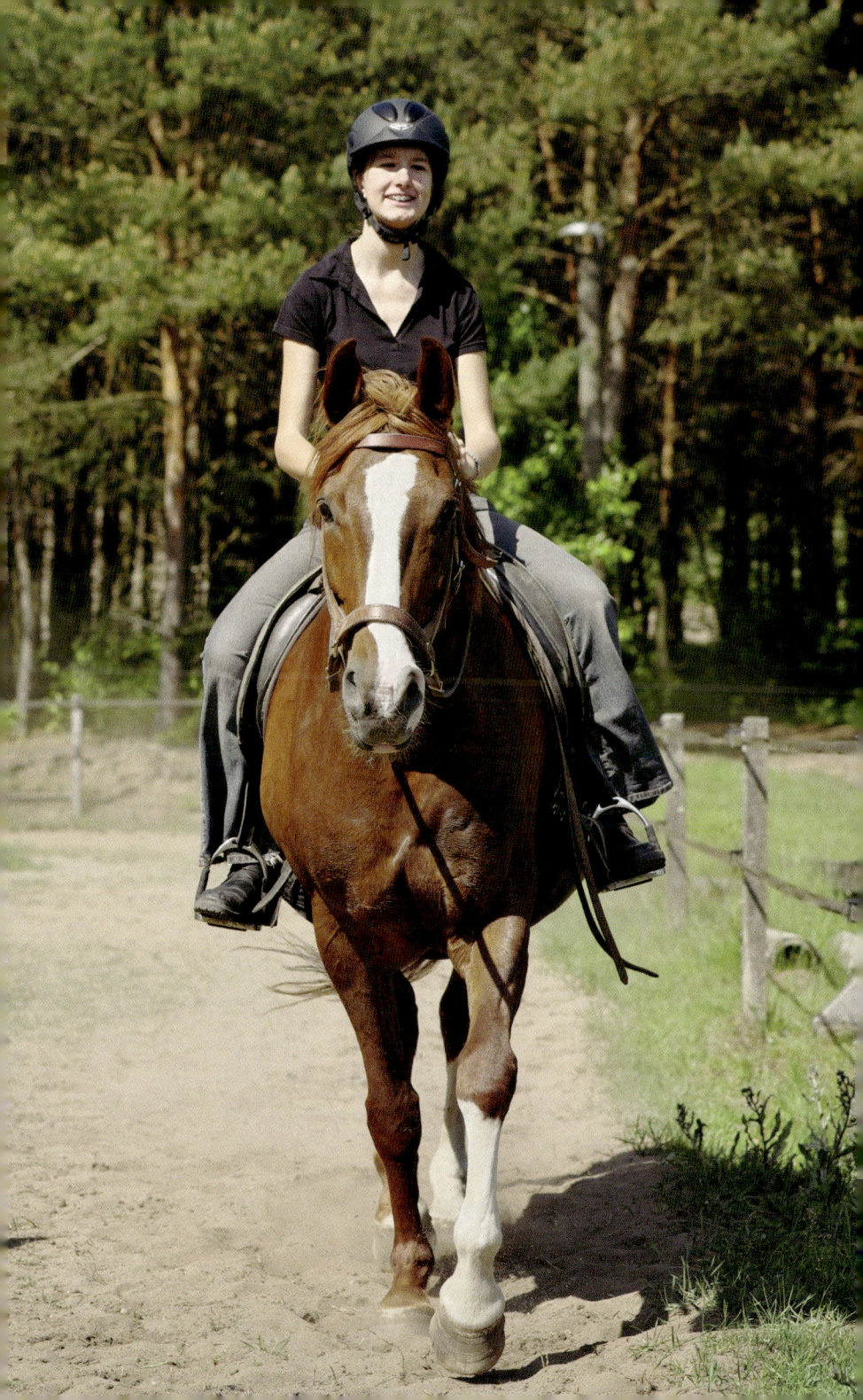

not the photographer. You can minimize the focus time (reducing the lag between pressing the shutter button and capturing the exposure) and increase the likelihood of a successful AF search by priming the camera and lens before the critical moment: press the shutter button halfway down to set the focus at the distance you anticipate for your moving subject at the moment when you would like to capture it.

You can also try to use the autofocus trick in tandem with the AF-C focus mode. If you choose this route, you will be limited to using the crosshair at the center of your frame as the position for your subject. This method, in other words, limits your choices when it comes to composing your shot.

Option 2: Pre-focusing on the Action

When using the autofocus trick, the photographer doesn't actually have the final say about when exactly the camera should capture an image; therefore it's better suited for situations when the exact timing is less critical than a sharp exposure.

If you would like to have control over the exact moment of exposure or if you're shooting a subject that's moving at a greater velocity, you can focus on the action in advance and then use the viewfinder to decide when the right moment to release the shutter is. Pre-focusing is best accomplished by using the MF mode to focus on an object that is approximately at the same distance from the camera as the subject you'd like to photograph. To reduce the trigger lag, press the shutter button halfway shortly before the exposure and hold it in that position until the right moment.

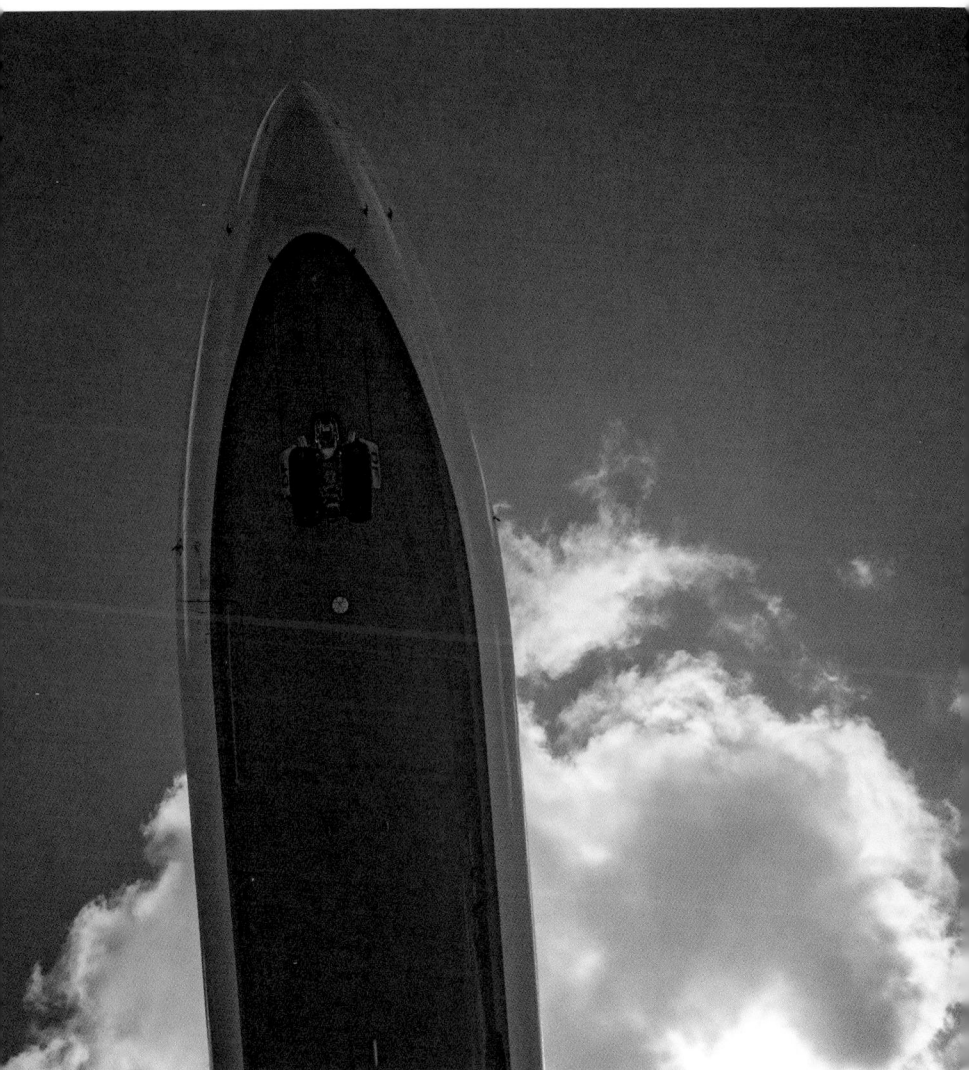

Figure 99: Focusing ahead of time: This shot of an Airbus A330 some 15 yards above my head as it came in for landing on the Caribbean island of St. Maarten came down to tiny fractions of a second. To successfully capture the moment with the XF18mmF2 R lens, I used the OVF of my X-Pro1 in combination with manual focus, which I set in advance by focusing on a beach hut that was also about 15 yards away from me. I tracked the approaching jet in the OVF, pressed the shutter button halfway to establish the metering and exposure shortly before the critical moment, and then pressed it down the rest of the way at just the right time. Exposure parameters: shutter-priority mode, f/4.5, 1/4000 second, ISO 200.

Option 3: Zone Focusing

Zone focusing is a variation of option 2. This method also calls for the use of manual focus. Instead of focusing on a specific distance, however, you focus on a range of the depth of field scale. In other words, you stop down the aperture until the depth of field is large enough to cover the zone in which you anticipate the action to occur.

This method of focusing is particularly popular among street photographers, and it was and still is often used with traditional rangefinder cameras. The depth of field indicator of an X-E1 or X-Pro1, however, is too conservative for many photographers. If that's the case, it makes sense to rely less on the depth of field indicator in the viewfinder and more on your experience and gut feeling. Or use one of the many DOF calculators that are available on the Internet and as smartphone apps.

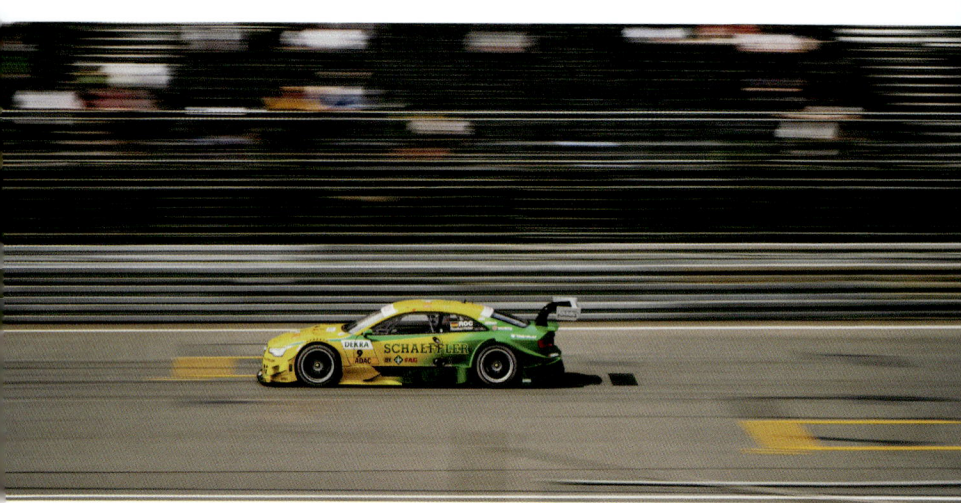

Figure 100: **In the zone:** The OVF of my X-Pro1 was very helpful in creating this classic spectator-capture at the DTM race at the Norisring. I shot in shutter-priority mode with a preset shutter speed of 1/60 second. The camera calculated an aperture of f/20. These settings in combination with the XF60mmF2.4 R Macro lens provided more than enough depth of field to cover a long stretch of the racetrack.

2.5 ISO, DETAIL, AND IMAGE NOISE

The image sensor in the X-Pro1 and X-E1 has a nominal sensitivity of ISO 200, making it twice as sensitive as standard sensors, which typically exhibit a sensitivity of ISO 100. You're probably familiar with ISO values from the world of analog photography, where they refer to film sensitivity. The more sensitive the film, the less light it requires for a properly exposed image. Sensitive films with high ISO numbers are therefore ideal for shooting at night or in poor lighting conditions. Their disadvantage is that they show both an increase in visible image grain and a decrease in resolution and dynamic range (i.e., the range of brightness tones). Photographers therefore use highly sensitive film only when necessary.

Digital cameras work similarly to film cameras in this regard, but you can't swap out the fixed image sensor with one that's more sensitive and able to use less light. Your camera's image sensor retains its nominal sensitivity of ISO 200 for every exposure, regardless of the ISO value you have set. If you set your camera to ISO 400, for example, the exposures captured by the image sensor will be underexposed by one exposure value, or in other words one f-stop. Selecting ISO 800 corresponds to an underexposure of two f-stops, ISO 1600 to three, ISO 3200 to four, and so on. In a similar manner, selecting ISO 100 means the sensor will capture an exposure that's overexposed by one f-stop.

If this is the case, why do our images appear to be correctly exposed regardless of the selected ISO setting? The camera manages this by carrying out signal amplification: it boosts the weak (i.e., underexposed) signal for the image by an amount that depends on the ISO setting you (or your camera) chose. This signal amplification inevitably results in a loss of image quality. It intensifies the desirable parts of the signal (the image data) as well as any noise or flaws. Increased ISO values, and their progressively stronger signal amplifications, make the blemishes in your images more clear.

The amplification of the captured image data can happen by analog and digital means. Fujifilm and other manufacturers use a combination of both methods: up to a certain ISO value, the camera uses the analog process and thereafter, the digital one. Then these data are saved in the RAW file. For still higher ISO values, the image data saved in the RAW file are digitally multiplied in the (internal or external) RAW converter. In each case, the brightness of the final image corresponds to the ISO "sensitivity" programmed on your camera.

By the way, the actual sensitivity of the image sensor in the X-Pro1 and X-E1 deviates a bit from its nominal sensitivity. Measurements from the well-respected website dpreview.com reveal that the image sensor's actual sensitivity is not at ISO 200, but is approximately 1/3 to 1/2 f-stop lower, corresponding to a sensitivity more along the lines of ISO 160. This won't affect your day-to-day shooting unless you're using an external exposure meter, in which case you'll want to configure it accordingly—by either using a lower ISO value or adjusting it with another correction.

The generous rounding up of the nominal sensitivity is something of a tradition with Fujifilm. The slide film Velvia 50, which was very popular in the 1990s, supposedly had a nominal sensitivity of ISO 50 but in reality was more like ISO 40. Ambitious photographers knew this and adjusted their cameras and exposure meters to ISO 40 to expose their images a bit more to counteract the weaker sensitivity of the film.

When shooting in the FINE+RAW mode, you can choose ISO values between 200 and 6400. But again, if you opt for an ISO value greater than 200 (either by pressing the Q button or by programming the Fn button to serve this purpose), you're not actually increasing the sensitivity of the sensor. Instead, you are reducing the exposure window and/or using a smaller aperture to lessen the amount of incident light that will reach the sensor. This necessitates a subsequent amplification of the reduced signal, which leads to a reduction in image quality.

How drastic is this loss in quality, and what does it mean for your photography? On this particular issue, you're in luck with your camera. Exposing images at high ISO values is among its greatest strengths. While other cameras with an APS-C sensor produce images with noticeable noise or an unfortunate loss of detail resolution, your camera can still produce truly respectable results.

Three factors contribute to this:

- The sensor benefits from new technology, and each new generation of sensors demonstrates better performance when it comes to image noise.

- The sensor's X-Trans color array weights the primary colors differently from the traditional Bayer pattern, improving the signal-noise-ratio.

- The internal RAW converter is very good. This affects not only the camera's representation of color, but also its noise reduction and detail reproduction.

The combination of these factors lets you create images with your camera and its APS-C sensor that are on par with those created by DSLR cameras that have substantially larger sensors, such as the Nikon D700 and the Canon EOS 5D Mark II.

ISO SETTING AND IMAGE QUALITY

Let's examine the image quality at various ISO settings with a test subject: a kitschy and particularly dusty Christmas figurine that's perfect for detecting image noise and detail reproduction.

The retention of detail and the reduction of noise are adversaries, and the RAW converter needs to strike a compromise between them. You can't have both in an image with a high ISO setting (i.e., a strong sensor signal amplification); either the noise can be reduced at the expense of fine details, or the subtle details can remain at the expense of an effective noise reduction. The critical factor is how well the camera's internal RAW converter is able to broker this compromise. Laboratory measurements only tell half the story here, because image quality in this case doesn't just depend on how measurable the reduction of noise is; it also depends on how visibly attractive or unattractive it looks to the human eye.

Attractive noise? The idea isn't so far-fetched when you consider that image-editing software allows you to simulate the effect of image grain characteristic of film to give digital exposures a more analog and organic look. Image grain—the analog equivalent of digital image noise—is sometimes desirable. If a camera can make the unavoidable image noise present in exposures taken at high ISO values have the appearance of grain, then it won't look as bad to a critical eye.

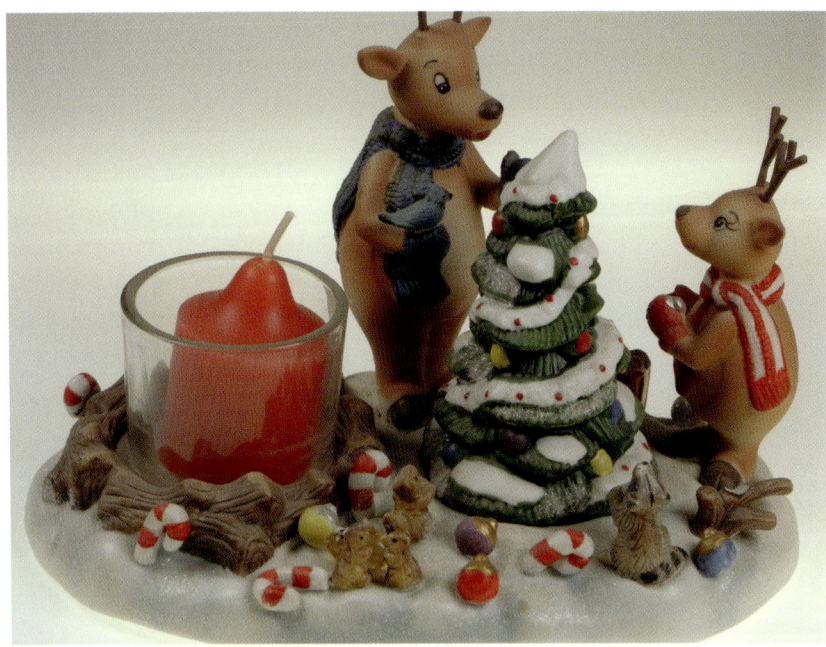

Figure 101: **ISO test series:** I chose this dusty test subject because it's well suited to demonstrating image noise (color surfaces, shadow areas), detail reproduction (fine particles of dust), and dynamic range (blown-out highlights) at different ISO levels (the example here shows ISO 200). The images were taken with the default JPEG settings and are available to view in higher resolution online at: www.dpunkt.de/XPro1/Abbildungen.

While many cameras with an APS-C sensor already produce visible image interference at ISO 3200, it's smooth sailing for the X-Pro1 and X-E1. Even exposures at ISO 6400 lend themselves pretty well to standard print and presentation sizes.

The camera also offers a so-called extended ISO range with values of ISO 12800 and ISO 25600, but you won't be able to save these images as RAW files. This extended range is only available when the RAW option is disabled and your camera is set to JPEG-only mode.

Why is this the case? What's hiding behind the extended ISO range? Not much, actually. At these two high ISO settings, the camera exposes RAW images at ISO 6400, but underexposes them by one or two exposure values and then boosts the exposure again when the image data is converted to a JPEG. You can achieve the same effect by setting your camera to ISO 6400, turning the compensation dial to −1 EV or −2 EV, and then using the internal or an external RAW converter to "push" the image one or two exposure values.

Employing the extended ISO values results in an unavoidable loss of quality, so you should only use them in emergencies. You actually retain more flexibility if you underexpose your image while shooting with ISO 6400 and FINE+RAW and then plan on adjusting the exposure manually during the RAW conversion.

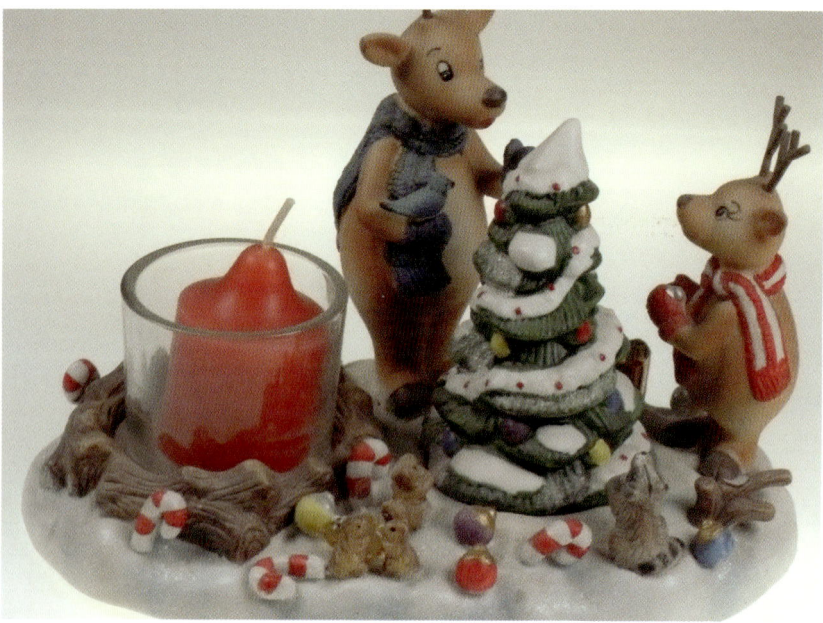

Figure 102: The test subject with ISO 25600: You can see that as long as you don't overly en-large the picture, this for-emergencies-only mode still offers quite acceptable results. Again, you can inspect the full ISO series in full resolution online at www.dpunkt.de/XPro1/Abbildungen.

The extended ISO range also includes the option of shoot-ing at ISO 100, which is only an option if you are shooting exclusively in JPEGs. Here the process is inverted: the camera captures an image at ISO 200 and overexposes the RAW data by one exposure value. Then during the RAW conversion, it brings the exposure down by one exposure value. This process—the opposite of "pushing" an exposure—is called pull development.

This method produces images with minimal noise and a high degree of detail, particularly in the shadow areas, which comes at the expense of the high end of the dynamic range. The highlights, or bright tones, suffer dramatically, making ISO 100 another setting for use only in emergencies and for images that don't feature high contrast or important highlight details.

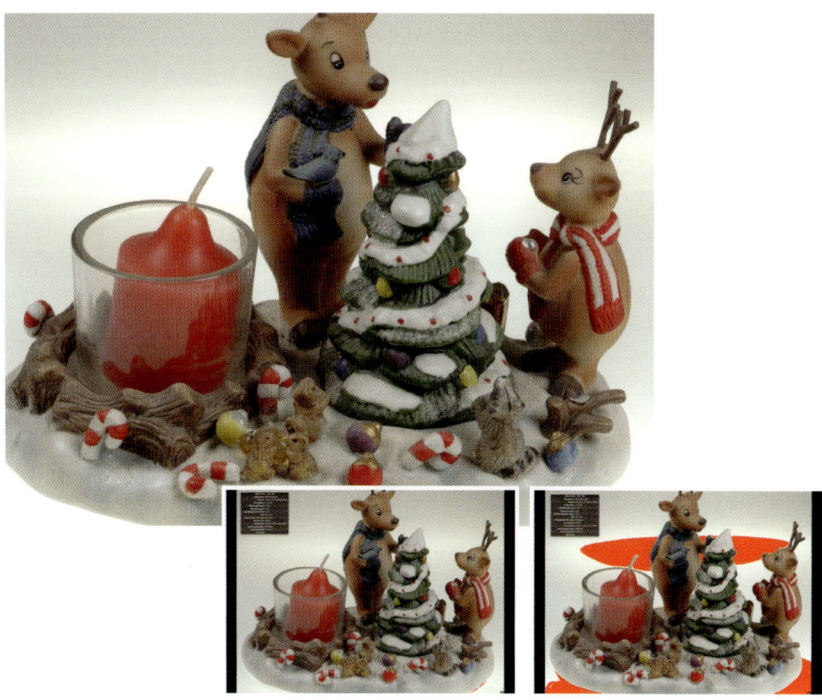

Figure 103: The test subject with ISO 100: The loss of dynamic range at the high end of the spectrum is easy to spot: the highlights here are partially blown out. The exposure warning (indicated by the red-marked areas in the two small images below) in the image-editing software Aperture shows the difference even more clearly: the left image shows the subject shot at ISO 200, the right with ISO 100.

SUMMARY

At high ISO settings, which often cause big problems with other cameras, the X-Pro1 and X-E1 still deliver excellent results. Nevertheless, you should only stray beyond the range between ISO 200 and ISO 6400 when there's no other option. ISO 100 results in a reduced dynamic range for highlights and ISO 12800 and ISO 25600 lead to very visible interference and a loss of detail. Moreover, these three settings of the "extended ISO range" are available only when your camera is programmed to save JPEGs only—retaining RAW files is not an option with these settings.

PRACTICAL ISO TIPS

There are four methods for changing the camera's ISO setting:

- Go to SHOOTING MENU > ISO and select your desired ISO setting.

- Press the Q button and program your desired ISO setting in the Quick Menu.

- The ISO setting is one of the parameters you can save in the camera's seven custom shooting profiles. You can change the current ISO setting by selecting a shooting profile that has a different ISO setting. To select or edit a shooting profile, hold the Q button until the appropriate menu pops up on the display.

- Set the Fn button to access the ISO menu. This is actually the factory-programmed function of this button. To program the function of the Fn button, simply hold it down until the assignment menu appears.

As a rule, lower ISO values produce better photographic results. You'll get the best image quality at ISO 200. Avoid ISO 100, opting instead to stop down the aperture, shorten the exposure time, or use an ND gray filter.

But don't be afraid of high ISO values! At ISO 400 and ISO 800, the camera produces almost the same image quality that it does at ISO 200. This is especially true when you make use of the DR function (discussed in section 2.6), which enables you to extend the camera's dynamic range one or two f-stops upward. Not to jump too far ahead, but the DR function—depending on how it's set—requires a minimum ISO setting of 400 or 800. In addition, the result when using this feature is often more pleasing than if you were simply to expose your image at ISO 200 without using the DR extension.

Also keep in mind that you should try to optimize your image quality by using low ISO values only when it doesn't adversely affect your settings for aperture and/or shutter speed. What good does shooting at ISO 200 do if you have to extend the shutter window so long that camera shake or unwanted motion blur mars your shot? And what good does a low ISO setting do if you have to open the aperture so much that critical details of your image are no longer in the exposure's depth of field?

In other words, rather than setting the ISO independently of your other settings, choose it while considering them. These other exposure settings will ultimately have a greater influence on your result than whatever camera sensitivity level you choose—as we already know, this really only concerns the degree to which the signal from the sensor is amplified.

In this regard, your camera is particularly capable: in most cases, the human eye won't be able to detect a difference between images taken at ISO 200 and ISO 1600 when they're not significantly enlarged. For this reason, many photographers use the auto ISO setting and allow the camera to determine the most fitting ISO value by itself.

AUTOMATIC ISO

If you choose any of the options in the ISO menu that have the word AUTO, then the camera will use the lowest possible ISO setting (i.e., ISO 200 or higher). On a case-by-case basis, the camera will raise the ISO as needed, but it won't ever overstep the upper limit that you define. If you select AUTO (800), for example, the camera will use ISO settings between 200 and 800. When set at AUTO (6400), the camera uses ISO values between 200 and 6400.

So far, so good. But what concrete rules does the camera follow when selecting an ISO value between these two limits? Here's the basic rule: the camera doesn't attempt to raise the ISO until it no longer has any leeway to adjust the aperture and shutter speed to make the exposure work.

With the aperture, it's straightforward: in the **P** and **S** exposure modes, the upper limit is the maximum aperture of whichever lens is currently attached. In the **A** and **M** modes, the camera uses the aperture value that is selected by the user.

Determining shutter speeds is a bit more complicated. In principle, the camera could allow the exposure window to run up to 30 seconds in the **P** and **S** exposure modes before it has to bump up the ISO setting even a smidgen. This would be entirely impractical and unrealistic, though, which is why it makes sense to establish a realistic minimum shutter speed.

While many cameras, including the Fujifilm X100S and X20, allow users to set the minimum shutter speed for their auto ISO settings, the X-Pro1 and X-E1 determine this value automatically. An old and trusted rule from the world of 35mm photography comes into play here to help you avoid unwanted camera shake in your images: *minimum shutter speed = the inverse of the focal length.*

Since the X-Pro1 and X-E1 aren't 35mm cameras—they have an APS-C sensor—you must also include a conversion factor of 1.5 in the equation, making the minimum shutter speed in seconds = (1/[focal length x 1.5]). With the 18mm lens, the X-system minimum shutter speed (when the auto ISO is activated) is 1/27 second; with the 35mm lens, 1/52 second; and with the 60mm lens, 1/90 second. Please note that this basic rule applies only to prime lenses without optical image stabilization.

Such a rigid rule, as you can imagine, won't be able to accommodate many everyday photography situations. While 1/52 second may be short enough for most photographers to take handheld shots with the 35mm lens without camera shake, if you're shooting moving subjects (like a running child), you'll want to use a much faster shutter speed. Conversely, if you set your camera and lens on a tripod for a landscape photo, 1/52 second is much too short—1/20 or 1/8 second would be more fitting.

Many photographers wish that the camera allowed users to change the minimum shutter speed used with auto ISO. The obvious solution is to use the **S** exposure mode and set the exposure time yourself with the shutter-speed dial. In practice, this works very well; however, you are also at the mercy of Fuji's wide-aperture lenses. As you will remember, auto ISO only bumps up the camera's ISO setting when the maximum aperture doesn't suffice to take a correctly exposed image. With the 35mm f/1.4 lens, this of course means an aperture of f/1.4, which will produce a depth of field that is too shallow for many situations.

Why not then use auto ISO in tandem with the **M** exposure mode to set your desired shutter speed and your desired aperture? This actually works. Switching your exposure mode to manual when using the automatic ISO selector will allow what I call misomatic shooting:

automatic ISO in combination with a manually selected shutter speed and aperture. It would seem logical that you could give your camera as much freedom as possible and select AUTO (6400) from the ISO menu. Sounds too good to be true? It is! The misomatic solution has a significant catch: the camera's exposure compensation dial is useless in **M** mode, which is also true when the auto ISO is active.

In other words, in misomatic mode, you're entirely dependent on the camera's automatic exposure metering, because you are unable to make any exposure corrections manually.

How can you compensate for this disadvantage?

- Change the light metering mode. While the multi metering method tends to expose liberally (brighter), the average metering method exposes conservatively (darker). This will help you to avoid overexposed areas in your images.

- Use the spot metering method. With experience, you'll start to develop a sense for which element in your image you should target for the light metering in order to expose your image successfully.

- If you want to expose your image darker than the camera normally would, first meter an image frame that's brighter than the frame you actually want to expose and then temporarily save the exposure settings by pressing the shutter button halfway. Conversely, if you want to expose on the brighter side, first expose a darker frame and follow the same process.

- Use the camera's automatic exposure bracketing feature! As long as you are shooting something that can't run away from you—a landscape, for example—it's never a bad idea to expose multiple versions of it, from which you can later select the best. To activate this function, press the DRIVE button and select AE BKT.

• If blown-out highlights are your biggest concern when using the misomatic mode, you can counteract them by enabling the DR function. Go to SHOOTING MENU > DYNAMIC RANGE and then select either DR200% or DR400%. These settings will lead to RAW files that are underexposed by one or two f-stops, respectively. When you develop your image data into JPEGs, either by using the internal RAW converter or an external one, you can balance this exposure. This method will give you one or even two aperture stops of wiggle room with your highlights. You can read more about the DR function in section 2.6.

IMPORTANT

Remember that the misomatic mode only appears to be an automatic exposure mode on the surface. In reality, you're still in manual mode even with the auto ISO activated. You are ultimately responsible for making sure the exposure of your images is correct. For this reason, the camera won't give you an exposure warning if it can't find an appropriate ISO value to match your manually selected aperture and shutter speed. Instead the camera shows the resulting over- or underexposure of your shot in the exposure indicator on the left side of the display.

As you can see, the seemingly simple concept of an automatic ISO function quickly becomes complicated in certain circumstances. In situations where the auto ISO function doesn't offer an acceptable aperture and/or shutter speed setting in the **P**, **A**, or **S** exposure mode, the best solution is often to turn off the automatic function and select an appropriate ISO value yourself. Sometimes the simplest solution is also the best.

ISO BRACKETING

As an alternative to conventional automatic exposure bracketing (see section 2.3.2), you can use ISO exposure bracketing. When using this function, the camera creates three differently exposed images, and the largest exposure variance between each image is ±1 EV. In contrast to the regular exposure bracketing, however, the three images are created not with different combinations of aperture and shutter speed, but with sensor signal amplifications of varying degrees—or, in other words, different ISO settings. The camera doesn't need to take three different exposures in short succession when executing this type of exposure bracketing. The sensor data from a single exposure will suffice; the camera develops the same data into three different JPEGs.

One advantage of this method is that all three exposures are identical in terms of the elements within the image frame, so you don't have to worry about ghosting artifacts when compositing an HDR image on your computer. ISO bracketing therefore lends itself well to HDR subjects that feature moving objects.

To enable this function, press the DRIVE button and select ISO BKT. You can then set the range of exposure values for the sequence (±1/3 EV, ±2/3 EV, or ±1 EV).

Figure 104: With the automatic ISO bracketing feature, ▶ the camera develops three different JPEGs from the same RAW data. With this variant of exposure bracketing, the maximum variance between each JPEG is also ±1 EV. I used Photomatix Pro to composite the HDR example shown here out of the three JPEGs that resulted from the ISO bracketing feature (±1 EV = ISO 200, 400, and 100).

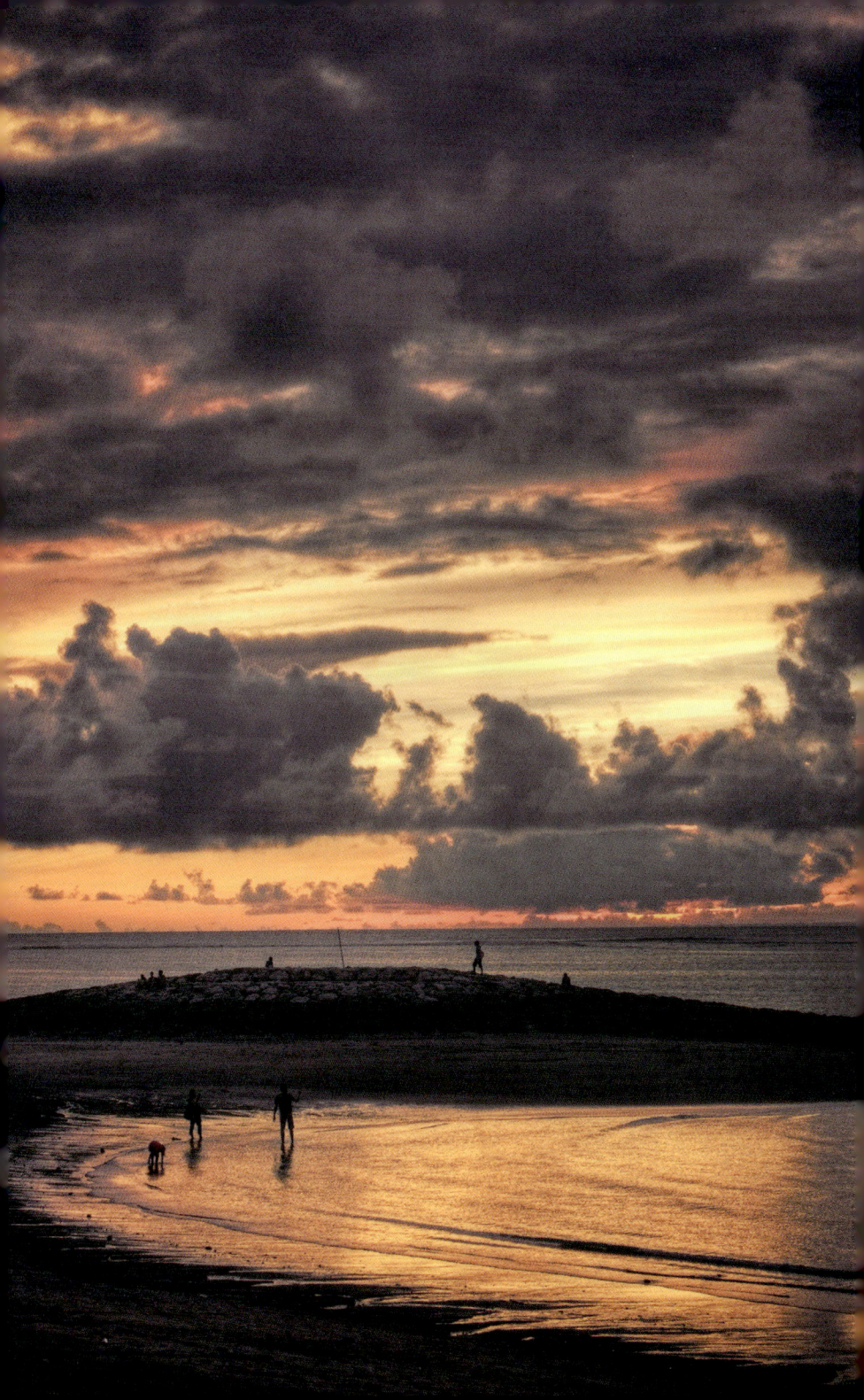

HINT

Please note that the camera does not write a RAW file to the memory card when running the ISO bracketing feature. Instead, it saves three different JPEG files that are identical in terms of the photo's subject matter as well as the aperture and shutter speed used to expose the shot. The only difference between the images is the strength of the ISO amplification.

ISO bracketing is possible with any ISO setting between 200 and 6400, including all of the auto ISO options. You can also use this feature in all four of the camera's exposure modes and in combination with the misomatic mode. When you can live with a JPEG and no RAW file, the ISO bracketing function can work as a makeshift replacement of the exposure compensation dial, which is useless when shooting with misomatic settings.

IMPORTANT

The automatic ISO bracketing feature uses push/pull methods to "develop" the image captured by the sensor. You can achieve the same results by taking a RAW file that has been conventionally exposed and using the internal or an external RAW converter to produce two additional "prints," one with the corresponding overexposure and one with the corresponding underexposure.

2.6 EXTENDING THE DYNAMIC RANGE

Does the following scenario sound familiar? You take a picture of a landscape that looks wonderfully beautiful to the naked eye only to find out later that in your image the blue sky no longer looks blue and the fascinating cloud formations are just white blobs. The reason for this and similar disappointments is that the scene captured in the image has a larger dynamic range than the camera.

Every camera sensor is capable of capturing only a certain range of contrast—that is, a limited range between the brightest and the darkest parts of an image. With standard JPEG output, your camera covers about 9.5 f-stops or exposure values. In other words, there are 9.5 EV between the minimum amount of light required for the sensor to depict something more than black pixels and the maximum quantity of light beyond which the sensor registers white pixels. This is the dynamic range of the camera. Within this range, the X-Pro1 and X-E1 can depict levels of brightness between pure black and pure white.

Unfortunately, the world doesn't abide by these limits, and many subjects exhibit a larger dynamic range than the camera is capable of capturing. We see these limitations, for example, in backlit situations and when people are standing in the shadow of an entrance. Professional photographers (and film directors) reduce the dynamic range of their subjects by using additional light. That's why you'll see an entire arsenal of floodlights and reflectors on large film sets even on bright days.

Only the luckiest photographers have the luxury of elaborate lighting equipment. Most of us have to make do with natural lighting, which often produces contrast in our subjects that exceeds a range of 9.5 EV. When you try to photograph these subjects with your camera, your images will have either blown-out white areas or blocked-up shadows, regardless of the combination of aperture and shutter speed you choose. They may even have both! Contrasts that the human eye (or more accurately, the human brain) seems to process without any trouble pose near-impossible challenges for even the best camera sensors.

This section could end here on a frustrating note, but there are several approaches for dealing with this common problem. I already discussed one solution in section 2.3 under "Metering": high dynamic range (HDR). With this method, you take several shots of the same subject at different exposure settings. Then you (or your camera) can work to composite this series of exposures into one image, taking the dark areas (shadows) from the overexposed images and the bright areas (highlights) from the underexposed ones.

The X-Pro1 and X-E1 do not offer an HDR mode, so you will need to patch together your images on your computer using a software program designed for this purpose, such as HDR Efex Pro or Photomatix Pro.

HDR technology doesn't lend itself to all high-contrast subjects, though. For this reason, many photographers instead opt for a compromise: they base the exposure on the brightest element in their frame and accept the ensuing underexposure in darker areas. While it's impossible to restore information to blown-out highlights, effective post-processing can generally rescue blocked-up shadows.

This method is called tone mapping, and it consists of a reassignment of brightness values. Tone mapping is the same function as the "fill-light" slider in our modern image-editing programs for external RAW development: it brightens the shadows and dark midtones of images that we intentionally exposed too dark until the relative levels of brightness throughout the image appear balanced. The drawback of this method is increased image noise in the shadows as well as a decreased number of brightness levels in these darker areas. In general, this cost is well worth the gain: you can retain detail in the bright areas of your image that otherwise would be lost.

Extending the dynamic range is actually a method of "dynamic range compression": when we intentionally underexpose an image (i.e., base the exposure settings on the brightest part of the frame), its middle and dark tones are shifted further to the left and piled up there on the histogram. The decompression happens when you map the tones in your images, bringing the dark and middle tones to lighter and more appropriate levels of brightness. And voilà: the results suggest that you've extended your camera's dynamic range. That's technically exactly what happened, although admittedly the expense is a bit more noise, and fewer nuances in the dark areas.

If you go to SHOOTING MENU > DYNAMIC RANGE and select AUTO to switch on the camera's automatic DR function, it takes care of this process for you with the following steps:

1. The camera analyzes the subject and determines whether or not its range of contrast exceeds the sensor's dynamic range.

2. If it does, the camera exposes the image one (DR200%) or two (DR400%) f-stops darker than normal in order to retain detail in the bright areas of the image (highlights). This is why it's necessary to have an ISO setting of at least 400 for DR200% and an ISO setting of at least 800 for DR400%.

3. The camera develops the JPEG by remapping the tones in the RAW data that was intentionally exposed too dark to bring the shadows and middle tones back to normal. In turn, the amplification of the sensor signal is reduced by one (DR200%) or two (DR400%) exposure values.

IMAGE 1

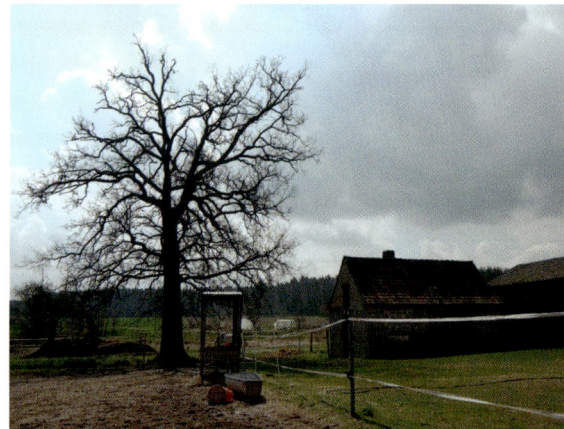

IMAGE 2

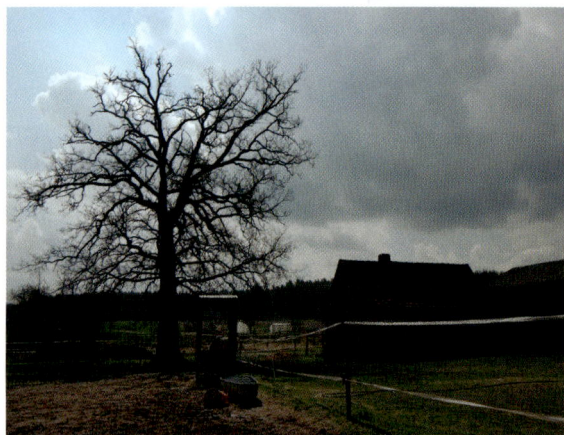

IMAGE 3

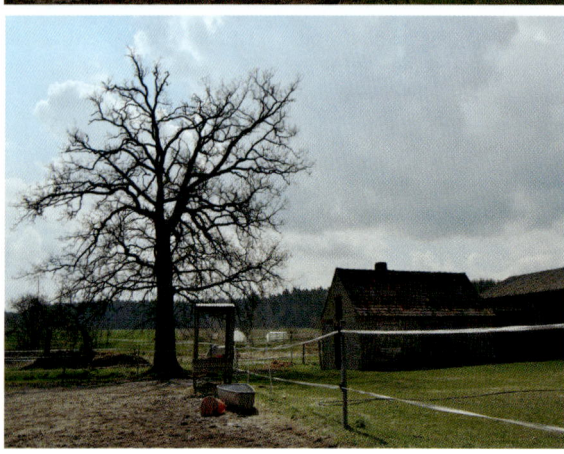

IMAGE 4

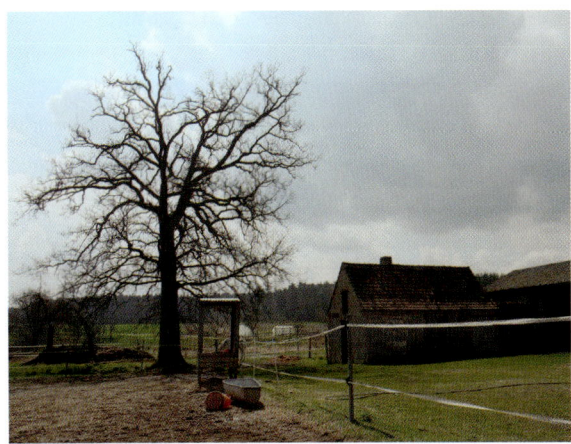

Figure 105: **Extending the camera's dynamic range:** This example illustrates how to rescue the bright areas of an image (highlights) that are beyond the sensor's dynamic range. This would normally require a manual process in which the photographer would purposefully underexpose an image and then make the appropriate adjustments when developing the image in a RAW converter. The DR function automates this process.

Image 1 (left, above) is a JPEG of the test subject taken with the camera's standard settings (DR100%) and without an extended dynamic range. Here you can see that the shadows and dark midtones are correctly exposed, but the sky has lost its color and the bright parts of the clouds have lost all of their detail. The sensor's blue channel has been overwhelmed: during the exposure, it was bombarded with more photons than it was capable of absorbing.

Image 2 (left, middle) has been manually underexposed by one aperture stop. The sky and the clouds now look okay. They've been rescued: the darker exposure meant that fewer photons hit the sensor and its capacity was sufficient for the bright parts of the image. This also has the effect of making the dark areas of the image look underexposed—and that's exactly what they are. We've shifted the problem from the bright to the dark areas of the image.

Image 3 (left, below) shows the image after the shadows have been restored. I've taken the RAW file for image 2 and used Silkypix to edit it, using fill light to conduct tone mapping. The highlights retain their detail, while the shadows now look as they did in image 1 (left, above). The dynamic range has effectively been extended.

Image 4 (right, above) shows the results of allowing the camera to rescue the highlights of the image by itself using the DR function. With auto DR activated, the camera selected DR400%, exposed the RAW file two aperture stops (exposure values) dimmer than normal, and remapped the brightness tones appropriately when developing the JPEG file. Measured in exposure values, the camera's dynamic range (based on its JPEG output) effectively increased from approximately 9.5 EV to 11.5 EV.

Above all, the DR function is practical and simple. It automatically handles nontrivial work that photographers would otherwise have to do themselves in order to prevent the loss of detail in bright areas.

For photographers who don't work with RAW files and instead demand that their camera produce finished JPEGs, the DR function is essential. While the camera can capture images with 12 bits or 4,096 brightness levels, a finished JPEG is in 8-bit format with only 256 brightness levels. An intentionally underexposed JPEG (i.e., an exposure based on highlights) is much more difficult to correct with tone mapping than a RAW file that was exposed in the same manner. In particular, JPEGs may only have a handful of brightness levels available in the darker regions of an image, meaning the tone mapping process of raising and spreading out these levels can lead to undesirable results.

For JPEG photographers, the DR function is a genuine plus, because when the camera conducts the dynamic compression and decompression by itself, it works with the RAW data captured by the sensor—all 4,096 brightness levels. Only after the camera maps the tones does it convert the image to 8-bit format and produce a JPEG with 256 brightness levels.

QUESTIONS AND ANSWERS ABOUT THE DR FUNCTION

The DR function tends to cause some confusion, which is why I've included a few of the most common questions and my attempts to answer them.

When should I use the dynamic range function?

The DR function is ideal for circumstances in which the subject of an image exhibits a larger range of contrast than the camera is capable of capturing. When AUTO is set for the DR function, the camera will extend the dynamic range as needed based on the detected range of contrast in the subject. It will choose either DR200% (an extension of the dynamic range by one exposure value) or DR400% (an extension by two exposure values). You can alternatively select both of these options manually. The automatic function tends to operate rather liberally—it sometimes selects a higher DR setting than is necessary.

Why shouldn't I always leave DR200% or DR400% active?
The DR function is a compromise: it extends the dynamic range at the cost of more noise and a reduced tonal range in the shadow areas of your images. You should only turn it on when the benefits outweigh the costs and when you really need an extended range.

How can I tell if the range of contrast in my subject will overwhelm the camera's sensor?
If you see cropped peaks piled up at the right edge of the histogram, it's a good indication that the bright parts of your image will lose their detail. If those parts of the frame are important to your image, you should attempt to rescue them—either by purposefully underexposing the shot (perhaps with the help of the exposure compensation dial) and then mapping the tones when developing the RAW file or by entrusting this work to the camera by availing yourself of the DR function.

What is meant by "important parts of an image"?
Sometimes you want to intentionally play with extreme contrasts or allow portions of your image to be blown out. In these cases, you shouldn't rely on the camera's automatic dynamic range extension. The camera cannot think, and doesn't know what makes for a good image. It simply measures the exposure and dynamic range and uses these values to make its decisions. Don't let the camera dictate what your images look like; create

IMAGE 1

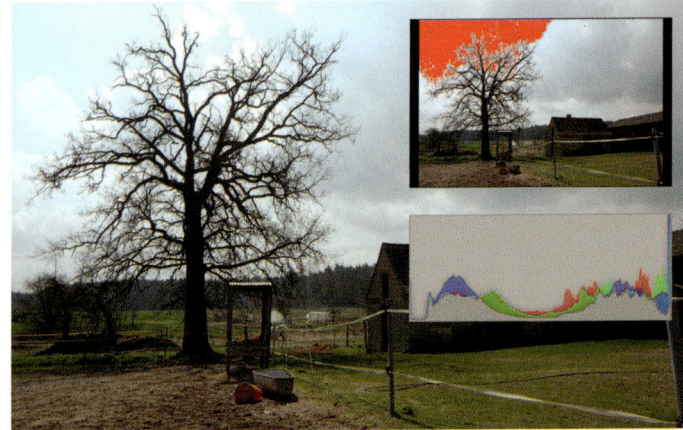

IMAGE 2

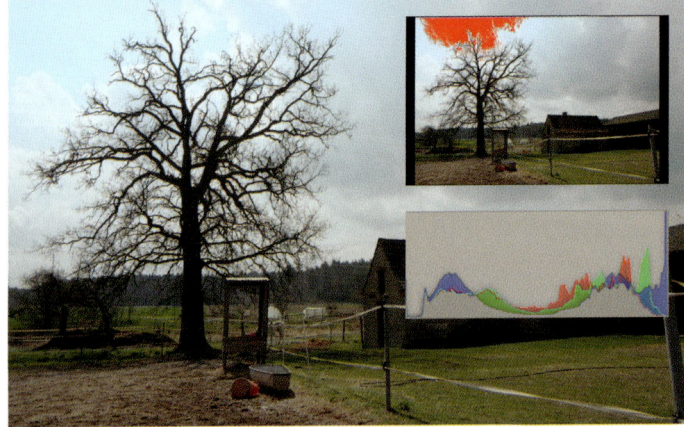

IMAGE 3

IMAGE 4

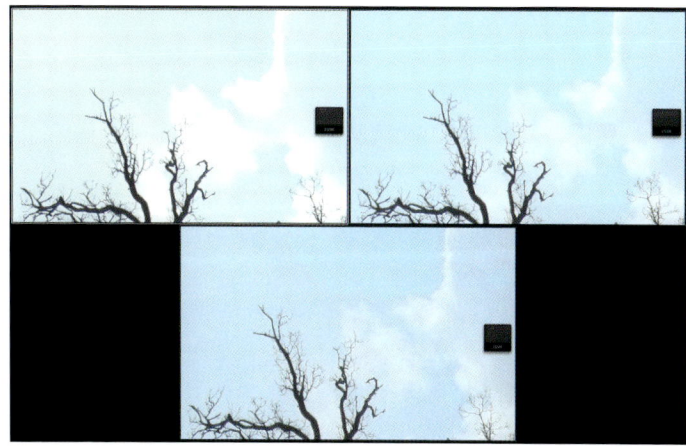

Figure 106: The DR function in action: The three JPEGs on the left illustrate the effect of the DR function on a high-contrast subject. Image 1 is the baseline image with the extended DR disabled (DR100%). Image 2 is the result of shooting in DR200%, and Image 3 DR400%. You can see how the piled-up highlights at the right edge of the histogram are rescued from one image to the next—something you can also tell by the decreasing size of the red area indicating an exposure warning. The details in Image 4 clearly illustrate the process's positive effect on the image's highlights—in this example, the sky and clouds.

them yourself! If you want a stark contrast, set the camera to DR100% and expose the image according to the elements in it that are important to you.

How do the DR function and the ISO value mesh together?

For the camera to underexpose the RAW file by 1 EV (DR200%) or 2 EV (DR400%), it must also use ISO settings of at least 400 or 800, respectively. When these ISO settings are used, the camera normally amplifies the sensor signal. This boost is left out, however, when the DR function is enabled. In its place, the process of tone mapping must be used in the development of the RAW file. So make sure you set your camera to at least ISO 400 or 800—or better yet, to AUTO (800) or higher.

If you manually program an ISO value that won't work with the selected DR setting, the camera will automatically bring the DR setting down. If you have set the dynamic range to DR400% and the ISO to 400, for example, the camera will adjust the dynamic range setting down to DR200%. If you were to set ISO 200, it would go to DR100%. When this happens, the current DR setting appears yellow and remains so until you bump up the ISO to an operative level. In other words, your manually selected ISO value has priority over the DR setting. But the DR settings do have priority over automatically selected ISO values. This is why I recommend that you use the DR function in tandem with AUTO (800) or higher.

How does the DR function affect RAW files?

It should be clear by now that the DR function can help produce attractive JPEGs for high-contrast subjects. But what about RAW files? The image data in these files are underexposed by one exposure value with DR200% and two exposure values with DR400%. If you develop your RAW files with your camera, the internal RAW converter will compensate for this condition automatically. If you use external RAW converters, it depends on the specific program. Silkypix, Lightroom, and Capture One also automatically detect the DR function and adjust the exposure settings accordingly. The results will vary from those produced by the camera, which isn't to say that one is better than the other. With RAW converters, you also have the opportunity to tackle the task yourself and manage the editing based on your specific preferences.

Figure 107: **Light and shadow:** This image was ▶ shot at DR400% and developed from the RAW file with Adobe Lightroom 4. Exposure parameters: X-E1 with 18–55mm kit zoom, f/5, 1/40 second, ISO 800, DR400%.

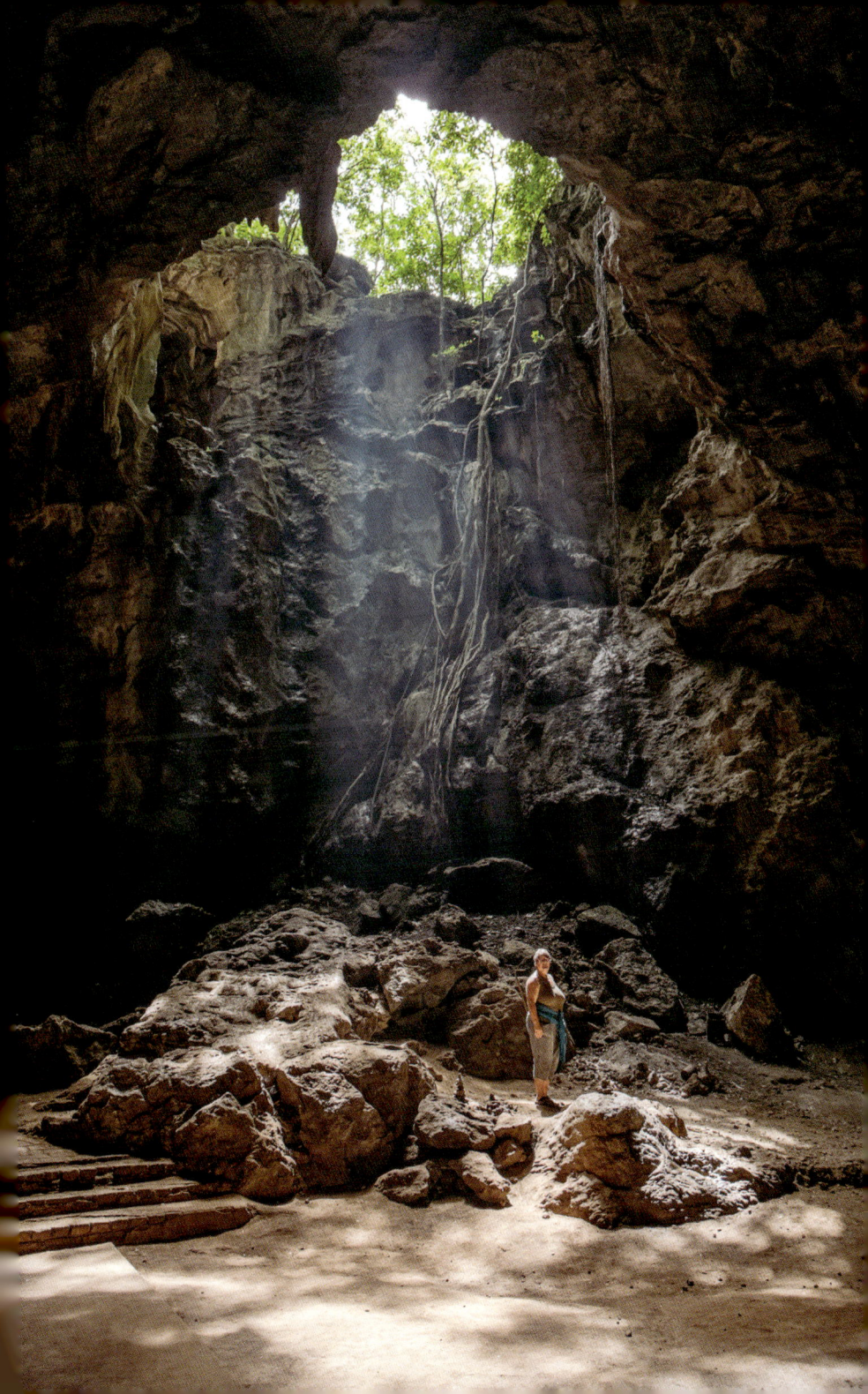

Should I use the DR function if I plan on working with the RAW files?

This is a tricky one, because the answer depends on your personal habits. If you plan to exclusively use RAW files and you don't plan on using the JPEGs prepared by the camera at all, then I recommend not using the DR function (i.e., set it to DR100%). Instead, use the live histogram to monitor your exposure levels while shooting and to make sure that no important elements in your image are crammed up against its right border. The benefits of this manual method are that your work can be more precise than the camera's automatic methods and you can control the tone mapping with all of your personal tricks and preferences in an external RAW converter.

Conversely, if you are mainly interested in the camera's JPEGs (for their "Fuji colors"), you'll want to enable the DR function to make them as attractive and balanced as possible. The RAW files will then be exposed one or two exposure values darker. Silkypix (including the free version of RAW File Converter EX) and Lightroom/ACR can balance this underexposure automatically when reading the RAW files. On the other hand, Apple's RAW processing, and hence Aperture 3, handles such RAW files rather badly.

You can undoubtedly manually underexpose your images much more precisely than the camera can on its own. The automatic DR procedure is limited to crude steps of 1 EV and 2 EV. Experienced RAW shooters who prefer to have full control over the photographic process generally turn the automatic dynamic range off (DR100%).

Figure 108: After the rain: ▶
Exposure parameters: X-Pro1, XF35mmF1.4
R, f/13, 1/400 second, ISO 800, DR400%.
Developed from the RAW file with Silkypix 4;
finished with Aperture.

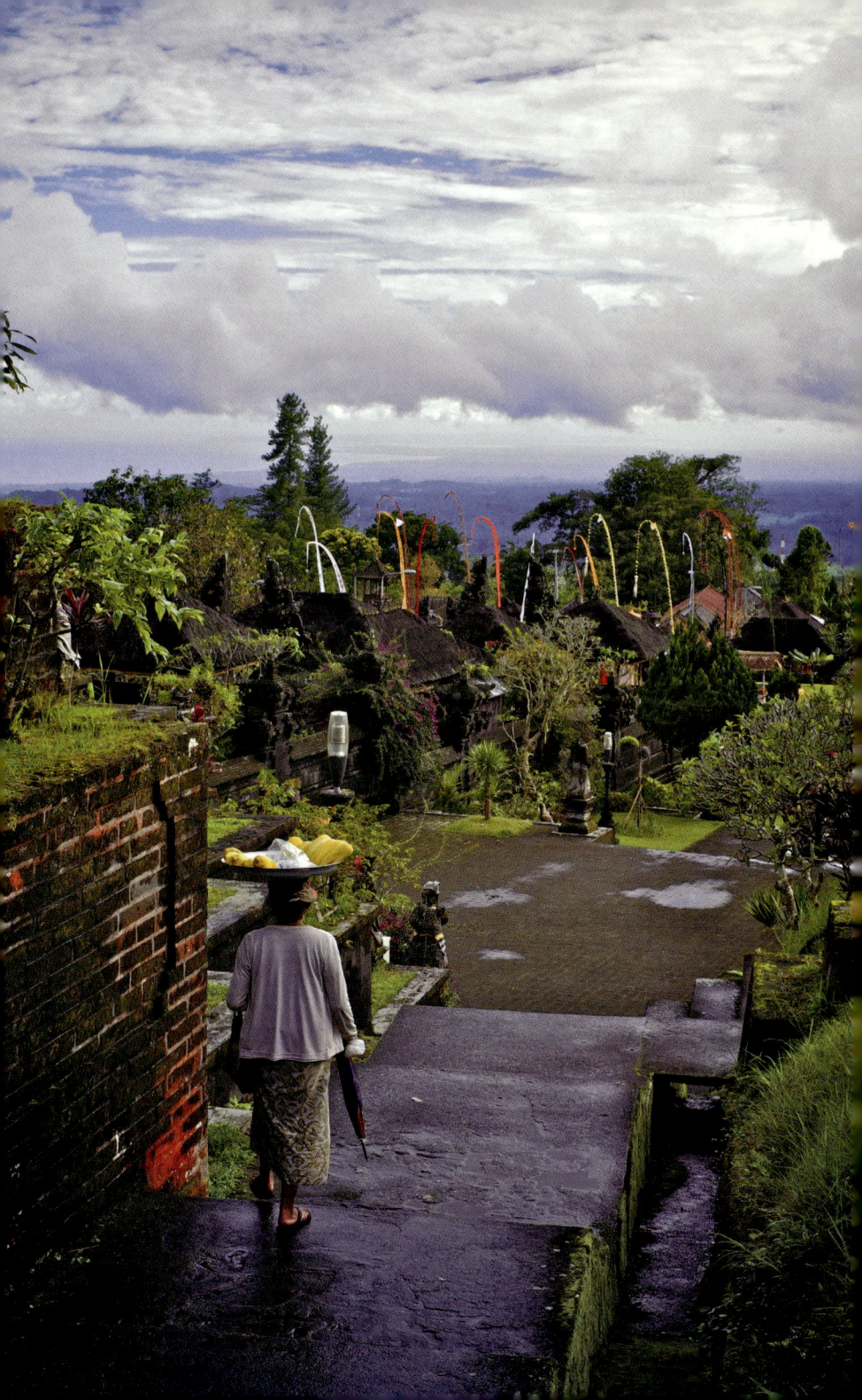

What do I personally do? It depends on the day and my intentions. If I want to squeeze every last drop of quality out of my camera and sensor, I work exclusively with an external RAW workflow, shoot at DR100%, and expose as precisely as possible.

IMPORTANT

The camera's live histogram always works independently of the DR function and is not influenced by the dynamic range setting. Please remember to rely on the live histogram only when using DR100%.

TIPS FOR HANDLING THE DR FUNCTION

There are four ways to change the DR settings of your camera:

- Go to SHOOTING MENU > DYNAMIC RANGE, where you can select from AUTO, DR100%, DR200%, and DR400%. If AUTO is selected, the camera will choose from the three other options: DR100% turns the dynamic range exstension off; DR200% extends the dynamic range by one exposure value; DR400% extends it by two exposure values.

- Press the Q button and select the dynamic range directly from the Quick Menu.

- The DR function is one of the parameters that you can save in your custom shooting profiles. Therefore you can indirectly adjust the DR settings by choosing a different shooting profile. As a reminder, you can select or edit these profiles by pressing the Q button until the desired menu comes up on the camera's display.

- Assign an Fn button to control the DR setting. Remember, to change the function of an Fn button, hold it down until the menu for assigning its function pops up.

IMPORTANT

Remember that DR200% will only be available if your ISO is set to at least 400, and for DR400% the minimum ISO is 800. For this reason, I recommend selecting AUTO (800) or higher for the ISO when you plan to use the DR function.

The camera prioritizes your manually defined ISO values over the DR. When you're using the variable auto ISO feature, the camera can and will adjust the ISO to the level needed for the DR function to work properly.

Which DR setting should you use? Pay attention to the live histogram. If there are cropped peaks crammed in at the right side of the histogram, you have areas in your image frame that are overexposed. If this is something you don't want in your JPEGs, then definitely use the DR function—either DR200% or DR400%, based on the contrast range of your subject. When in doubt, opt for AUTO and leave the decision-making up to the camera.

DR BRACKETING

If you would like to see three different dynamic range versions of the same subject, press the DRIVE button and select DYNAMIC RANGE BKT. The camera will then capture three images when you press the shutter button, at DR100%, DR200%, and DR400%.

The drawback of this method is that the camera only writes JPEGs to the memory card; it doesn't save any RAW files. Moreover, the JPEGs will only be captured at the lowest possible ISO setting (i.e., the best possible quality) if you've turned on auto ISO. For photographers who value RAW files, this function doesn't have much to offer. In any case, it's useful to test how the three differ-ent DR settings look with different subjects. You can get

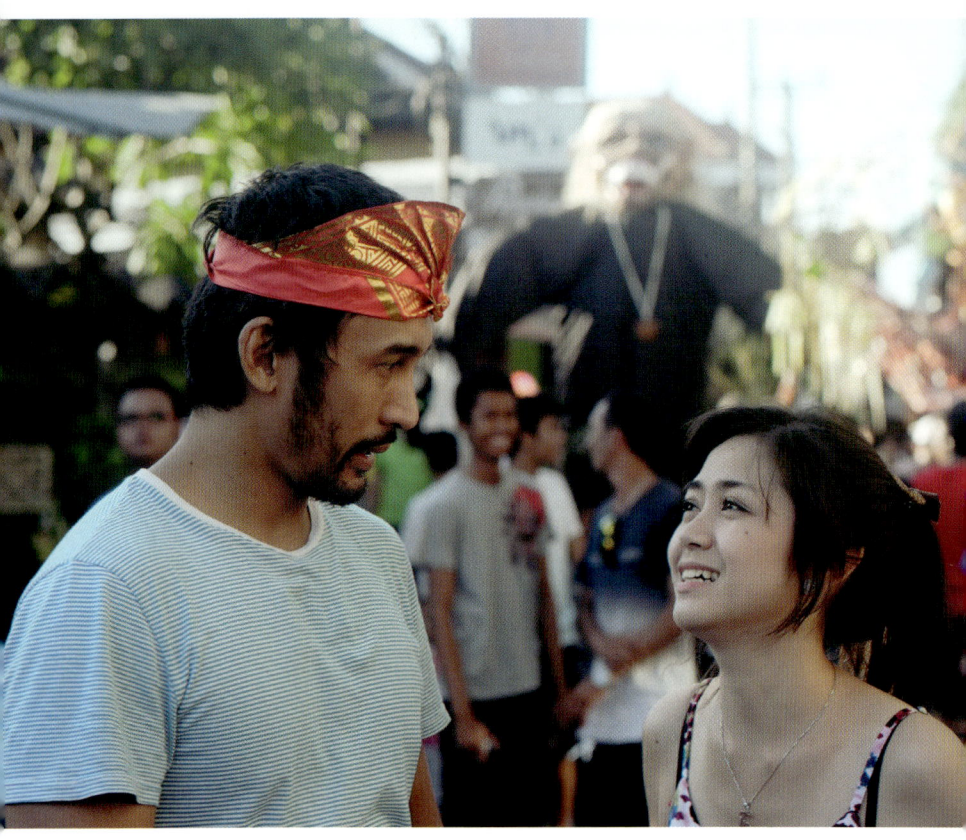

Figure 109: Ogoh-Ogoh Festival: The X-Pro1's internal RAW converter developed this JPEG, which (aside from cropping) is unedited. Exposure parameters: XF60mmF2.4 R Macro, f/4, 1/800 second, ISO 800, DR400%. JPEG conversion parameters that deviate from the default settings: white balance 5300K, push/pull processing +1/3 EV, film simulation PRO Neg. Hi, color m-high, sharpness m-hard, shadow tone m-hard, noise reduction m-low.

almost the same effect by exposing an image at DR400% and then developing the RAW file with the internal RAW converter into two more versions: one at DR200% and one at DR100%. To use the RAW converter, go to PLAY-BACK MENU > RAW CONVERSION.

2.7 WHITE BALANCE AND JPEG SETTINGS

The X-Pro1 and X-E1 offer a practical feature regarding white balance, film simulation, contrast settings, color saturation, image sharpness, noise reduction, and the selection of a color space: not only can you define these settings before you capture an image; you can also change them afterward! The only requirement is saving the RAW file in addition to the JPEG so the camera's internal RAW converter has something to work with. This is another reason to choose SHOOTING MENU > IMAGE QUALITY > FINE+RAW as your default image-quality setting.

This is great news for photographers who are interested in getting finished JPEGs from their camera. Instead of agonizing over the perfect settings before every exposure, you can concentrate on your subject, the focus, and the actual exposure while shooting. You can try out different variations to optimize your images with the aforementioned parameters later. That sounds like exciting and stress-free photography to me.

White balance and the various JPEG settings control how the camera interprets the RAW data collected during an exposure. The RAW file—the digital negative—remains unchanged during this conversion process. This section focuses on settings that can influence the "prints" that the camera develops from these negatives. It also explains how the camera can continue to make new and different JPEGs from the same RAW files, just as you can with real negatives.

2.7.1 SETTING THE WHITE BALANCE

Light exhibits certain color temperatures that give objects a hue. Without taking a proper white balance, a gray object shown in a warm light (e.g., the light of an incandescent bulb) will appear orange and in a cold light (e.g., a camera flash), bluish. The color of the object itself is actually neither orange nor blue—it's plain gray.

To ensure that gray objects appear gray in all lighting conditions, the camera needs to measure the color temperature of the light for each exposure and compensate for any detectable hues. The camera does this not only automatically, but also very precisely and with remarkably few errors.

Some problems arise for the automatic white balance when a scene features multiple light sources, each emitting a different color temperature. Which color temperature should the camera use as the baseline in such a case? It has no choice but to settle on a compromise—one that likely won't work for every situation and won't satisfy every viewer.

This isn't the end of the world, though, because you always have the option of adjusting the white balance—even afterward—using the internal RAW converter or a software program on your PC.

To set the white balance, go to SHOOTING MENU > WHITE BALANCE and choose from the menu options there. As is the case with the DR function and the ISO setting, you can set the white balance by accessing the Quick Menu (Q button), by changing the custom shooting profile, or by programming the Fn button accordingly.

Any setting you select from the WHITE BALANCE shooting menu will apply only to the JPEGs that the camera produces, so it won't affect the data of the RAW files. The white balance is, however, stored in the so-called metadata of the RAW file, so that a RAW converter can detect how the camera (or photographer) set the white balance at the time of exposure. When developing the RAW file later, the RAW converter will use the stored white balance information as a starting point.

As with most settings that affect how the JPEGs are rede-red, the effect of your white balance setting will be visible in the live image displayed on the camera's LCD monitor or in the electronic viewfinder. Having this practical advantage means you won't have to make a complete stab in the dark when choosing the white balance. You can get a rough idea of how your selection or adjustments to the white balance (or any other JPEG settings) will affect your shot.

AUTOMATIC WHITE BALANCE

The default setting for the white balance is SHOOTING MENU > WHITE BALANCE > AUTO. With this option set, the camera will measure the ambient color temperature automatically before each exposure and adjust itself accordingly. This process functions so well that many of you will rarely use a setting other than AUTO—especially because you can continue to make additional changes and adjustments to the RAW file afterward.

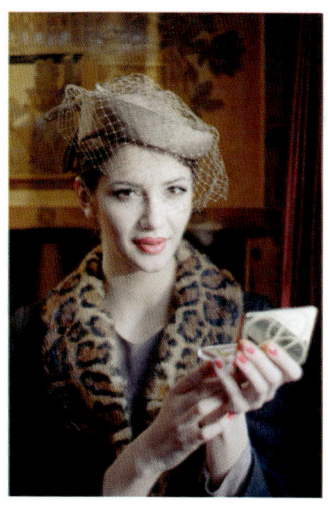

Figure 110: Automatic white balance: The camera's default white balance setting delivers excellent results, even in complex lighting conditions. This example image features a blend of natural light from the right and artificial light from the upper left. The JPEG you see here came directly from the camera and didn't receive any post-processing at all.

WHITE BALANCE PRESETS

When you plan to shoot a series of exposures under constant lighting conditions (e.g., sunny or overcast skies), it can be practical to use an appropriate preset. This reduces the chance of misinterpreting the color temperature, and ensures that different JPEGs in the series will be exposed with the exact same (predefined) color temperature setting.

The following seven presets are available in the WHITE BALANCE menu:

- FINE: for subjects in sunlight

- SHADE: for subjects in shadow

- FLUORESCENT LIGHT-1: for exposures under "daylight" fluorescents

- FLUORESCENT LIGHT-2: for warm white light

- FLUORESCENT LIGHT-3: for cool white light

- INCANDESCENT: for use with incandescent bulbs

- UNDERWATER: for underwater exposures or pictures of fish in large aquarium tanks and oceanariums

2.7.2 FILM SIMULATION

If you recall the days of film photography, you'll remember that different films often produce different results. A roll of Fujichrome Velvia 50 slide film is miles apart from Fujicolor Pro 160C in terms of colors, saturation, and contrast.

Digital cameras, on the other hand, have only one sensor, which doesn't vary in character. Fujifilm, however, offers various film simulations so that you can bring the look of color films into the world of digital photography. You can set these either in the shooting menu or when using the RAW converter in the playback menu. As an alternative, you can change the film simulation by accessing the Quick Menu, changing the custom shooting profile, or programming the Fn button accordingly.

In addition to the five color film choices, the camera is able to create sepia and black-and-white digital images with various virtual color filters (red, yellow, green, neutral).

COLOR FILMS

Your camera allows you to choose from three slide films (PROVIA, ASTIA, VELVIA) and two color negative films (PRO NEG. STD and PRO NEG. HI).

- Provia exhibits the weakest contrast and is the most neutral of the film simulations. It's also the camera's default setting. Its color saturation is understated and can therefore appear flat.

- Astia is soft with the highlights and offers noticeably more contrast in the shadows than Provia. The colors are livelier and produce the typical look of "Fuji Colors" with pleasant skin tones. Astia is one of the most popular film simulations among photographers.

- Velvia delivers very saturated and striking colors with stronger contrast. This option is less suited for portraiture but is great for nature and landscape photography.

- PRO Neg. Std is an excellent choice for neutral portraits, because it exhibits soft contrast, modest color saturation, and excellent skin tones. This is a logical choice for situations with controlled light, such as in a studio.

- PRO Neg. Hi is the contrast-rich version of PRO Neg. Std, with stronger colors and more pep. This setting provides accurate and attractive skin tones.

Remember that the selected film simulation affects the live image display when in shooting mode. It also affects the live histogram in the EVF or on the LCD monitor. This applies to all other JPEG settings described in this chapter, too. The viewfinder, monitor, and histogram all reflect your current JPEG settings. Independent of the settings you use when you expose an image, you can also adjust the JPEG parameters afterward in playback mode by using the RAW converter—as long as you save the RAW file.

After white balance, the selection of a film simulation will have the greatest effect on the look of your image. Before you devote any thought to the contrast or color settings of your image, you'll want to decide on a film simulation, and then set the other JPEG parameters accordingly.

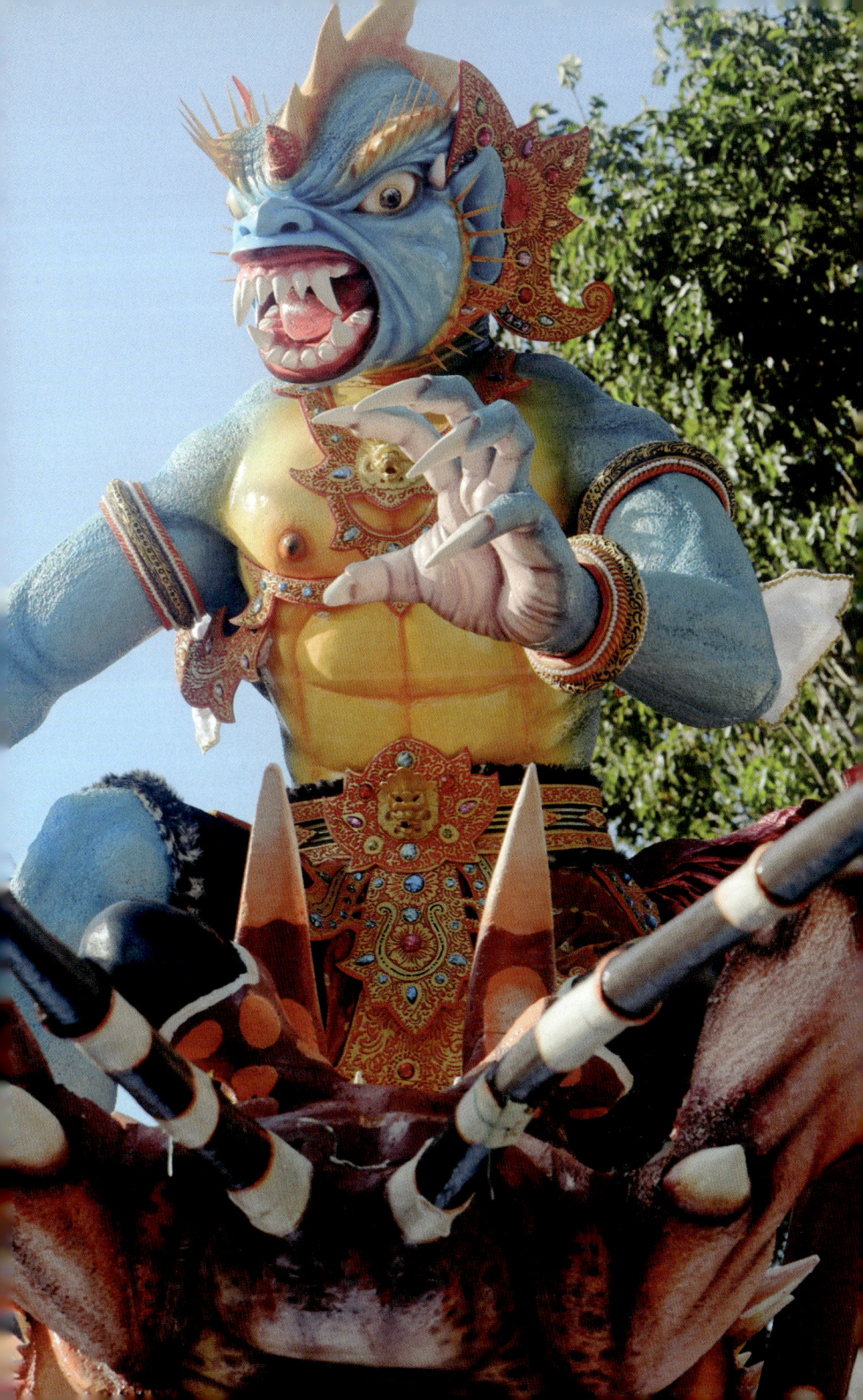

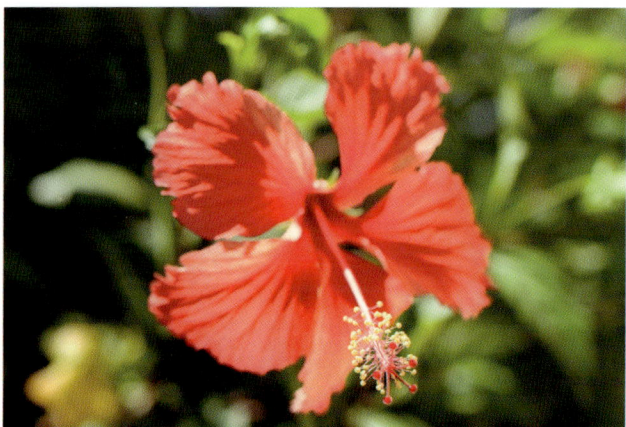

PROVIA

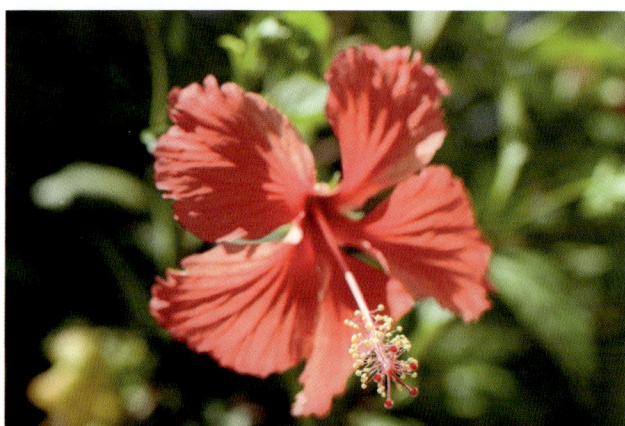

PRO NEG. STD

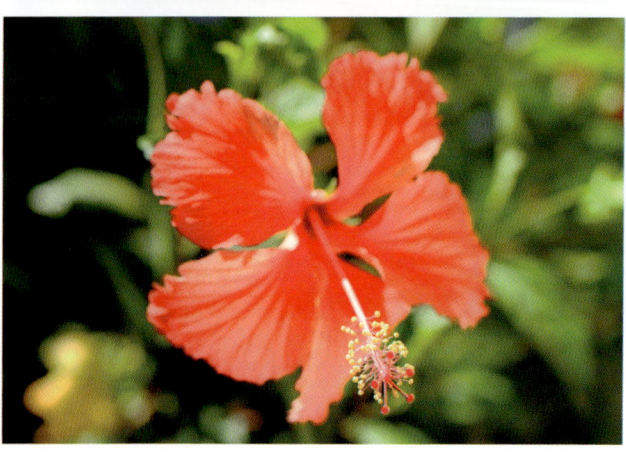

VELVIA

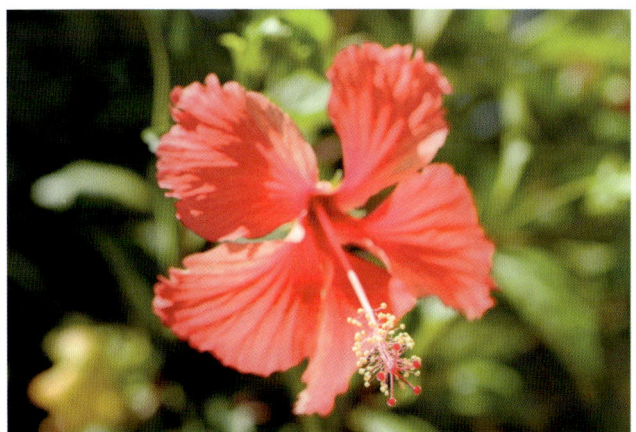

ASTIA

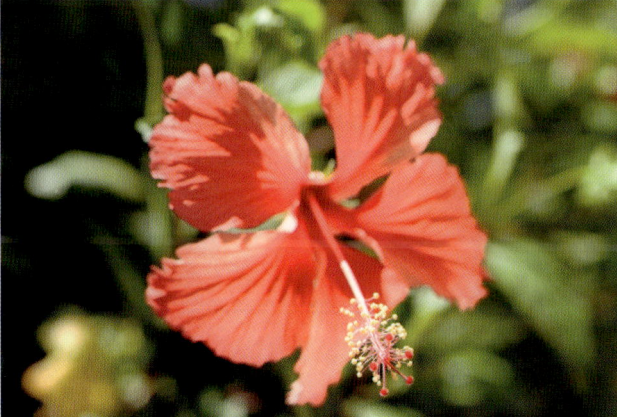

PRO NEG. HI

Figure 114: **Comparing color slide and color negative simulations:** Provia (top left) exhibits a conventional and realistic look. Astia (top right) is bolder and leans toward purple a bit. PRO Neg. Std (middle left) is generally unsaturated and stays away from bright colors. PRO Neg. Hi (middle right) is a bit more daring in this regard, but less so than the three slide film simulations. As expected, Velvia (bottom left) takes the cake here—its colors almost appear overloaded. You can inspect these and other full-size samples online at: www.dpunkt.de/XPro1/Abbildungen.

BLACK-AND-WHITE CONVERSION

In addition to the five color film modes, the camera can produce black-and-white JPEGs. You can create conventional black-and-white images or pair them with virtual color filters (when shooting black-and-white images with film you'd have to screw these filters to the end of the lens). Conventional conversions of color tones to gray values based on their luminosity (brightness) often produce boring results. A pronounced contrast between a dark red and a dark blue area in the original image could quickly become a gray mush with an unfiltered black-and-white conversion.

Color filters are used in black-and-white photography to retain these pronounced contrasts of color during the conversion process. A red filter darkens a blue sky so that it will appear dark gray or nearly black in contrast to the bright white clouds. Without this filter, you would end up with bright gray clouds on a bright gray sky. The camera simulates this effect by running the RAW file (which is always in color) through a virtual color filter when it develops a JPEG. You have five black-and-white options available:

- MONOCHROME executes a conventional black-and-white conversion of the color RAW file.

- MONOCHROME + Ye FILTER produces a general boost in contrast for many subjects and is accordingly a good compromise.

- MONOCHROME + R FILTER darkens blue tones (e.g., a blue sky) and brightens faces and red lips.

- MONOCHROME + G FILTER differentiates green tones in images of natural settings, darkens faces and red lips, and emphasizes any blemishes of the skin.

- SEPIA tints the black-and-white conversion with sepia, giving the image an antiquated feel.

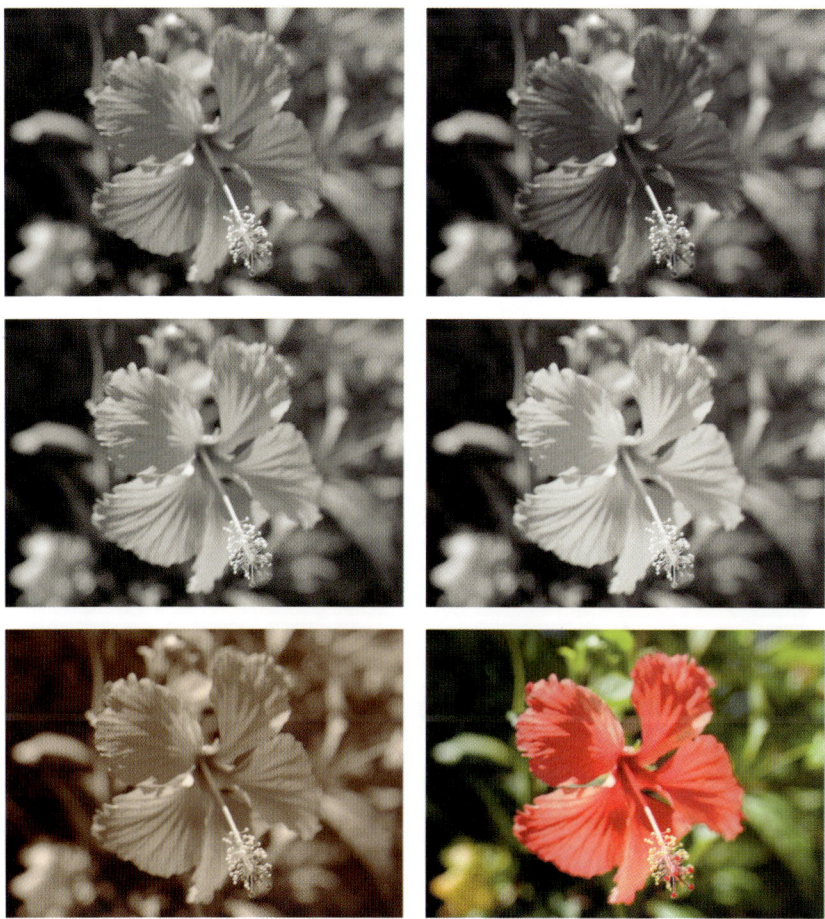

Figure 115: **Using filters with black-and-white conversions:**
The conventional MONOCHROME conversion (top left) is markedly different from a conversion that employed the G FILTER (top right): the filter darkened the red petals drastically. The Ye FILTER (middle left) produced a general increase in contrast, and the R FILTER (middle right) brightened up the naturally red blossom. The SEPIA (bottom left) conversion recalls the early days of film photography, and on the bottom right you can see the color source for these conversions, depicted with the Provia film simulation.

Unlike the color film simulations, the black-and-white conversions do not have the distinctive contrast curves typical of film. The conversion tends to be much more flat and unobtrusive so that the black-and-white images produced by the camera can still withstand a manual contrast adjustment on your computer.

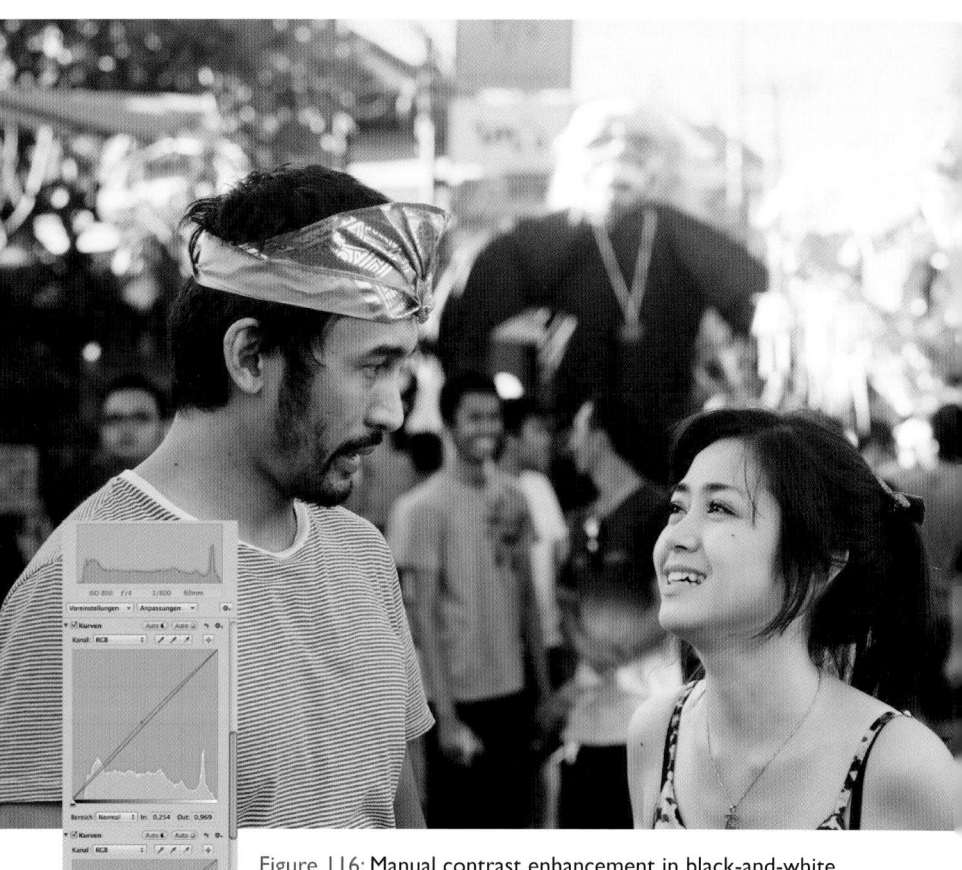

Figure 116: **Manual contrast enhancement in black-and-white conversions:** The camera converted the JPEG here with the MONOCHROME + R FILTER. I then edited the image in Apple Aperture 3 by applying a contrast curve typical for black-and-white film.

The X-Pro1 and X-E1 aren't black-and-white cameras. As with nearly every other digital camera, they capture subjects in color, save this data as color RAW files, and then later develop the images in black-and-white during the RAW conversion. Along with the usual suspects of Lightroom, Photoshop, and Aperture, there are also highly specialized programs such as Nik Silver Efex Pro and Topaz B&W Effects that offer many more possibilities than the camera's comparatively rudimentary internal black-and-white options.

Nevertheless, it can still be useful for experienced black-and-white photographers to use the black-and-white film simulation mode. If nothing else, it will provide you with a preview image in the EVF and on the LCD monitor that can inform your later decisions and methods. In addition, it can be useful to save the JPEG produced by the camera as a reference when executing the external RAW conversion. You lose nothing by switching your camera into black-and-white mode, because at any time you can go in and reconvert the RAW data files into color versions with one of the five color film simulations.

FILM SIMULATION BRACKETING

If you would like to get a quick overview of what the different film simulations would look like with a given subject, you can press the DRIVE button and select the option FILM SIMULATION BKT. When this feature is active, the camera will produce three JPEGs each time you release the shutter. You can control which three simulations the camera uses by going to SHOOTING MENU > FILM SIMULATION BKT.

In principle this is a practical option for anyone who can't decide which simulation to use, or who would like to have more than one result from which to choose. However, the camera does not save any RAW files when this mode is activated. Selecting this option means foregoing the opportunity to develop and optimize your exposures again later with either the internal or an external RAW converter.

For this reason, I recommend that you generally avoid this mode and instead shoot with the FINE+RAW image quality setting so you will always have access to the RAW files. Snap your exposures with the film simulation that you are most likely to prefer. Then, if needed, use the internal RAW converter to produce alternate options (PLAYBACK MENU > RAW CONVERSION).

2.7.3 COLOR

The color setting allows you to control the color saturation of your JPEGs. The intensity of the colors can be either dialed up or toned down. To do this, go to SHOOTING MENU > COLOR and select one of the five available levels from (−2) LOW to (+2) HIGH.

As with most other JPEG settings, you can change the COLOR setting by pressing the Q button or switching the custom shooting profile. This setting cannot be assigned to the Fn button, however.

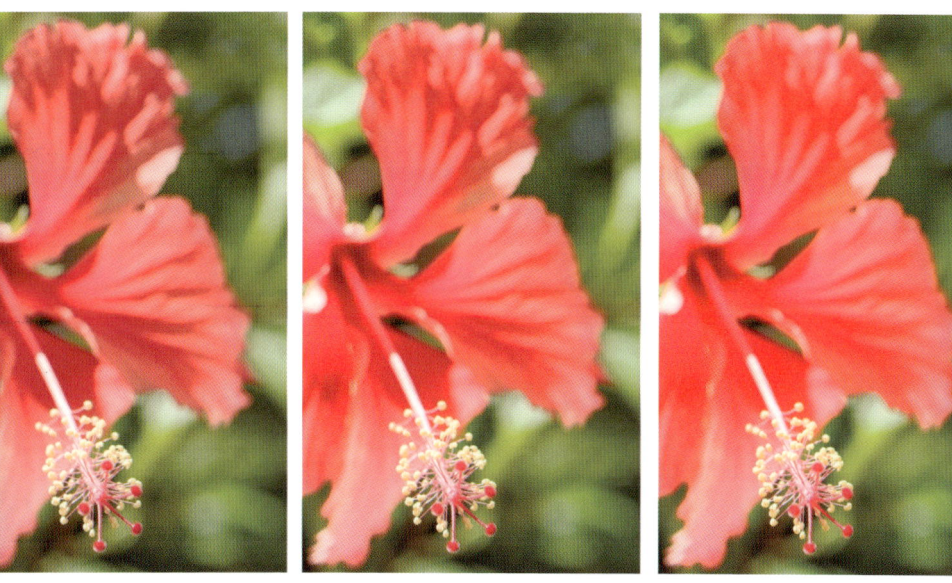

Figure 117: **Color saturation:** The JPEG setting COLOR regulates the intensity of color reproduction. The setting you choose works in combination with the color profile for whichever film simulation you're using. Using Provia in combination with (+2) HIGH for the COLOR still produces less saturated colors than Velvia does with a neutral COLOR setting. This illustration shows the film simulation Astia at three different color levels: COLOR (–2) LOW (left), COLOR (0) STANDARD (middle), and COLOR (+2) HIGH (right).

The color setting—as with most other JPEG settings—is something you don't really need to think about until after your exposure. With the help of the internal RAW converter (PLAYBACK MENU > RAW CONVERSION) you can increase or decrease the saturation as needed. In the end, color is a matter of taste, but you should make sure that dialing up the color saturation doesn't result in an overflow of a particular color channel (and the ensuing loss of tone values).

2.7.4 CONTRAST

Every image has three rough areas of tonal values: shadows, midtones, and highlights. When you increase the brightness of the highlights while decreasing the brightness of the shadows, you are increasing the contrast of the exposure. When working in an image-editing program, you can adjust the contrast control or apply an appropriate gradation curve to achieve this effect.

The camera allows you to modulate the bright and dark tonal values—the highlights and shadows—independently. By brightening or darkening these image areas separately, you can roughly influence the gradation curve of the JPEG produced by the camera.

CONTROLLING THE HIGHLIGHTS

By going to SHOOTING MENU 2 > HIGHLIGHT TONE you can control the areas of bright tonal values in your images. Here also you have five levels at your disposal, ranging from (−2) SOFT to (+2) HARD. You can also adjust this setting by opening up the Quick Menu (Q button) or changing the custom shooting profile.

Settings on the SOFT side will darken your highlights, and settings on the HARD side will brighten them. STANDARD produces a neutral result.

Figure 118: The HIGHLIGHT TONE setting: This contrast setting ▶ regulates the reproduction in the bright areas of your images: SOFT darkens the highlights, STANDARD keeps their normal brightness, and HARD makes them even brighter. In this illustration, you can spot the effect of the highlight tone setting clearly on the roof of the car, on the bright collar of the shirt, and in the sky. As you can see, you should adjust this setting with caution. Increasing the contrast too much can cause the highlights to blow out, resulting in a loss of image detail. Conversely, images for which the contrast is too soft appear unattractively flat. As with other settings, it's best to adjust the highlight tone with the internal RAW converter afterward to try out different options.

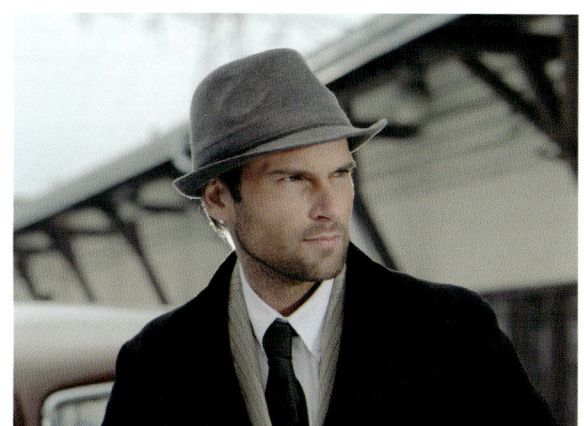

HIGHLIGHT TONE
(–2) SOFT

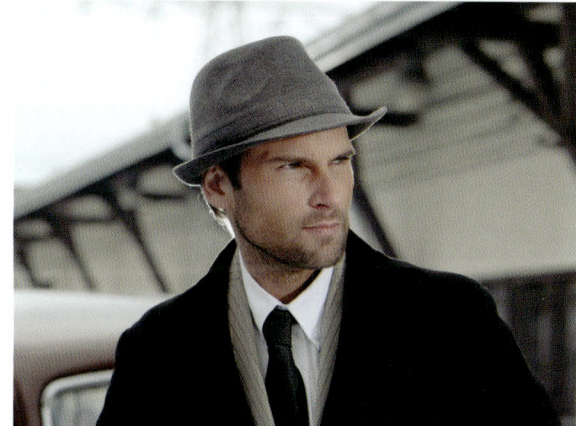

HIGHLIGHT TONE
(0) STANDARD

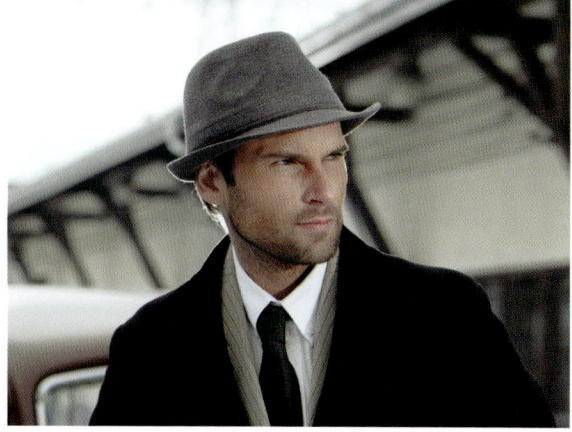

HIGHLIGHT TONE
(+2) HARD

CONTROLLING THE SHADOWS

The counterparts to the highlights in an image can be
controlled by going to SHOOTING MENU > SHADOW
TONE. This setting controls the contrast in the dark parts
of your images. Five levels are available, from (−2) SOFT
to (+2) HARD. Adjusting your image with values on the
SOFT end of the scale will result in brighter shadows,
and values on the HARD side will result in darker shadow
tones. You can also change this setting by pressing the Q
button or changing the shooting profile.

Figure 119: The SHADOW TONE setting: This setting controls the ▶
reproduction of shadows when the camera produces JPEG files. SOFT
brightens the shadows and HARD darkens them. This effect can be seen
clearly in the overcoat in this photo. The coat's different levels of brightness are much easier to see when the shadow tone is set to SOFT. The
coat and the tie are blocked up when the shadow tone is set to HARD.
This is another reason to err on the side of setting this parameter conservatively to avoid the unwanted loss of tonal values.

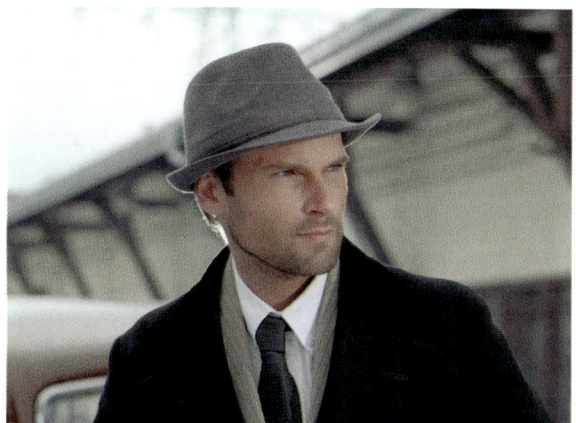

SHADOW TONE
(−2) SOFT

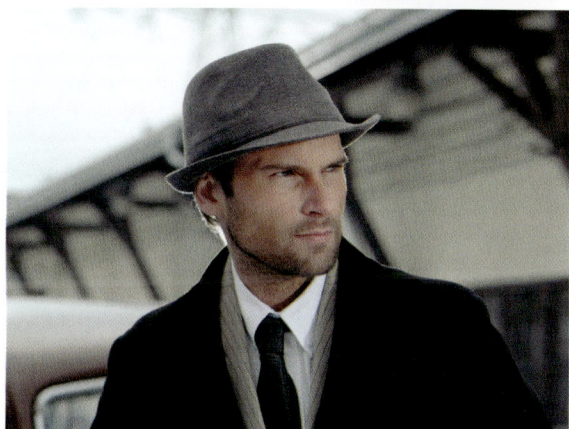

SHADOW TONE
(0) STANDARD

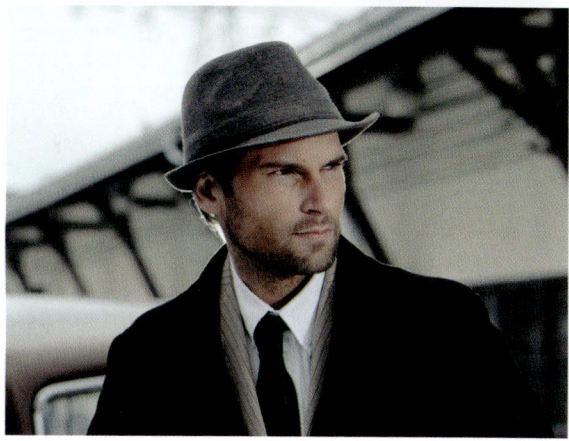

SHADOW TONE
(+2) HARD

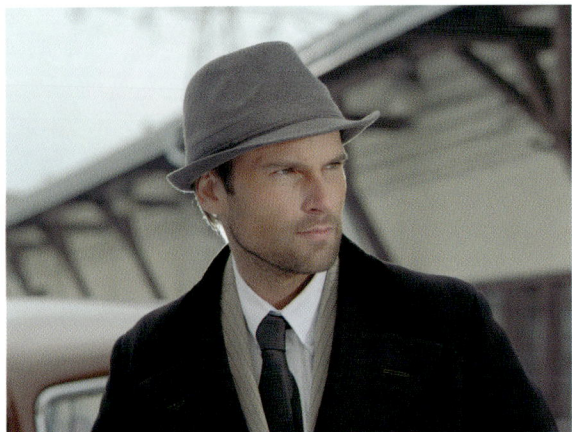

SOFT–SOFT

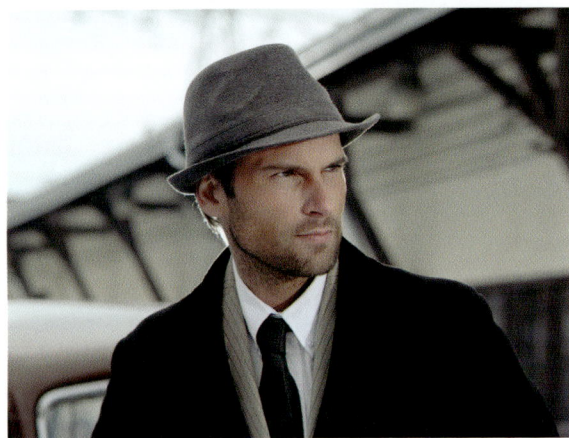

STANDARD–STANDARD

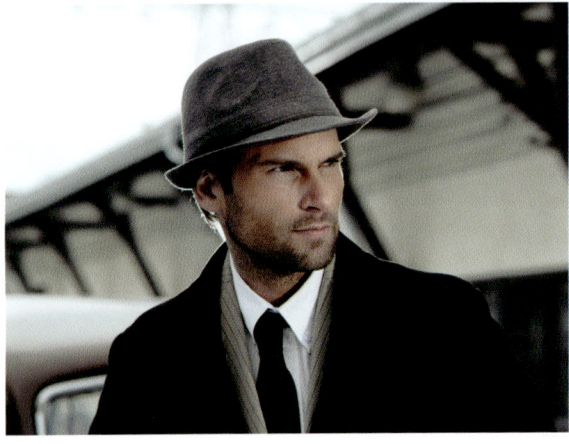

HARD–HARD

Being able to regulate the highlights and the shadows separately gives you more flexibility than a conventional contrast control does. You can, for example, brighten the dark areas of an image without blowing out the highlights.

You can also use these contrast controls to simulate a traditional contrast control by adjusting the highlights and shadows in the same direction. Setting the tonal values in both areas to SOFT, for example, will reduce the contrast in your image, and setting them both to HARD will increase it.

Since these contrast settings greatly affect the appearance of your images, it's generally best to play it safe and avoid the extreme settings when exposing your image. You can always experiment with less conservative settings afterward by using the internal RAW converter to redevelop your images.

◄ Figure 120: Traditional contrast control: By adjusting the highlight tone and shadow tone in parallel, you can adjust the contrast of your exposures by conventional means. To do this, simply set the parameters identically for both areas of tonal values. The image shows the same exposure three times, with both the shadow and highlight tones set at SOFT, then at STANDARD, and finally at HARD.

2.7.5 SHARPNESS

If you ask a layperson whether he or she prefers images that are sharper or less sharp, the answer is likely to be, "Sharper, of course!" But in regard to image sharpness, or better yet, the sharpening of an image, the answer isn't so simple.

Sharpening an image accentuates details, making them easier to discern. At the same time, however, the process causes the smallest details to be lost. This is why it's best to apply the sharpness setting in a measured fashion. Fortunately, this setting is available when you're using the internal RAW converter, so you can try out several different settings and choose the best after capturing your image.

In addition to bringing up the sharpness options when using the RAW converter, you can pull them up in shooting mode by going to SHOOTING MENU > SHARPNESS. The camera again offers five steps of intensity, ranging from (–2) SOFT to (+2) HARD. You can also open the Quick Menu to adjust the sharpness with the Q button, or program custom shooting profiles with varying sharpness levels.

HINT

Different contrast settings can often give the impression of increased (or decreased) image sharpness. The stronger the contrast is, the stronger the impression of sharpness. A popular method of achieving this effect is to increase the microcontrast in the midtones of an image. The much-loved clarity slider in Adobe Lightroom is capable of doing this. Many photographers like to set their sharpness to a softer level, preferring to adjust it on their computer, perhaps by using an unsharp mask or a specific software program such as Nik Sharpener Pro. The truth is, you can sharpen an image at any time; it's much more difficult to remove excess sharpness after the fact.

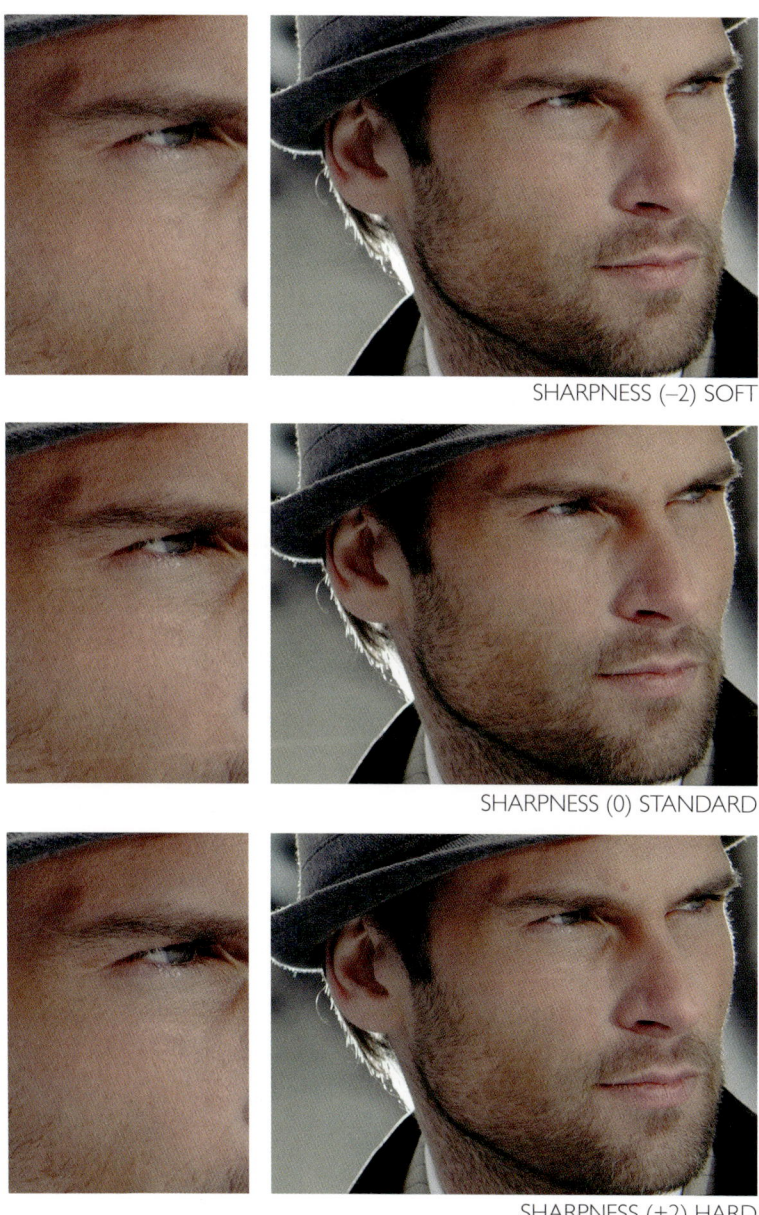

SHARPNESS (−2) SOFT

SHARPNESS (0) STANDARD

SHARPNESS (+2) HARD

Figure 121: **Sharpness setting:** This image demonstrates the effect of the SHARPNESS setting when programmed to SOFT, STANDARD, and HARD. With increasing hardness, the setting accentuates the contours of individual details, thereby giving the impression of a greater overall sharpness.

2.7.6 NOISE REDUCTION

Image noise most commonly arises at very high ISO values. One way to keep image noise in check is by using the noise reduction function when converting your JPEGs. This method has a catch, though: the stronger you apply this setting, the more image details are lost. Applying noise reduction is a balance of retaining details while doing away with visual interference.

The X-Pro1 and X-E1 excel at this function, and SHOOTING MENU > NOISE REDUCTION offers five different settings—ranging again from (–2) LOW to (+2) HIGH—to help you strike the optimal balance. This is another instance in which you should delay worrying about the perfect setting until after you've exposed your image and are ready to process it with the camera's internal RAW converter.

As with most of the other JPEG parameters, you can define the noise reduction setting in the Quick Menu as well as in the custom shooting profiles.

HINT

Many photographers prefer to carry out their own noise reduction with image-editing software on their computers, rather than trust the camera to do the job. In this case, set the NOISE REDUCTION to LOW. Since noise reduction is a setting that affects only JPEG files, you would need to attend to noise reduction anyway when developing your images in an external RAW conversion program or when using a specialized program such as Nik Dfine or Topaz DeNoise. The camera's X-Trans sensor captures images with so little noise, however, that distracting image noise is likely to surface only at ISO settings above ISO 3200.

The STANDARD (0) setting is, in most cases, a decent compromise. The camera's noise reduction technology is so good, actually, that some external editing programs can't hold a candle to it. But this too is a matter of personal taste and ultimately depends on your subject. In particular, when using the black-and-white conversion feature, you can almost always set the noise reduction to LOW (–2).

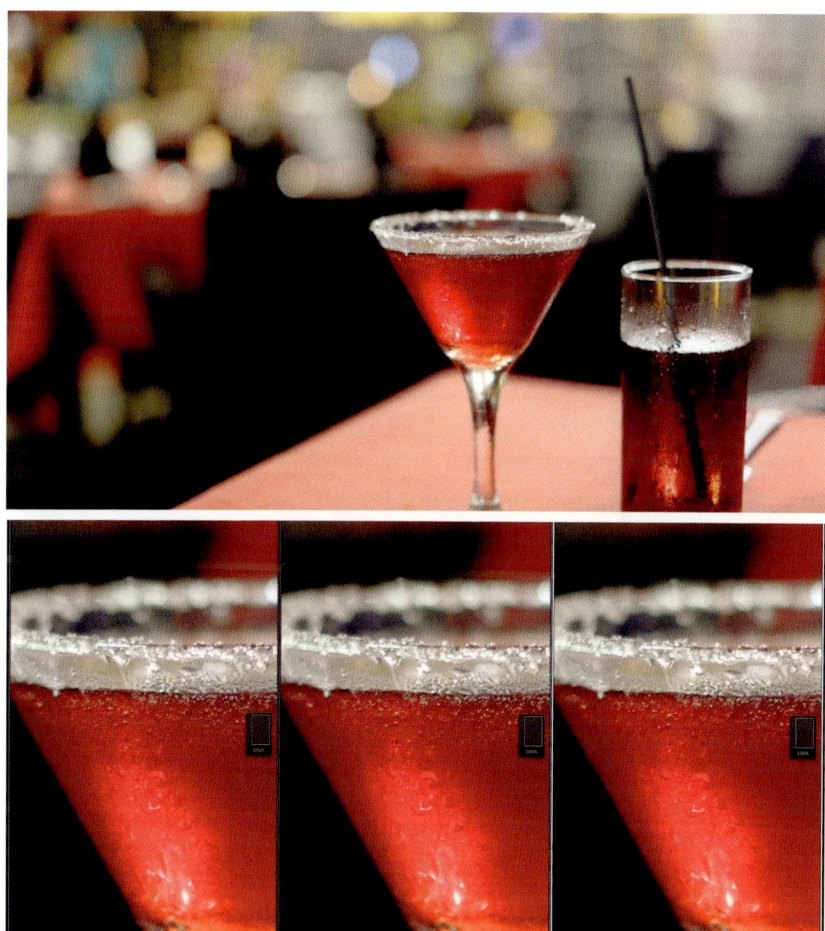

Figure 122: **Noise reduction setting:** This image, snapped at ISO 3200, shows just how effective the camera is at eliminating disturbing image noise while retaining desirable details when creating JPEGs. The three enlarged portions of the image show the results of applying the LOW, STANDARD, and HIGH noise reduction settings. Even in the lowest setting (left) you can see that the color noise is in no way bothersome. The standard setting in the middle is a decent compromise, but the HIGH setting washes out a few details and is thus not ideal for this situation.

2.7.7 CUSTOM SHOOTING PROFILES

As we've seen, the X-Pro1 and X-E1 offer a plethora of setting options: ISO, DR function, white balance, film simulation, color, contrast (highlights and shadows), sharpness, noise reduction. You may be wondering, "How am I supposed to adjust all of these settings quickly when I'm ready to snap an image? I want to take pictures; I don't want to stand around fumbling with my camera!"

Here is where the seven custom shooting profiles come into play. They allow you to program each variable independently and then save all of the settings together in a bundle. Then you can switch back and forth quickly among your predefined profiles.

CREATING AND CHANGING CUSTOM PROFILES

To set up or change a custom profile, go to SHOOTING MENU > EDIT/SAVE CUSTOM SETTING and select one of the seven profiles (CUSTOM 1 to 7). You can either import your current camera settings to one of the profiles (SAVE CURRENT SETTINGS) or input new parameters for ISO, DYNAMIC RANGE, FILM SIMULATION, WHITE BALANCE, COLOR, SHARPNESS, HIGHLIGHT TONE, SHADOW TONE, and NOISE REDUCTION.

You can also use a combination of the two methods by first saving the current settings and then adjusting them accordingly. When you're finished and you press the DISP/BACK button, the camera will ask if you'd like to save your settings. When the answer is yes, select OK; if you'd like to continue editing the selected custom profile, select CANCEL.

TIP

The Q button offers a shortcut to editing or changing your shooting profile. Press and hold the Q button until the EDIT/SAVE CUSTOM SETTING menu appears on the camera's active display.

RECALLING A CUSTOM PROFILE

To activate one of the seven saved custom profiles, go to SHOOTING MENU > SELECT CUSTOM SETTING and choose your desired profile.

The Q button can also save you some time here: tap the Q button to bring up the Quick Menu and then select from C1 to C7 in the setting field in the top left. The shooting settings associated with each profile will display in the Quick Menu so you can get an overview of the definitions for each setting.

The third option to switch between custom profiles quickly is to program an Fn button to serve this purpose. Hold the Fn button until the configuration menu appears and then assign SELECT CUSTOM SETTING.

IMPORTANT

The camera always operates with its current settings, also known as BASIC in the Quick Menu display. Custom profiles are just storage spaces that you can quickly recall and copy into the camera's current settings. Don't confuse custom profiles with modes. Instead, regard them as a quick way to change your current camera settings by selecting and copying predefined sets of shooting parameters into your camera's current settings. This also means that one of your custom profiles (typically C1) should hold your preferred default camera settings, so you can always quickly revert to this important configuration.

EXAMPLES OF CUSTOM PROFILES

Which profiles should you save? Only you can answer this question for yourself—photographers not only have individual requirements and aims, but they also have their own stylistic preferences. This is exactly why your camera offers so many different programming possibilities. If there were one optimal universal setting, Fujifilm could have done away with the various options. Nevertheless, here are a few recommendations for potentially useful custom profiles:

- **All-around profile:** In this profile, I save my personal default settings that generally apply to everyday situations and quick snapshots with preferred JPEG output. The typical settings for my all-around profile are automatic white balance, auto ISO, auto DR, Astia, and occasionally a decreased noise reduction set at medium low.

- **DR100% profile:** This is a variation on the all-around profile with the dynamic range setting fixed at DR100%. This profile allows me to use the live histogram for correcting the exposure and targeting the brighter areas of my image more accurately when defining the exposure settings.

- **Black-and-white profile:** I use this profile anytime I imagine a shot would look good in black-and-white, which includes the black-and-white film simulation, increased contrast settings and minimal noise reduction. The electronic viewfinder gives me a practical black-and-white preview of my subject.

- **Special profile:** I generally reserve one profile for special situations such as shooting in a studio or taking infrared images, when it is practical to shoot with a color temperature setting predefined in Kelvin.

- **"RAW shooter" profile:** I use this profile when I know in advance that I will probably want to expose the image very carefully so that I can develop and edit it with an external RAW converter.

A JPEG PROFILE FOR RAW SHOOTERS

No, the idea of a JPEG profile for RAW shooters is not a joke. While JPEG settings have no effect on RAW files, they do affect what image you can see in the electronic viewfinder (EVF) and on the LCD. Moreover, the data for the live histogram is derived from the image that appears in the live view—in other words, it too is affected by your current JPEG settings.

What does this mean in practice? If you select VELVIA as your film simulation, for example, not only will you have a brightly colored JPEG; you'll also have a more brightly colored live view preview with pronounced contrast. This image preview is reflected in the live histogram as well, and the Velvia simulation will cause the peaks of exposure to shift to either the left or the right limits more quickly than if Provia were used instead.

The same goes for the contrast settings (HIGHLIGHT TONE and SHADOW TONE): if both parameters are set to HARD, then the highlights and shadows will shift beyond the right and left limits of the histogram faster than they would if both were set to SOFT.

As I've already said, the RAW file itself isn't affected by any of this—it collects all of the image information that the sensor is capable of capturing. Conversely, JPEGs rely on only a portion of the RAW data.

Do you see where this is going? The objective here is setting the JPEG parameters in a way that allows you to see the largest possible portion of the RAW data, because this is the information that interests us as RAW shooters. We want to squeeze everything possible out of our camera and its sensor, to get the absolute maximum and leave nothing behind. We want to explore the limits of the dynamic range and expose as close as possible to its borders. And we want the live histogram to inform us as precisely as possible of where these limits are.

The JPEG settings influence how we expose and adjust our images because we make our decisions about exposure using the information we can gather from the histogram and the live image. We therefore want JPEG settings that produce the softest contrast in order to obtain a histogram that reveals the most useful information about dynamic range for RAW files. Here are my recommendations for this JPEG profile:

- DYNAMIC RANGE > DR100%. The live histogram supplies meaningful information only with this DR setting, and we don't want our RAW files to end up underexposed by 1 or 2 EV due to the camera choosing DR200% or DR400%.

- FILM SIMULATION > PROVIA. This is the most neutral film simulation and also has the softest contrast. This setting will prevent highlights and shadows from unnecessarily being cropped at either end of the histogram.

- HIGHLIGHT TONE > (–2) SOFT. In the RAW format, the sensor has a highlight exposure reserve of at least 0.4 EV in comparison to the processed JPEG format. You can access this reserve with an external RAW converter. The live histogram should be set to SOFT at its edges to prevent RAW shooters from exposing their images to be too dark.

- SHADOW TONE > (–2) SOFT. When you use DR100% with high-contrast subjects in order to use the live histogram to base your exposure on the bright areas of your image, the dark areas often end up appearing as blocked-up black areas. This SHADOW TONE setting of (–2) SOFT counteracts the problem, since it brightens the dark tonal values in the viewfinder (and in the live histogram).

ETTR—EXPOSE TO THE RIGHT

The ETTR exposure technique is popular among RAW shooters because it takes into account the technical characteristics of the camera's sensor. The ETTR rule suggests that you should expose every image (regardless of its dynamic range) as far to the right of the histogram as possible without allowing any valuable highlight areas to become overexposed. The reasoning behind this is technical: since the X-Pro1 and X-E1 are 12-bit cameras, they can differentiate 4,096 (= 2^{12}) tonal values that they must pack into some nine exposure values. Since the brightness gets cut in half for each exposure value, the brightest exposure value contains 2,048 (=4,096/2) tonal values, the second brightest has only 1,024, and so on. The lowest exposure value of the camera can only record eight different tones.

If you expose your images as brightly as possible, you will be relying on a greater number of tonal values. This will give you more tolerance when editing your images, especially since you can take an image that's been exposed to the right and shift it back to the left when developing the RAW file and using a software program's exposure control feature.

The noise behavior of the sensor provides an additional reason for following the ETTR line of thinking. Noise is much more of a problem in the shadows because the signal-to-noise ratio is much worse for darker tonal values. For subjects that are very dark and have weak contrast (e.g., a black cat on a black street), it makes sense to forgo attempting to expose your image realistically as black, and instead to brighten it up and expose it as gray, knowing that you can correct the exposure later with the RAW conversion. This method allows you to have more tone values and less noise.

ETTR often leads to misunderstandings. It does not suggest that you should expose your images in such a way that you end up with overexposed areas and lost tonal values above the sensor's upper limit. Correctly applying ETTR methodology actually often requires that you shift the image left to make sure that any significant highlights aren't blown, but are located directly at the right limit of the histogram. The highlights should just touch the right border; they shouldn't go far beyond it!

▶

▶ Finally, keep in mind that shifting a dark and low-contrast image to the right inevitably leads to slower shutter speeds and/or lower f-numbers. ETTR only makes sense when the subject is well suited to adjustments in the exposure parameters. It's no good, for example, if you need to raise the ISO, or if you allow your camera to do so with auto ISO, in order to expose to the right. You're only making extra work for yourself, because any benefits will be counterbalanced by the cost of needing a stronger signal amplification.

It's also important to note that shifting a RAW image to the left in an external RAW converter can lead to color shifts, meaning the resulting image can look different from a "correctly" exposed shot. To be safe, you may want to record a second (darker) RAW file or use the camera's exposure bracketing feature (DRIVE button).

Figure 123: A storm is coming: Looking out of my ▶ apartment window in Bangkok, I saw this quite impressive buildup of clouds. In order to capture them without blowing important highlights, I set the camera to ISO 200 and used the live histogram to properly expose the shot. The resulting RAW file was processed in Lightroom 4 and Apple Aperture. Exposure parameters: X-E1 with 18–55mm kit zoom, 18mm, f/5, 1/50 second.

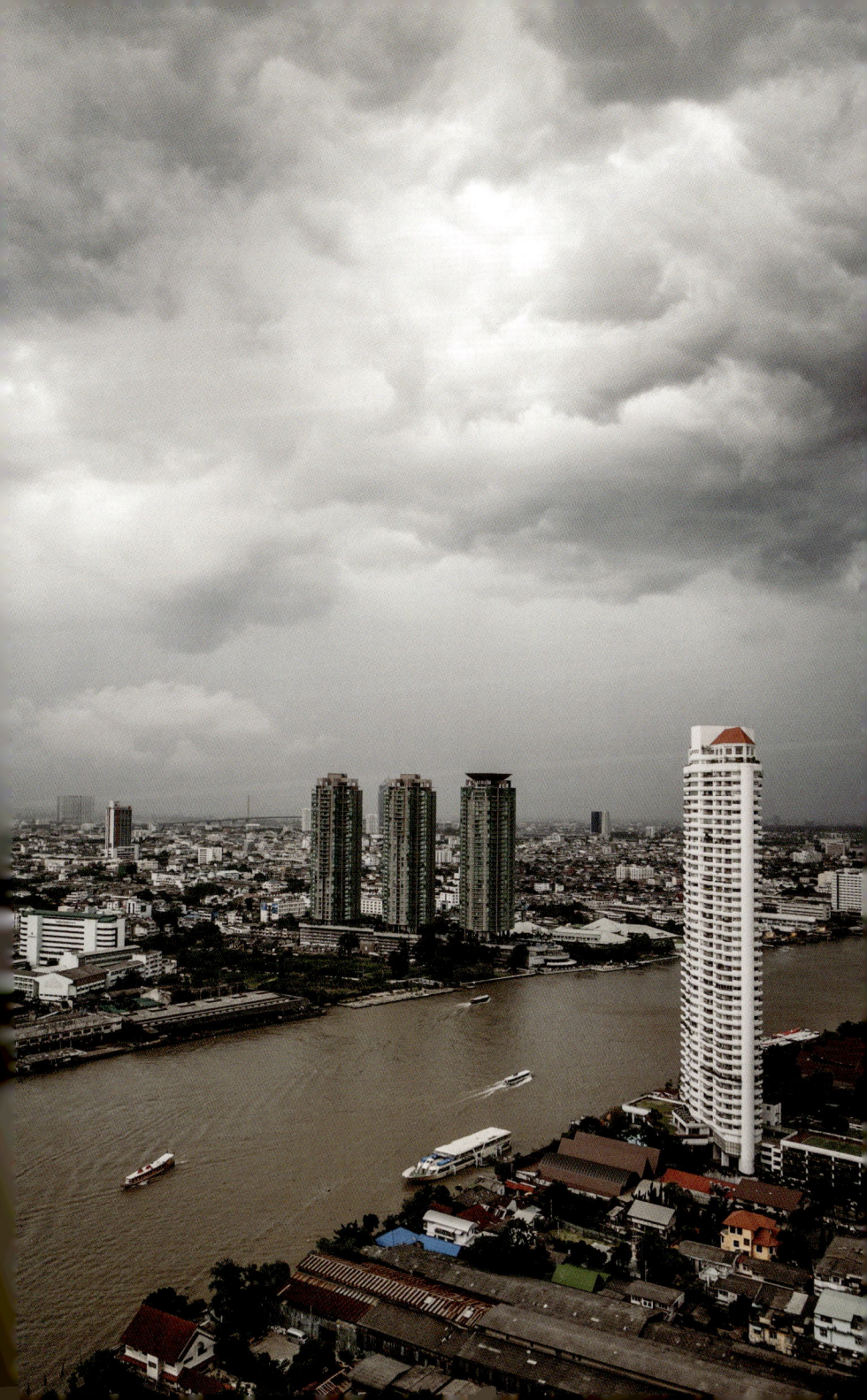

2.7.8 INTERNAL VS. EXTERNAL RAW CONVERSION

The X-Pro1 and X-E1 make a RAW shooter out of every-
one to some degree. This is because the camera's internal RAW converter allows even the most dedicated JPEG
photographers to develop new and improved JPEGs from
already-exposed images with just a few simple steps. As
a user of these cameras, you can be a relaxed specta-
tor to the fervid wars fought in Internet forums on the
subject of "RAW vs. JPEG." By using the recommended
FINE+RAW setting, you're always on the right side and
have all of your options available:

- You can hold onto the JPEG that the camera produces
  immediately after exposure when you are satisfied with
  the JPEG settings that you used.

- You can use the camera's internal RAW converter to
  develop the RAW file into alternate versions of the
  original JPEG file.

- You can transfer the RAW file to a computer and use an
  external RAW converter such as Lightroom, Silkypix or
  Aperture to develop and edit JPEGs.

- You can also transfer the JPEGs you produced with the
  first two options to your computer and continue to edit
  them there. The robust JPEGs that the camera produces
  are intended to allow post-processing. With that said, the
  compressed 8-bit JPEG image format (256 different tonal
  values) does have certain technical limits, putting it at an
  obvious disadvantage in comparison to the 16-bit files
  from external RAW converters.

Figure 124: **External RAW conversion:** When shooting with the X-E1 and X-Pro1, you can ▶
attain maximum sharpness, detail resolution, and control over colors and contrast with the
help of an external RAW workflow. This example benefited from the use of RPP 64, Adobe
Lightroom, Apple Aperture, and VSCO Film. Exposure parameters: XF60mmF2.4 R Macro,
f/8, 0.4 second, ISO 200, automatic white balance.

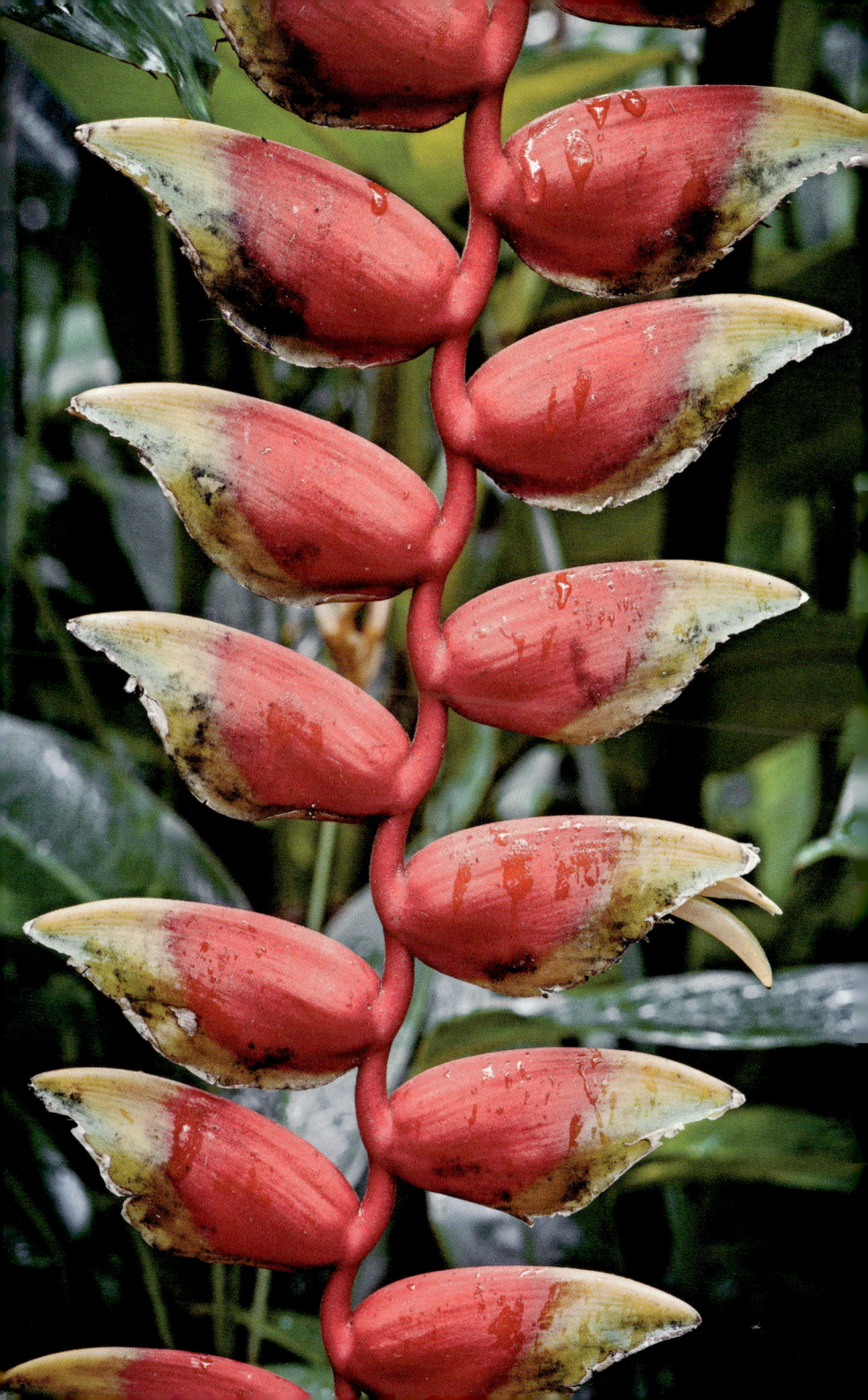

When should you develop RAW files internally and when should you rely on an external RAW converter? This is ultimately a question of purpose and quality. Just to be clear: the camera's internal RAW converter produces excellent results as well as the much-loved Fuji colors. For most situations, the internal converter is more than adequate. Configuring your camera in the manner I've just discussed will allow the X-Pro1 or X-E1 to develop robust, attractive JPEGs that you can optimize on your computer without any trouble.

If you are interested in pushing the camera to its quality and resolution limits, though, I recommend that you use an external RAW converter. With the right settings, these programs are capable of producing fantastic results.

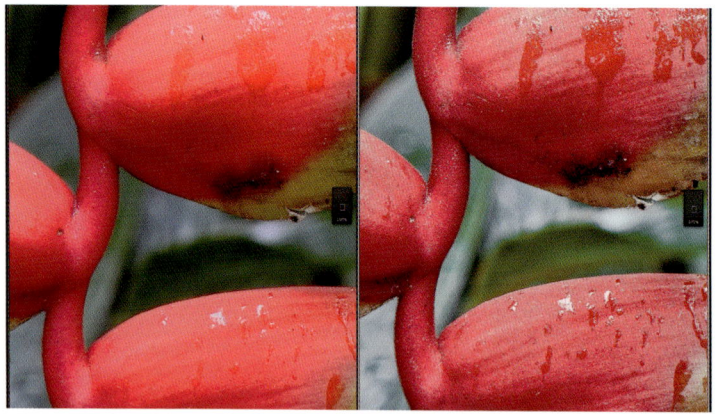

Figure 125: RAW (internal) vs. RAW (external)—comparing outputs:
To get the maximum performance from the camera sensor, you need not only competent post-processing, but also proper exposure technique. This means that exposing your images perfectly with ISO 200 and ETTR isn't enough if you want to explore the limits of the X-Trans sensor: you also need to shoot without any camera shake by using a stable tripod as well as a remote trigger or timer release, and you need to use an aperture that falls in the "sweet spot" of the lens (usually between f/5.6 and f/11). With this setup, there are noticeable differences between images created with the internal RAW converter and with a thorough external RAW development process. You can simply get more from the RAW data with an external converter—just set aside some time for it. This figure shows two outputs from the previous image: the left is a Velvia image produced directly by the camera; the right is the product of an external RAW workflow.

OPTICAL LENS CORRECTIONS

When the camera produces a JPEG file for you to review immediately after snapping an exposure, it applies several corrections (to distortion, vignetting, and chromatic aberrations) based on the optics of the lens, and saves information about these corrections as metadata in the RAW file. External RAW converters such as Silkypix and Lightroom can access the metadata and apply the necessary corrections automatically when developing an image. The corrections applied by external RAW converters aren't always identical to those applied by the camera itself, however. The RAW conversion programs RPP and AccuRaw lack the ability to apply any optical corrections. Instead, they output files with a full 16.3 megapixels of resolution, whereas the camera's internal engine and most commercial third-party converters (like Lightroom, Silkypix, Aperture, and Capture One) will deliver optically corrected files with only 16.0 megapixels.

You can think about the optical correction information saved in the RAW files as stage directions that different actors interpret in different ways. In the case of RPP and AccuRaw, there simply aren't any actors available.

2.7.9 COLOR SPACE

One other—and final—JPEG setting for the camera is COLOR SPACE. This JPEG setting is something of an anomaly because you won't find it in the shooting menu: it's located in the SET-UP menu. It also isn't available in the Quick Menu and you can't assign it to an Fn button or save it in the custom shooting profiles.

The camera allows you to save JPEGs in two different color spaces: sRGB and Adobe RGB. Both color spaces have the same number of colors, but those colors aren't the same.

• sRGB is based on the technology of standard computer screens and is accordingly suitable for any images that you plan to post on the web (e.g., on Flickr) or in social networks (e.g., Facebook), or view on a desktop computer, laptop, iPad, or smartphone.

• Adobe RGB offers a larger range of colors than sRGB (with larger gaps between individual colors) and includes colors that are specific to commercial four-color printing (CMYK).

Which color space you should use depends entirely on what you intend to do with your images. For most applications, sRGB will be the better choice (for compatibility reasons). sRGB is the color space that the LCD monitor and EVF use, and it is also the color space of most computer screens, laptops, and smartphones. If you do decide to use Adobe RGB, you should definitely use a wide gamut monitor that offers an extended color space display to edit your images. Only with a special monitor of this sort can you actually display the colors in the extended range that are not available in the sRGB color space. Without a monitor designed for this purpose, editing Adobe RGB images is similar to flying blind.

In addition to sRGB and Adobe RGB, there are several other extended color spaces. Modern image-editing programs often support more than a half dozen varieties. If you take your images to a service provider for printing, you should ask ahead of time what color space it prefers (usually it is sRGB). Anyone who works with laptops or monitors or plans to present his or her images online or in a digital format is best served by sRGB. I personally save all of my images exclusively in sRGB format.

This question about color space doesn't affect just the JPEGs that the camera produces; it also has implications for external RAW conversion. While RAW files themselves aren't saved in a specific color space, eventually you will have to save the converted RAW file, and then you will need to make a decision.

The camera adds an additional underscore to the file name of any JPEG file saved in Adobe RGB format. For example, if the file DSCF4064.JPG were saved in Adobe RGB, it would be saved as _DSF4064.JPG. This also goes for the RAW file associated with a JPEG, as long as the camera was set in Adobe RGB when the image was exposed (e.g., _DSF4064.RAF). This convention isn't specific to Fuji products; it's an industry standard. For every JPEG you develop from a RAW file using the camera's internal RAW converter, you can select a color space anew. The camera then uses the file naming convention described here.

2.7.10 USING THE INTERNAL RAW CONVERTER

As you already know, your camera has its own internal RAW converter for developing JPEGs from RAW files at any time. This converter gives you complete control over the various JPEG parameters, the white balance, and the color space of the final output. The internal converter not only delivers the popular Fuji colors; it allows you to operate independent of external software that may be either difficult to use or not (yet) compatible with the camera's cutting-edge RAW format.

When in playback mode, you can go to PLAYBACK MENU > RAW CONVERSION to bring up the internal RAW converter and use it to develop the selected RAW file. You will then have the following options available:

- With PUSH/PULL PROCESSING you can retroactively correct the exposure upward or downward in steps of 1/3 EV. This function is analogous to the exposure control slider of an external RAW conversion program.

- DYNAMIC RANGE allows you to raise the highlight brightness in an image that was exposed at DR200%

or DR400% by one or two aperture stops, for example, in order to raise its contrast.

- FILM SIMULATION allows you to choose from the camera's ten different color and black-and-white film modes.

- WHITE BALANCE gives you access to the various white balance presets and lets you manually select a color temperature in Kelvin (K).

- WB SHIFT brings up the color shift matrix for the white balance, where you can use the selector keys to tweak the color tone within the selected white balance setting.

- COLOR controls the color saturation of the conversion.

- With SHARPNESS, you can choose from five levels that will affect the degree of sharpness processing that the conversion will include.

- HIGHLIGHT TONE and SHADOW TONE independently determine the contrast settings (tone curve) for the bright and dark areas of an image, respectively.

- NOISE REDUCTION regulates the strength of the noise suppression that the converter uses when producing a JPEG.

- With COLOR SPACE, you can decide on the color space for the finished JPEG.

The options available in the RAW converter correspond to those in the shooting menu. Unfortunately, however, some of the descriptions vary slightly. For example, the option (−1) MEDIUM SOFT is called M-SOFT in the RAW converter.

If you'd like to develop a JPEG using exactly the same settings that you had in place when you exposed the image, simply press REFLECT SHOOTING COND.

What should you do if you want to develop a RAW file that is no longer saved on your camera's memory card?

No problem: you can copy RAW files created with an X-Pro1 or X-E1 (they don't have to be from your own camera) back onto an SD card at any time and then use the camera's internal converter to develop them.

IMPORTANT

The X-E1 will not develop RAW files from an X-Pro1 and vice versa.

Here's how it works: Copy the RAW file (complete with the recognizable filename extension .RAF) into the subfolder on the memory card to which your camera currently saves new image files. The directory path could be, for example, MEMORY CARD > DCIM > 104_FUJI. The number preceding the word FUJI is variable and dependent on the number of exposures that you have created with your camera.

If you have recently formatted your memory card and it doesn't yet have the proper file architecture, simply take a new exposure first and the camera will automatically create the appropriate directories. Then you can insert the memory card into your computer's reader and copy the RAW file that you would like to develop later to the appropriate image folder.

IMPORTANT

Transferring images from a computer to your camera is not possible with the included USB cable. You need to treat the memory card as an external drive and connect it directly to your computer. Then you can copy the desired images to the image folder.

2.8 CONTINUOUS SHOOTING, PANORAMAS, MOVIES, DOUBLE EXPOSURES, AND THE SELF-TIMER

The DRIVE button allows you to set the camera in several different exposure modes. You're already well acquainted with STILL IMAGE, the camera's standard setting. In this mode, the camera captures one single frame when you press the shutter button all the way down.

As long as the camera's buffer doesn't fill up, you can snap several frames in STILL IMAGE mode in quick succession. The buffer memory can hold about 11 exposures shot at the FINE+RAW quality setting. Since the image data is written to the memory card in the background, the X-E1 or X-Pro1 is always ready to shoot.

The camera's various bracketing options should also be familiar from the previous chapters. A quick review:

• AE BKT produces three images at different levels of exposure. The corresponding RAW files are saved in this mode, as long as the image quality setting dictates they should be (see section 2.3.2).

• ISO BKT produces three JPEG files at different ISO values from one exposure. No RAW files are saved (see section 2.5).

• FILM SIMULATION BKT produces three JPEGs with different film simulations from one exposure. Here too, the camera does not save any RAW files (see "Film Simulation" in section 2.7).

• DYNAMIC RANGE BKT creates three exposures at different DR settings and similarly saves no RAW files (see section 2.6).

IMPORTANT

> One unfortunate quality of the exposure bracketing func-
> tion is that the camera disables the shutter button until all
> of the image data for the three images is completely saved
> to the memory card.

The DRIVE button is also home to a few other handy
features:

• CONTINUOUS shooting

• MOTION PANORAMA

• MOVIE

Furthermore, the camera allows you to meld two images
exposed in quick succession into a single double-exposure with the MULTIPLE EXPOSURE feature. Inexplica-
bly, you can't access this feature by pressing the DRIVE
button—you have to go to the SHOOTING MENU.

CONTINUOUS SHOOTING (BURST MODE)

When the CONTINUOUS mode is selected from the
DRIVE-button options, the camera takes several exposures in a burst. You can choose between three and six
images per second. The camera will snap images at the
rate you determine for as long as you keep the shutter button fully depressed—or until the buffer memory
reaches its limit. If you're saving RAW files, the buffer
reaches its limit at about 11 exposures, but if you're
only saving JPEGs, you can shoot up to about 19. Once
the buffer memory fills up, the camera will still (spo-
radically) capture additional images, depending on
when older exposures are successfully transferred from
the buffer to the memory card. With a very fast memory card, you can basically shoot as many JPEGs as you
like and still retain a decent burst speed.

When using the CONTINUOUS mode, the camera applies the exposure, autofocus, and white balance settings that are in place for the initial exposure to the entire series. These settings are not reconfigured or adjusted for each individual capture.

The CONTINUOUS mode has some characteristics typical of Fuji:

• The file naming convention for the images captured in this mode is different from regular exposures: the file names for images in a continuous burst start with the letter S, for example: S0063422.RAF. If you import photos that are sorted alphabetically according to file name into your computer's image management software, any images belonging to a continuous series will pop up at the bottom of the list.

• Images that are part of a continuous series are treated differently from still images in the camera's playback mode: only the first image of the series is shown at the full size of the display. The rest of the exposures are displayed in a small window in the manner of a flip-book. To examine the individual images in a series, you must press the down selector key. Then you can browse the series' images as you normally would, using the selector keys or the command dial.

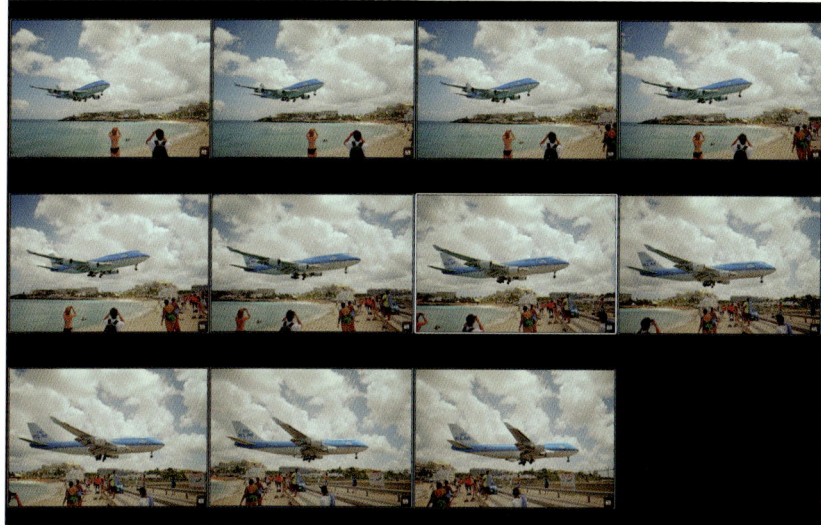

Figure 126: Continuous shooting mode: Even when saving RAW files, the camera can shoot up to six frames per second. The buffer memory, which can hold 11 RAW exposures, accordingly fills up in about 2 seconds. This means that good timing is critical for starting a series, because the actual window of time that the burst mode is fully functional is quite short. Also make sure to note the different file naming convention for images in a series: in contrast to other still images, the file names of images that are part of a series start with the letter S.

Figure 127: Playback of images in a series: When displaying a series of images in the playback mode, the camera presents the initial frame large and the others in a small flip-book preview. To examine the other images of the series more closely, you can use the down selector key and then browse through them as usual by using the selector keys or the command dial.

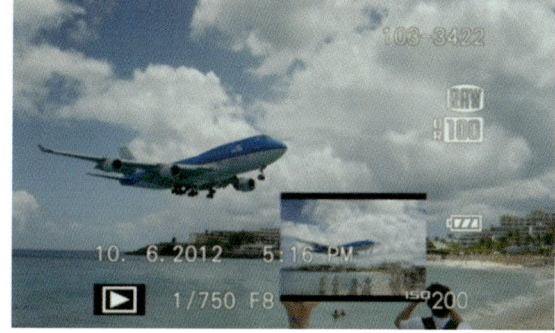

TIPS FOR WORKING IN BURST MODE

- Since the camera does not refocus or adjust the exposure or white balance after the first image in CONTINUOUS mode, it's a good idea to make sure you have these settings configured as accurately as possible before starting. Using the flash in burst mode is not possible.

- When you're using your camera's burst mode to track a moving subject, it's possible for the exposure situation to change drastically during the series. The first frame may be backlit, for example, while the remaining images in the series could be exposed with side light or reflected light. As another example, your moving subject may move from a shadowy area into direct sunlight. When you're trying to deal with circumstances such as these, opt for exposure settings that are a workable compromise for the entire series. You can set the exposure at an average setting by using AE lock (AE-L), by pressing the shutter button halfway, or by shooting in manual mode (**M**). The DR function also offers protection from blown-out highlights. If your subject exhibits a large dynamic range, consider using DR200% or DR400% to protect against overexposure.

- When using burst mode, set your focus in advance of the action and make sure to press the shutter button right before your subject reaches your desired focus point. You can also stop down the aperture to create a focus zone with a larger depth of field and then press the shutter button as soon as the subject moves into this zone. To avoid shutter lag owing to the autofocus, make sure to use the AF lock (AF-L), to store the focus by pressing the shutter button halfway, or focus manually.

- Since the camera's buffer can hold only 11 exposures at a time, you have just a brief two seconds for continuous shooting. This means your timing needs to be impeccable. You'll want to make sure that you have the shutter button pressed halfway down for at least a few fractions of a second before you actually want to start the burst; otherwise you run the risk of shutter lag ruining your shot.

• As an X-Pro1 user, you can also rely on the optical viewfinder (OVF) for fast-moving subjects, because it will allow you to perceive your subject without any time delay. This isn't true of the electronic viewfinder (EVF).

PANORAMA IMAGES

With the DRIVE-button option MOTION PANORAMA, you can create panorama exposures with dimensions of up to 7680 x 2160 pixels. The camera does most of the work, assembling the panorama image automatically from a series of still images. Your job as the photographer is to press the shutter button and evenly swivel the camera vertically or horizontally until the preset image angle is complete.

You can choose between two image angles, M and L, which correspond to 120 and 180 degrees, respectively, and can be applied either horizontally or vertically. In size L, the final size of the exposure in horizontal mode is 7680 x 1440 pixels, and in the vertical mode, 7680 x 2160 pixels. Size M ends up being 5120 x 1440 pixels with the horizontal setup and 5120 x 2160 pixels with the vertical. You can also use the vertical option to create a horizontal panorama—you'll just need to hold the camera on its side as you pivot it.

After you press the DRIVE button and select MOTION PANORAMA, the camera lets you define the direction you intend to move your camera with DIRECTION and the size of the panorama with ANGLE (M or L).

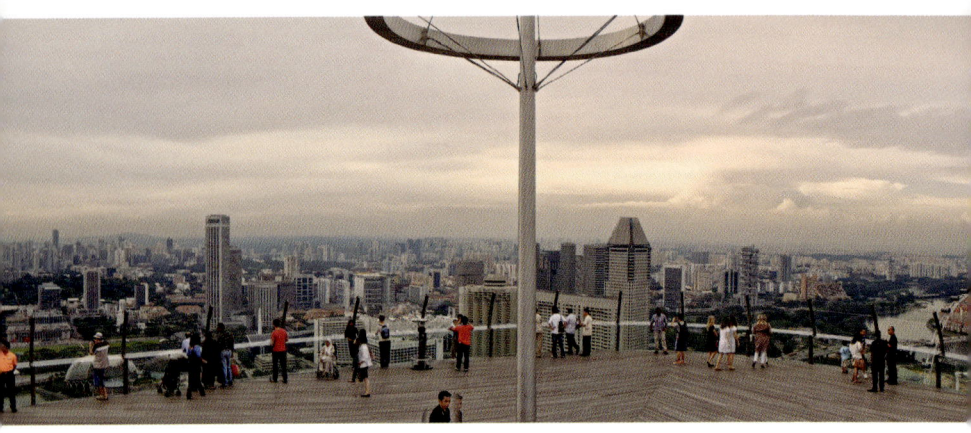

IMPORTANT

Using the MOTION PANORAMA option will not produce any RAW data; it only creates a large JPEG file. This means that you'll need to decide on a FILM SIMULATION and a WHITE BALANCE before you take the exposure. Neither setting can be changed afterward. Since panoramic images usually cover a large amount of subject matter with varying light conditions, you should set the white balance based on the most important area of your shot.

In a similar vein, the camera sets the exposure and the focus based on the first exposure in the series for panoramic images, so it also makes sense to set your focus and exposure in advance based on the most important part of your image—by focusing manually, or by storing the focus and exposure settings temporarily by pressing the shutter button halfway before you move the camera to its initial position and start to record the actual panorama.

Since panoramic images also tend to have a large dynamic range, it's often wise to avail yourself of the camera's DR function and select DR200% or DR400%. Since MOTION PANORAMA doesn't produce any RAW data and saves only a large JPEG file, ETTR won't do you any good. The camera doesn't provide you with any RAW file for you to map the tones afterward.

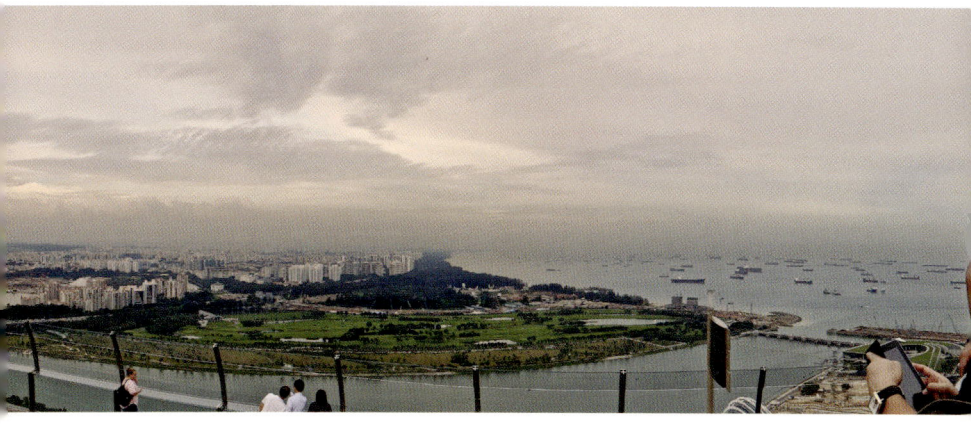

Figure 128: **Motion panorama:** This image shows a horizontal panorama of the larger size (L). The JPEG file has a size of 7680 × 1440 pixels. At first glance everything here looks to be in order, but upon closer inspection you'll discover a few ghosting artifacts (double images) of people who moved during the exposure window that lasted several seconds. Exposure parameters: XF18mmF2 R, f/10, 1/240 second, ISO 400.

As soon as you press the shutter button to start the MOTION PANORAMA, the camera will capture the still images it needs, as long as you evenly pivot the camera in the predetermined direction (indicated with an arrow in the viewfinder). You don't need to continue to hold the shutter button.

Once the camera has captured all of the images it needs to compose the panorama, it automatically stops. When you're creating a size M panorama, it can be irritating that the camera sometimes takes more images than are necessary. If that's the case, simply continue to pivot the camera until it ends the process by itself.

TIPS FOR WORKING WITH THE PANORAMA FUNCTION

- Avoid scenes with moving subjects, which will lead to undesirable ghosting artifacts when the function creates the composite image. For example, a person who walks through a scene while you're capturing it in a panorama could appear several times as fragments in the finished JPEG.

- Shoot with sufficient distance between your camera and your subject to avoid unsightly distortions and ensure that your entire subject will fall into your predetermined depth of field.

- Determine and set the focus, exposure, white balance, DR function, and film simulation settings before you capture a panorama—and be sure to base them all on the area of your image that you deem most important. Only in rare cases will the center of attention in a panorama fall within the initial (border) frame. Make use of the half-depressed shutter button to establish the focus and exposure settings based on the focal point of your image, and then move the camera to its appropriate starting position. Your camera uses the same focus, exposure, and white balance settings for the entire panorama. Don't forget that the exposure compensation dial also functions with panoramic images. You can use it to set the perfect exposure for your subject before you start to record the panorama.

- Pivot the camera with your eye to the EVF, not while looking at the LCD with your arm outstretched. The OVF of the X-Pro1 is not usable for shooting panoramas.

- Try to find a level ground for your panoramic exposures and align your body so that it's parallel with the middle of your planned exposure, not with the starting point of the panorama. This will help you avoid having to make unpleasant contortions, especially when creating L panoramas.

- When the camera is exposing a panorama, there's an increasing lag between what you will see in the viewfinder and the subject matter that is actually being captured. Don't let this bother you. It's also best to ignore the warning that pops up in the viewfinder telling you that you have deviated from the ideal line of horizon. When you see this warning, it's already too late for a correction (on account of the lag). Trying to correct the problem would lead to more problems. It's best to get used to pivoting the camera smoothly, in a straight line, and not allowing anything to break your concentration.

- Using fast shutter speeds with the X100 in panorama mode often leads to unsightly vertical stripes of varying brightness in the finished image. I have fortunately not had this experience with the X-Pro1 or X-E1, and have produced good results with quite short exposure times (even 1/500 second). Fast shutter speeds minimize the chance that individual images of a panorama will suffer from unwanted motion blur that can derive from the uniform pivoting of the camera. I should mention, however, that I've seen comments in Internet forums warning photographers to be cautious using short exposure times when creating panoramas with the X-Pro1 and X-E1 on account of these unpleasant vertical stripes. Since I can't exclude the possibility that your camera will exhibit this behavior under certain circumstances, you should at least keep this warning in mind. In other words, in the event that your finished panorama image ends up with vertical bands exhibiting differences in exposure, you can most likely solve the problem by using a slower shutter speed.

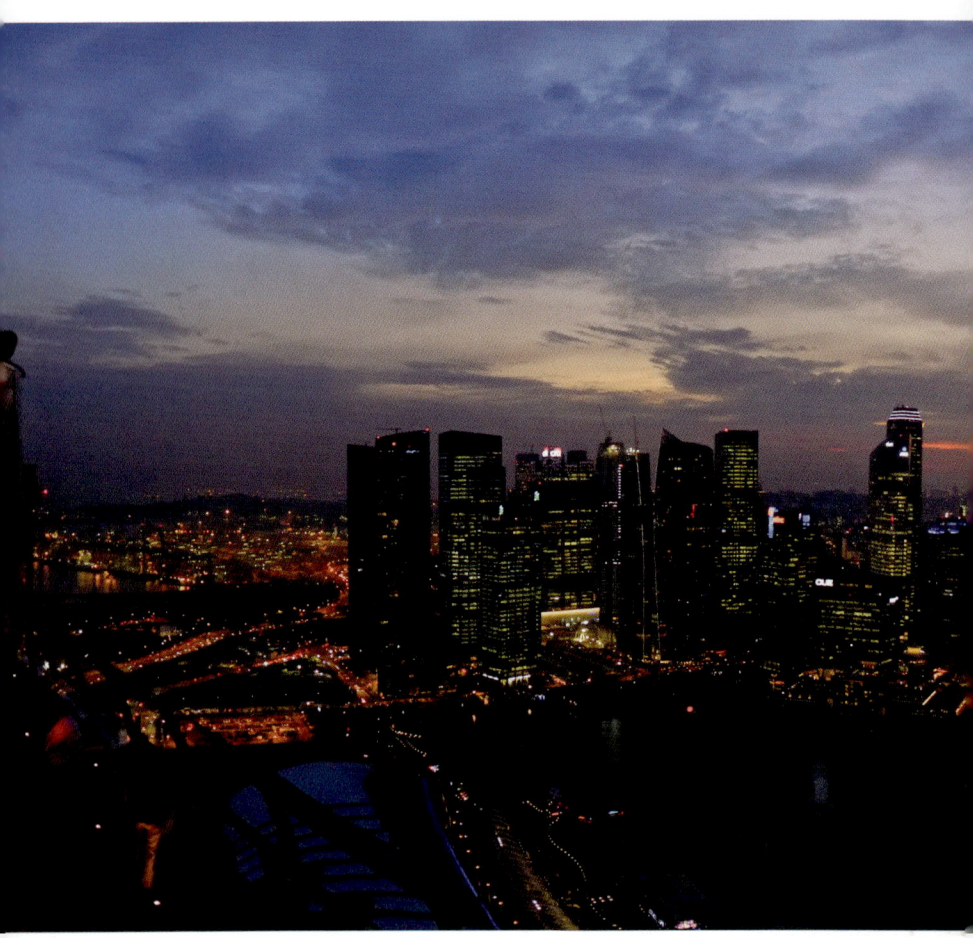

- If you would like to create a horizontal panorama with a higher resolution, select the vertical pan direction and hold your camera sideways as you pivot it horizontally.

- When you're using a tripod to create your panorama (which is generally advisable), you should align the camera parallel to the horizon before exposing your image. Since the electronic level is not available in panorama mode, you can temporarily switch into another mode to do this.

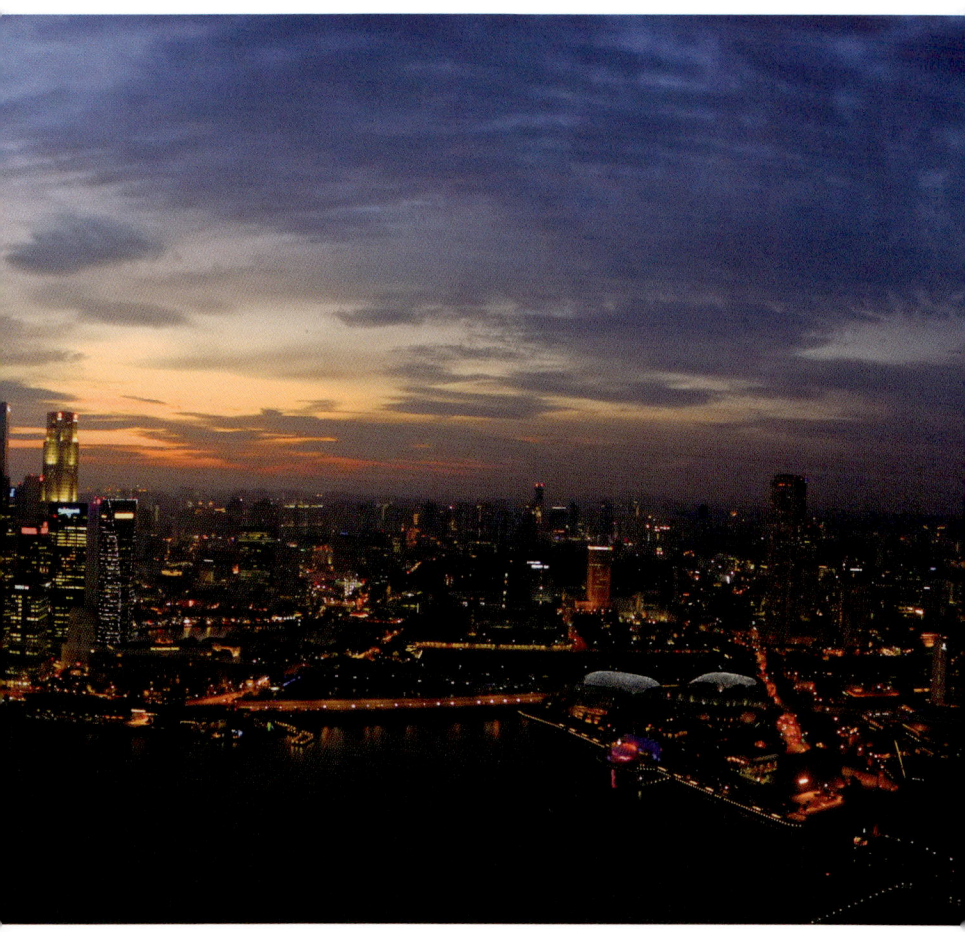

Figure 129: **Night Panorama at ISO 6400:** This picture was shot at ISO 6400 with an exposure time of 1/500 second as a vertical size M panorama (5120 × 2160 pixels). While panning this image, I simply held the camera upright. Exposure parameters: XF18mmF2 R, f/2, 1/500 second, ISO 6400.

- In general, use short focal lengths (e.g., 18mm or 35mm) with a sufficiently large depth of field. The longer the focal length, the harder it is to create a panorama by hand that is free from distortions and camera shake.

• Immediately after finishing your panorama, you should inspect it in playback mode and look for any compositing errors or ghosting artifacts. You can use the zoom buttons (the alternate functions of the AE and DRIVE buttons) or press the command dial to enlarge your panorama while viewing it on your camera. It's very frustrating to discover flaws in your panorama after you've gone home! In most cases you can repeat the shot to improve your results if you're aware of the problem at the scene.

MOVIES

The X-Pro1 and X-E1 are thoroughbred still-image cameras. Their video capturing capability (DRIVE > MOVIE) should be thought of as nothing more than a bonus, and little should be expected from it. In fact, it's best not to expect anything at all!

Nevertheless, they offer real "Full HD" (1080p) with 1920 x 1080 pixels. You can adjust this resolution in the video mode's shooting menu (MENU/OK button), which you can find under the submenu VIDEO MODE. Here you can alternatively select "normal" HD (720p) with 1280 x 720 pixels. The frame rate in both cases is 24 frames per second.

Other settings that you can select in the video menu before you start filming are FILM SIMULATION and WHITE BALANCE. The custom-defined white balance option (see "Manual White Balance" in section 2.7) is not available in this mode.

Even when its focus mode is set as AF-S, the camera always functions in AF-C mode when capturing movies and thus constantly tries to refine its focus. In practice, this is more often bad than it is good, because the contrast-driven autofocus is clearly not intended to be used this way. For this reason, I recommend you set the focus selector to M and manually focus with the AE-L/AF-L button and focus ring before filming. After you've started recording, the AE-L/AF-L button is functionless, but you can continue to adjust the focus with the focus ring.

Since the X-Pro1 lacks an external microphone jack, you're stuck using the integrated stereo microphone for sound capture. This unfortunately picks up the clicks, whirring sounds, and hums that the mechanical parts of the camera and lens emit. Using manual lenses from third parties tends to reduce this concert of distracting noise.

With the X-E1, you also have the option of connecting an external microphone, and you can manually adjust the (internal or external) microphone sensitivity level (SHOOTING MENU > MIC LEVEL ADJUSTMENT). You can also set the X-E1's microphone port to act either as a microphone input or as a remote shutter release port (see section 1.4).

With the appropriate lens adaptor, you can attach high-end video lenses to your camera. Capturing the video fully manually isn't possible, though, because the camera constantly attempts to adjust the exposure by itself. You can choose the aperture with the aperture ring in advance, but you can't set the ISO or shutter speed: the shutter-speed dial does not work in MOVIE mode.

If you preselect an aperture (you can't change this setting once the video has started to record), the camera will display aperture values that are appropriate for the scene in white. Apertures that would make what is in the frame too dark will be displayed in red. If you want the camera to automatically choose and adapt the aperture during recording, simply set the aperture of your lens to A.

If you use a lens with optical image stabilization (OIS), it's often useful to activate the OIS when shooting hand-held videos. This will reduce unwanted camera shake. You may want to turn the OIS off when operating the camera from a tripod.

TIP
Your camera doesn't feature a quick-start button that allows you to start and end a video easily. To begin recording a movie, you need to first activate the video mode (DRIVE button > MOVIE) and then use the shutter button to start and end the capture. If this is too inconvenient for you, assigning the movie mode to an Fn button is also an option. This allows you to jump back and forth between the still image and movie modes with the touch of a button.

DOUBLE EXPOSURES

The double-exposure function should be in the menu options for the DRIVE menu, but is instead located under SHOOTING MENU > MULTIPLE EXPOSURE > ON.

This function is quite simple. While several DSLR cameras offer various types of compositing, your camera offers only one.

In MULTIPLE EXPOSURE mode, the upper limit for the automatic ISO feature is 1600, and the DR function can only be set manually at DR100%, DR200%, or DR400%. This is a bit onerous if you usually shoot with the auto DR and ISO AUTO (6400), for example. When you activate the MULTIPLE EXPOSURE mode while in auto ISO AUTO (6400), the camera will automatically set the ISO to a fixed value of 1600 and the dynamic range to DR100%, which is probably not your ideal setup.

If you plan to use this feature frequently, it's a good idea to create a specific custom shooting profile (section 2.7) with more practical settings, such as ISO AUTO (1600). Then after you're finished with this function, you can revert back to your standard profile by accessing the Quick Menu. You can also assign the MULTIPLE EXPOSURE function to an Fn button, if that is desirable to you.

The operation of this feature is foolproof: take the first exposure and then follow the instructions on the display. One benefit of the feature is that it saves not only a JPEG of the finished double exposure, but also a corresponding RAW file (if the camera is currently programmed to save RAW files). Do note, however, that the composite image is the only one that the camera writes to the memory card—the two individual images will be available to you neither as JPEGs nor as RAW files.

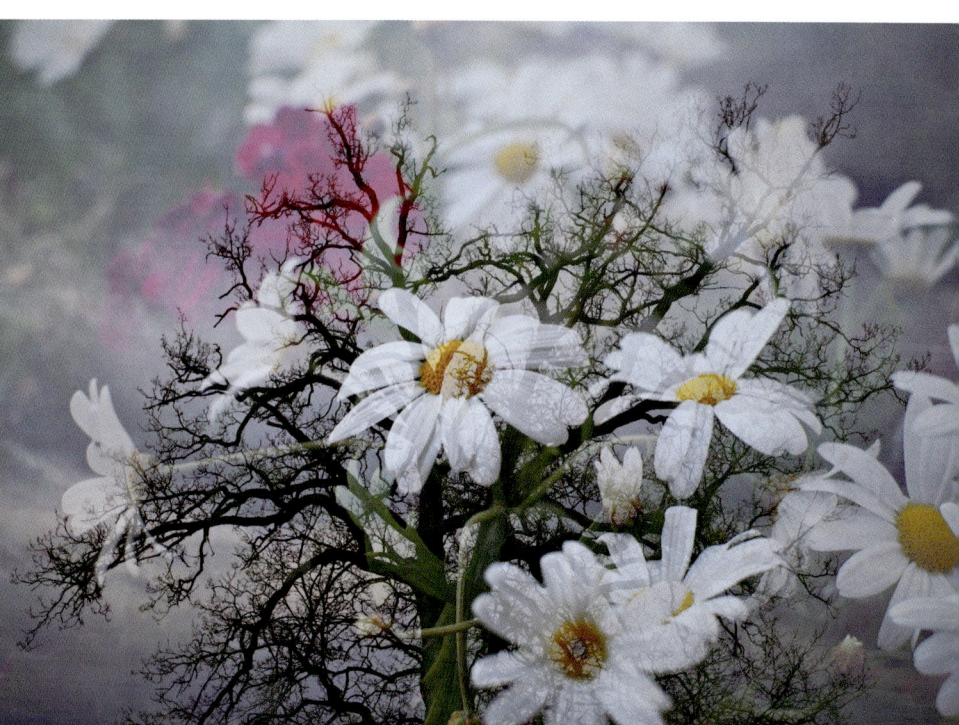

Figure 130: **Double exposure:** The MULTIPLE EXPOSURE feature allows the photographer to combine two consecutive shots by laying one on top of the other—something familiar from older film cameras.

SELF-TIMER

The camera has a self-timer that can be set to 10 or 2 seconds. To select a duration, go to SHOOTING MENU > SELF-TIMER. You can also use the Quick Menu or assign this function to an Fn button.

The 10-second option is intended to allow photographers enough time to move from behind the camera and get in the picture (as with self-portraits and group shots).

The shorter duration of 2 seconds is principally intended for situations in which you're using a tripod and want to avoid camera shake due to long exposure times. This method allows the camera to settle before it captures an image.

The self-timer remains active until you (or the camera) turn it off. In other words, it can be active for several consecutive exposures.

2.9 FLASH PHOTOGRAPHY

As of now, the X-Pro1 is the only camera from Fujifilm without an integrated flash. So flash photography with this camera requires the use of an external flash. The X-E1 also features a tiny integrated flash, and both cameras offer a TTL shoe mount. In addition, the X-Pro1 features a traditional sync terminal for connecting external (studio) flash units.

As long as you're comfortable modulating everything manually, you can use nearly every flash unit on the market with the X-Pro1 and X-E1, as well as most studio strobe devices and remote flash systems. If you want to hear about the experiences other photographers have had with a specific solution or combination of devices, the online sources listed in the appendix can be a good place to start.

In this book, I'll concentrate on the X-E1's integrated flash and the three system flash units that are compatible with both cameras: the EF-X20, EF-20, and EF-42 (see section 1.3). These flash units support the camera's TTL auto flash, with which the camera automatically modulates the amount of light that is emitted by the flash unit.

TTL stands for "through the lens" and means that the camera bases the flash exposure on the amount of light that shines through the lens and lands on the sensor. The camera sends a small pre-flash, meters the amount of reflected light, and then regulates the optimal flash output based on the results. The goal of this process is to create a natural balance between the ambient light and the light from the camera's flash.

If you attach a Fujifilm system flash unit to the camera and turn it on, there will be five flash modes available under SHOOTING MENU > FLASH MODE. These flash modes are not all available in every exposure mode (`P`, `A`, `S`, and `M`; see also section 2.3).

Here's a quick overview:

• Automatic flash (AUTO) / `P`

• Forced flash (FORCED FLASH) / `P`, `A`, `S`, `M`

• Slow sync (SLOW SYNCHRO) / `P`, `A`

• Synchronization with the second shutter curtain (2ND CURTAIN SYNC.) / `P`, `A`, `S`, `M`

• Suppressed flash (SUPPRESSED FLASH) / `P`, `A`, `S`, `M` (X-Pro1 only)

• Commander flash (COMMANDER) / `P`, `A`, `S`, `M` (X-E1 only)

You can also access these flash modes in the Quick Menu by pressing the Q button.

AUTOMATIC FLASH

In the AUTO flash mode, which is only available in the program automatic exposure mode, `P`, the camera determines whether the flash is needed by itself. You can tell that the camera has decided to use the flash for an exposure by the small flash symbol that appears in the viewfinder or on the LCD display as soon as you press the shutter button halfway. Please note that on the X-E1, the built-in flash won't pop up by itself. You have to manually release it by pressing the flash pop-up button next to the EVF.

When the camera uses the flash, the minimum shutter speed is determined by the well-known formula 1/(focal length x 1.5) or the minimum speed set by the active OIS system of your stabilized lens. For example, when you are using the 35mm lens, the camera always uses an exposure time of 1/52 second or less in AUTO flash mode, independent of the selected ISO setting.

This means that if you have the ISO set at a low value (perhaps ISO 200) and you're shooting in dim lighting conditions, the camera cannot adequately incorporate the natural light. You should either use a higher ISO value (or the auto ISO feature) or switch the flash mode to SLOW SYNCHRO (see below).

FORCED FLASH

FORCED FLASH functions exactly as the AUTO mode does except that it's available in all four exposure modes (**P**, **A**, **S**, **M**) and the flash always fires regardless of the lighting conditions. In the program automatic and aperture-priority modes (**P**, **A**), the minimum shutter speed rule for lenses without active OIS still applies: 1/(focal length x 1.5) or shorter. In **A** mode, it applies regardless of the aperture you have selected. Pay attention to the ISO setting in relation to the ambient light here, or switch the flash mode over to SLOW SYNCHRO.

In the **S** and **M** exposure modes you have control over the shutter speed and can incorporate more of the ambient light into your shot by choosing a longer exposure window. Don't overlook the risk of camera shake or unwanted motion blur with these slower shutter speeds. In exposure mode M, you have complete control over how much natural lighting affects your image. The TTL system contributes the appropriate amount of light from the flash automatically.

SLOW SYNCHRO

The flash mode SLOW SYNCHRO is available in the exposure modes P and A. This mode does away with the rule of thumb for the minimum shutter speed. Depending on the brightness of the subject, the camera uses an exposure window of up to 30 seconds (regardless of the focal length).

In the event that you don't want the parts of your image that are illuminated by the natural lighting to blur with such slow shutter speeds, you should use a tripod. Also keep in mind that the flash always fires immediately at the beginning of the exposure, just as the camera opens the shutter. In other words, the camera synchronizes the flash with the first shutter curtain. If you're trying to photograph a car driving by at night with a slow shutter speed, the light traces of the headlights will be recorded as ambient light. The car, which is much darker, will be illuminated by the light from the flash and appear to be more or less frozen in place.

The problem is, when the flash is synchronized with the first curtain, the light traces will continue forward in the direction of the car's travel. This creates an irritating impression because it looks as though the car were traveling in reverse. The solution? Synchronize the flash with the second shutter curtain!

SYNCHRONIZATION WITH THE SECOND SHUTTER CURTAIN

The flash mode 2ND CURTAIN SYNC functions identically to the forced flash, except that it delays firing the flash until the end of the exposure window, just before the

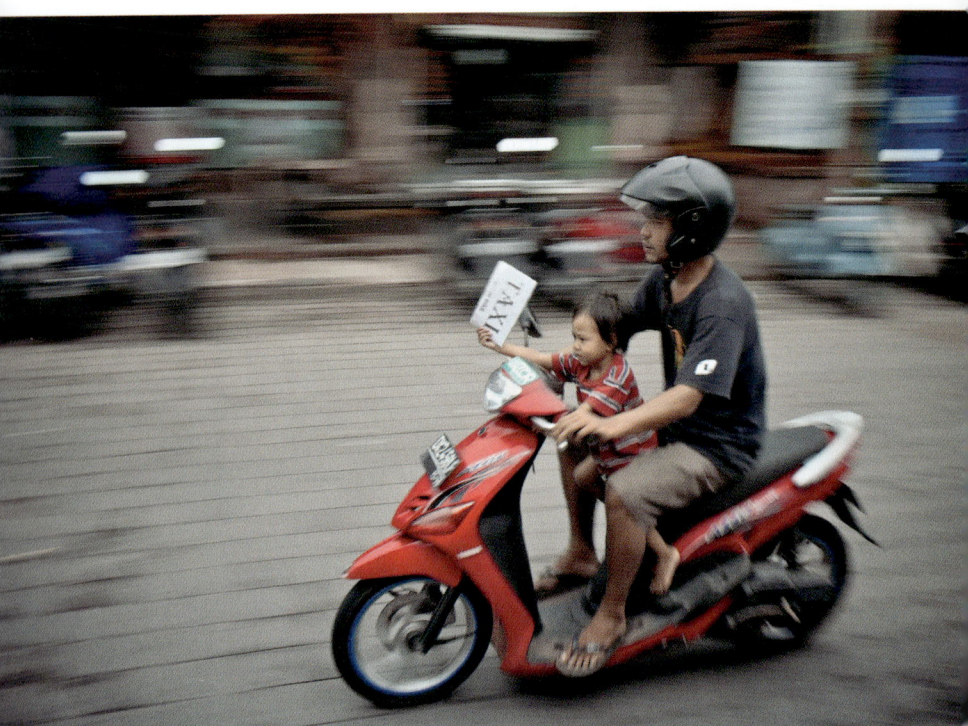

Figure 131: **Synchronizing with the second curtain:** Intentionally achieving motion blur can be an effective stylistic decision, but certain aspects of the image should often still appear mostly in focus. The use of light from a flash to complement the otherwise sufficient natural lighting conditions can be valuable, because it adds a second, brief flash during longer exposure windows. This method is not unlike a double exposure in that way. If you're photographing motor vehicles or other moving objects, it's advisable to synchronize the flash with the second shutter. Exposure parameters: XF18mmF2 R, f/16, 1/30 second, ISO 200, EF-20.

shutter closes. This method is known as second-curtain synchronization.

This flash mode is available in all four exposure modes (**P**, **A**, **S**, **M**) and the flash will fire regardless of the ambient lighting conditions. In the **P** and **A** modes the general rule once again applies for lenses without active OIS: minimum shutter speed = 1/(focal length x 1.5) or shorter. Again, in aperture-priority (**A**) this rule applies independently of the aperture you have selected.

In order to get the most from this feature, you should use it in combination with either the S or the M exposure mode so you can make use of longer exposure times.

SUPPRESSED FLASH (X-PRO1 ONLY)
The SUPRESSED FLASH setting disables the flash function entirely. It prevents any flash that is connected to your camera from discharging, even when it's turned on and ready to fire.

COMMANDER (X-E1 ONLY)
The COMMANDER setting lets you use the internal flash of the X-E1 as an optical trigger for (larger) manually set flash units. It will emit a burst of light that's strong enough to trigger the photodiodes of external slave flash units (like the EF-X20), and it doesn't emit a pre-flash.

> **IMPORTANT**
>
> Please note that when SILENT MODE is activated, all flash functions of your camera are also completely suppressed. To turn SILENT MODE on and off, press the DISP/BACK button for a few seconds.

RED-EYE CORRECTION
All of your camera's TTL flash modes can be used in combination with a red-eye removal feature. The problem of red-eye comes up frequently in portraiture as a result of the light from the flash reflecting off the retina. These reflections occur when the light from the flash discharges close to the optical axis. Put another way, you're likely to get red eyes if your shot is set up in a way that requires you to fire the flash directly in front of your subject, which is usually the case with most integrated and shoe-mount flash units. If you illuminate your subject

indirectly from above or from the side, this problem never or only rarely comes up.

To turn the red-eye correction feature on for all exposure modes, go to SHOOTING MENU > RED EYE REMOVAL > ON. The camera addresses the red-eye phenomenon in two ways:

- It prompts the flash unit to emit a pre-flash, which causes your subject's pupils, which normally would be dilated in the dim lighting conditions, to contract. This minimizes the amount of light reflected from the retina.

- It detects the presence of a face in an exposure and re-moves any remaining red-eye problems when it creates the JPEG file.

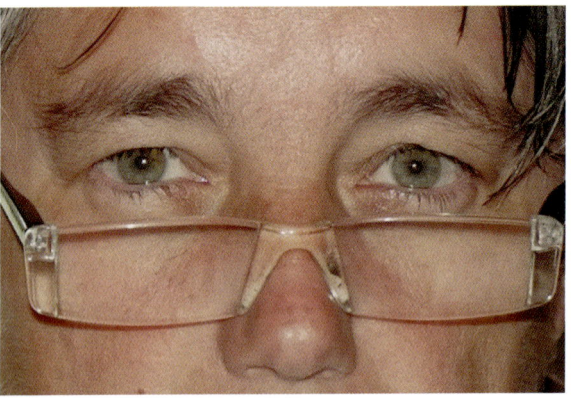

Figure 132: **Red-eye correction:** When this function is acti-vated, the camera emits a pre-flash and subsequently removes any remaining red-eye problems in the JPEG file. This process prevents reflections from the retina from showing up in your images or takes steps to remove them after the exposure.

TIP

> When the red-eye removal tool is active, you can program the camera to save the untouched JPEG in addition to the edited version. To do this, go to **SHOOTING MENU > SAVE ORG IMAGE > ON**. You can also use the camera's red-eye correction feature retroactively on images that have already been exposed. Find the problematic image in playback mode and then go to **PLAYBACK MENU > RED EYE REMOVAL**.

FASTEST FLASH SYNC SPEED

The official shortest exposure time that the X-Pro1 and X-E1 can use with a flash unit is 1/180 second. In practice, however, flash exposures without problematic shadowing effects are often possible at 1/250 second. Nevertheless, this technology-related restriction (the camera has a focal-plane shutter) is a blow to people used to the X100S or other leaf shutter cameras that have very fast flash sync speeds. For DSLR converts, this limitation should be business as usual.

In the exposure modes **P** and **A** the camera limits the exposure time to 1/180 second when the flash is activated—anything shorter is not possible. In the **S** and **M** exposure modes, conversely, you can set your own shutter speed, but at your own risk. The camera will obey, but for exposures that are shorter than 1/250 second, you may end up with visible shadowing effects and an uneven illumination of the exposure.

FLASH EXPOSURE CORRECTION

As mentioned, the TTL logic is designed to establish the ideal flash output for the camera based on a specific subject. Expecting it to work perfectly every time is wishful thinking, though. You will sometimes need to adjust the flash manually to attain a level of exposure that looks optimal to you, just as you would with regular exposures. The camera and the photographer don't always see eye to eye, and ultimately the photographer is always right.

One method of correcting flash exposure is to regulate the output of TTL flash units directly: the EF-20 allows you to adjust its output by ±1 EV in steps of 1/2 EV; with the EF-X20, it's also ±1 EV, but in steps of 1/3 EV. Another method is to control the flash through the camera. To do this, go to SHOOTING MENU > FLASH. There you have access to a correction range of ±2/3 EV in steps of 1/3 EV.

How do the two methods of controlling flash output interact? Quite simply, they add up. By using them together, you can adjust the TTL flash output up or down by a maximum of ±1 2/3 EV (±1.66 EV).

If you only use the built-in flash of your X-E1, the only way to control flash output is through the flash menu. Unfortunately, there's no option to quickly change this setting in the Quick Menu or to assign it to an Fn button.

CONTROLLING THE AMBIENT LIGHT
You can control the flash output with the flash exposure compensation techniques discussed above. At the same time, you can continue to control the parts of your image that are not affected by the flash in exposure modes **P**, **A**, and **S** with the exposure compensation dial. This dial has no direct effect on the amount of light fired by the flash. The interplay between the flash exposure compensation and the normal exposure compensation gives you a lot of control to reach your desired balance of artificial and natural light.

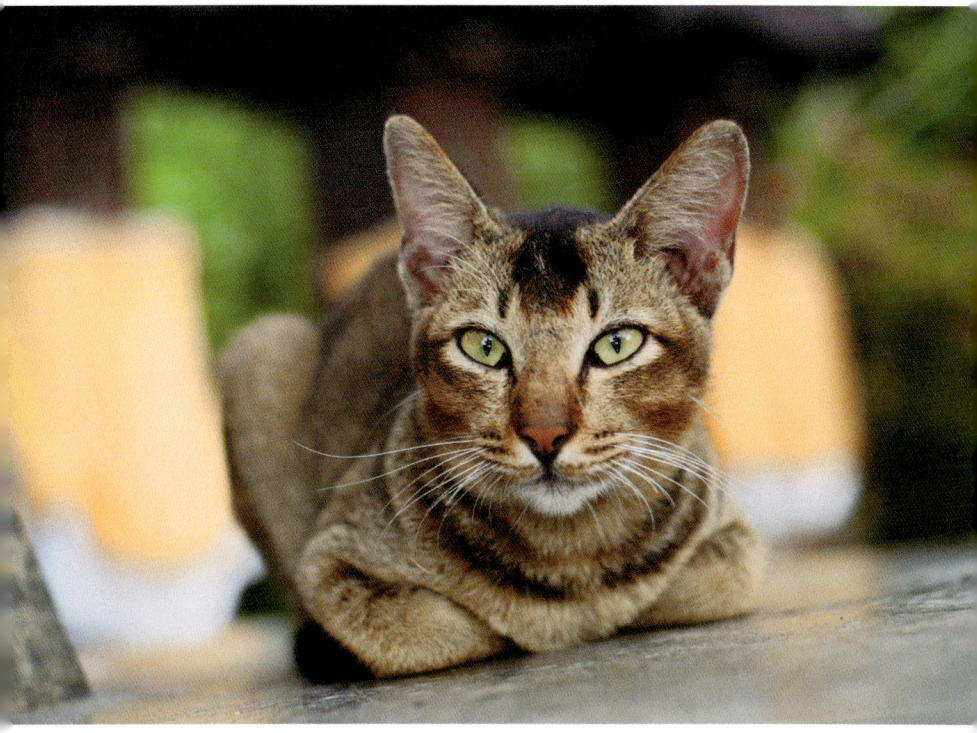

Figure 133: **Considering ambient light when using flash:** With many successful flash exposures, you don't even realize at first glance that flash was used. In this photo, the cat's eyes betray the use of a flash. Fuji's automatic TTL flash system is one of the best in the world and consistently delivers very good results. Since there's always room for improvement, though, be sure to make regular use of the compensation functions for both flash and ambient light. Exposure parameters: XF35mmF1.4 R, f/2.2, 1/125 second, ISO 400, EF-20.

TIPS FOR EXPOSING WITH FLASH

• When you attempt to meter a CUSTOM WHITE BALANCE (see "Manual White Balance" in section 2.7) with a flash that is ready to fire, the flash will go off, thereby affecting the camera's white balance measurement. Since different flash units exhibit different color temperatures (and since photographers often modify a neutral flash with color filters), this feature can be very useful.

- You can strike the right balance of flash light and ambient light by using flash exposure compensation to adjust the flash (go to SHOOTING MENU > FLASH and/or adjust the flash unit output directly on the device) and by using the exposure compensation dial to regulate the ambient light captured.

- If you want to keep the background sharp when using long exposure times, you should use a tripod even with a flash. Sometimes, however, you may want a blurry background. In this case, the flash will help to ensure that the subject in your exposure stands out frozen against the blurry background.

- As I mentioned above, the camera's official flash sync speed is 1/180 second, but in reality you can often get away with 1/250 second. Sometimes that's not enough, though—for example, if you're shooting a portrait in broad daylight and want to use a wide-open aperture to establish a shallow depth of field that will isolate your subject from the background. Before you reach for the last resort of ISO 100 (which probably wouldn't take care of this problem and would end up reducing the dynamic range), you should attach a neutral density (ND) filter to the lens to reduce the incident light by the equivalent of a few aperture stops.

- When shooting moving subjects with long exposure times, synchronize the flash with the second curtain. You can select the appropriate shutter speed for your purpose by using the **S** or **M** exposure mode.

- The camera is a marvel at high ISO settings. This makes using the flash unnecessary in many cases and allows you to rely on the ambient light, which may end up producing a better look in your final image. Don't flash your subjects to death—less is often more. It's true that in the studio you need to compose the light

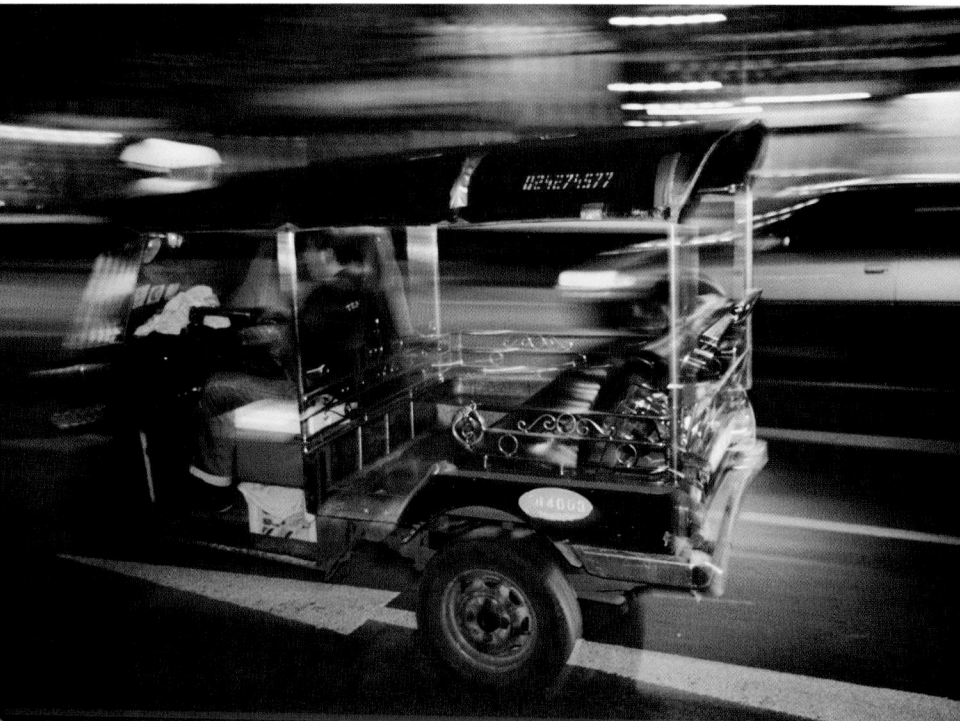

Figure 134: **Foreground and background:** I handheld this shot taken at night with a long exposure window of 1/15 second to capture some of the movement that was critical to the scene on the street. Thanks to ISO 3200, even the tiny built-in flash of my preproduction X-E1 was powerful enough to freeze part of the action in the foreground, while the background remains blurry with the motion of traffic and the panning of my camera. The flash was also synchronized with the second curtain here. Exposure parameters: X-E1 with 18–55mm kit zoom lens, 21.4mm, f/3.2, 1/15 second, ISO 3200. Processed with Silkypix and Apple Aperture.

for the entire scene, but the built-in flash of the X-E1 and the small EF-20 and EF-X20 flash units are first and foremost intended to be artificial brighteners, not the only sources of light for a scene.

- With the aid of a pin-compatible Canon TTL extension cord (see section 1.3) you can expose remotely when using the camera with Fujifilm system flash units. In other words, you can use the flash in TTL mode even when it's tethered to the camera. Important: You can also then use flash units from Canon, but not in TTL mode. You'll need to control them manually.

• The EF-X20 comes equipped with a slave mode that allows it to be optically triggered by another flash. This slave mode doesn't operate based on TTL control; you will need to configure it manually by defining the desired flash output directly on the flash unit. There are seven different levels of output, ranging from the 1/1 maximum to 1/64 of full power. The EF-X20 also reacts to a pre-flash from the master flash unit intended to reduce red-eye effects. If your trigger camera will fire a pre-flash, adjust the slide switch on the bottom of the EF-X20 that is serving as the slave to P-MODE; if no such pre-flash will occur, switch it to N-MODE. To return the flash back to its normal TTL operation controlled by the camera, set the switch back to X.

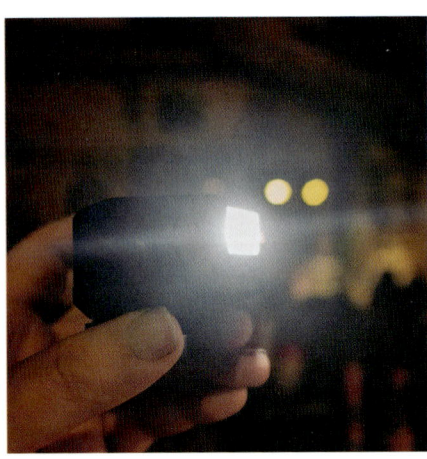

Figure 135: The EF-X20 in Slave Mode: The small EF-X20 system flash can be controlled wirelessly by another flash unit. When using it in this manner, you will need to set its output manually. In this image, the EF-X20 was triggered by a flash from a Fujifilm X100, which in turn captured the response.

- When using a wide-angle lens, remember to flick on your flash unit's wide-angle diffuser to make sure that your flash uniformly and completely illuminates your scene.

- Lens hoods are a good thing, but when using the EF-20 or EF-X20—especially for closeup and macro shots— they can lead to unwanted shadows. It's best to remove the hood for these particular situations or make use of a remote flash.

- In order to achieve softer flash lighting, it's often wise to flash indirectly, for example by bouncing the flash off a white ceiling. In TTL mode, this is possible with either the EF-20 or the EF-42, whose heads can be tilted upwards. By carefully pulling the built-in pop-up flash of the X-E1 backward with your finger, you can direct its light emission upwards too. The power of this flash is limited, so your results will vary.

IMPORTANT

Exposures taken in poorly lit circumstances with the auto ISO function active (e.g., at dusk) often end up being more than adequately illuminated or even overexposed. Adding extra light from a flash won't improve the image at all. In these cases, make sure to regulate the ambient light captured with the exposure compensation dial, so that your flash can produce the effect you desire.

Also keep in mind that the TTL flash system works well with the dynamic range options DR200% and DR400%. But be careful: the DR function's requirement for a higher ISO setting can lead to faster shutter speeds and/or larger f-numbers. Neither of these is desirable for flash photography, especially because the fastest official flash sync speed for the camera is 1/180 second.

2.10 USING THIRD-PARTY LENSES

One highlight of the X-mount system is undoubtedly
the small flange back distance of only 17.7mm. It allows you to attach practically any third-party lens from
another camera system—with the appropriate adaptor.
The Chinese manufacturer Kipon has already announced
X-mount-compatible adaptors for 42 third-party systems,
and Novoflex, a German manufacturer of high-quality
adaptors, has also dutifully created X-mount adaptors for
some 13 established third-party systems.

Unfortunately, when a lens is attached to the camera
with an adaptor, the auto ISO operates with a minimum
shutter speed of 1/30 second independently of the actual
focal length and what is defined in the lens adaptor
menu. This is too fast for many wide-angle lenses and
too slow for most normal and telephoto lenses.

The camera also sets the minimum flash sync speed
at 1/15 second when a third-party lens is attached, which
is largely useless for lenses with longer focal lengths. To
make matters even more frustrating, the camera has an
adaptor menu where you can input the focal length of
the lens currently attached. In other words, the camera
"knows" exactly what the current focal length is, but
doesn't do anything useful with this information.

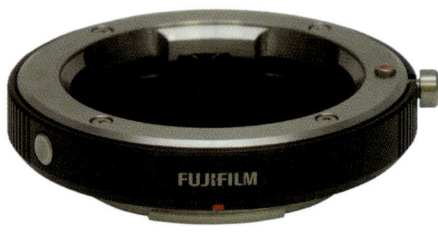

Figure 136: Fujifilm M-mount adaptor:
Fuji's own adaptor for lenses that feature
Leica's M connector includes X-mount
signal contacts as well as a function button on the adaptor ring that brings up
the adaptor menu on the monitor or in
the viewfinder. Furthermore, this adaptor
unlocks extra camera functions that allow
you to correct optical errors such as
vignetting, distortion, and color shifts at
the border of an image.

At least the bright frame of the X-Pro1's OVF uses the focal length setting selected in the adaptor menu (SHOOTING MENU > MOUNT ADAPTOR SETTING), as long as the setting stays between 18mm and 60mm. Focal lengths of less than 18mm are indicated in the optical viewfinder with yellow arrows in the corners; focal lengths of greater than 60mm are indicated with a red frame calibrated to 60mm.

Within the acceptable range of focal lengths for the OVF—18mm to 60mm—two frame indicators will appear in the viewfinder: one white, one blue. The white frame is corrected for parallax for objects at infinity, and the blue frame is corrected for objects at about two yards.

IMPORTANT

Third-party lenses attached to the X-Pro1 and X-E1 with a specific adaptor can only be focused manually. The only exposure modes that are available are the aperture-priority **A** and manual exposure **M** modes. Other functions such as auto ISO, TTL flash, and DR extension, however, are still available.

CONNECTING AND RECOGNIZING THIRD-PARTY LENSES

After you have mechanically attached a third-party lens to your camera with an adaptor, you should make sure that SHOOTING MENU > SHOOT WITHOUT LENS > ON is selected. Otherwise, your camera won't take any pictures.

Next go to SHOOTING MENU > MOUNT ADAPTOR SETTING. Here you will have six lens settings to choose from: four focal length presets (21mm, 24mm, 28mm, and 35mm) as well as LENS 5 and LENS 6, which are two focal lengths that you can set manually.

If you happen to be using an M-system adaptor from Fujifilm, you will also have a number of correction settings available, which I'll cover below.

FOCUSING WITH THIRD-PARTY LENSES

One way to focus precisely when using a third-party lens is to use the magnified display of the electronic viewfinder (EVF) or the LCD monitor. Your camera will need to be in manual focus (MF) mode, so turn the focus mode selector on the front of the camera to M. As usual, you can magnify the digital displays by pressing the command dial. Change the magnification level by turning the dial.

You can enhance this process by activating your camera's focus peaking function by choosing SHOOTING MENU > MF ASSIST > FOCUS PEAK HIGHLIGHT and picking one of two available strength levels.

To focus as precisely as possible, you'll want to open the aperture as wide as possible. The reduced depth of field will help you find the correct focus point. After you've found it, you can reset the aperture to your desired setting. The focus point should not move, but the depth of field should become larger. You can observe this effect in the EVF. The viewfinder's distance and depth of field indicators will be nonfunctional.

However, keep in mind that some lenses exhibit so-called *focus shift*: the plane of focus changes along with changes of the aperture. If your adapted lens is suffering from this syndrome, is may be wiser to manually focus the lens at the intended working aperture.

Figure 137: Voigtländer Heliar 75mmF1.8 with M adaptor: ▶
Numerous adaptors make it possible to attach nearly any new or old third-party lens to your camera. Especially popular are lenses that feature Leica's M connection, which are available from more brands than just Leica itself, including Zeiss and Voigtländer. This image was shot with a fast 75mm f/1.8 Heliar and the Fujifilm M adaptor—a lightweight telephoto lens for portraits with character. Exposure parameters: X-E1, Voigtländer Heliar 75mmF1.8, f/2.8, 1/125 second, ISO 1250, Profoto strobe. RAW file processed in Apple Aperture.

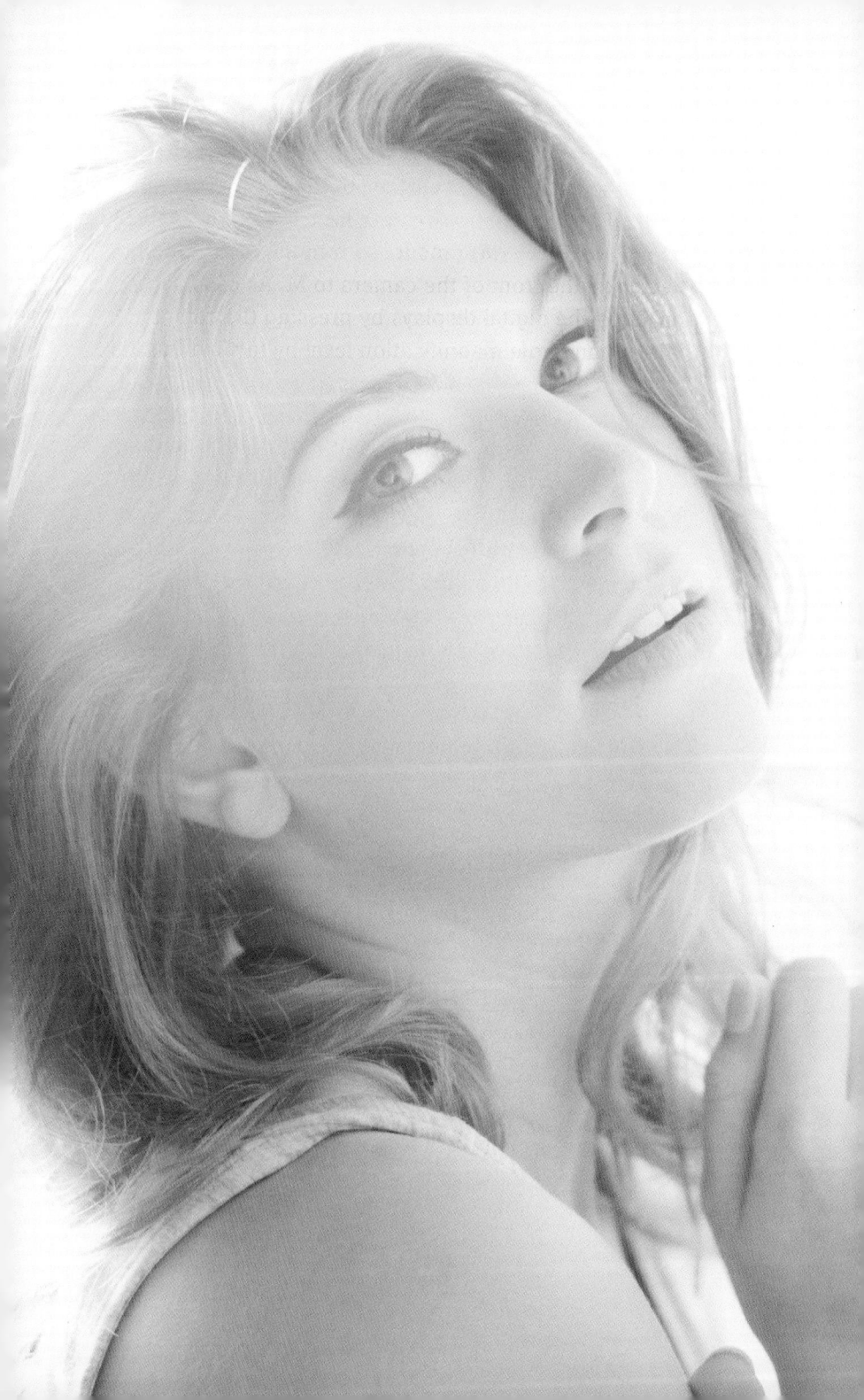

To refine your focus at any time, you can always reactivate the magnified digital display. Well, at *almost* any time: the magnified display will not be available while the camera is transferring data from the buffer memory to the memory card. As soon as that finishes, you can activate it again.

EXPOSING CORRECTLY WITH THIRD-PARTY LENSES

When a third-party lens is attached, the camera works exclusively in the aperture-priority (A) or manual (M) exposure mode. However, neither of these modes function exactly as they do with native (electronic) Fujinon and Zeiss lenses: while X-mount lenses don't set the aperture until the shutter button is pressed halfway in A and M modes, adapted third-party lenses reduce the aperture immediately after you set a larger f-number. This not only causes the depth of field to increase in the EVF display; it also causes the live view image to get darker, since less light is able to enter the lens and reach the sensor.

The camera attempts to counteract this loss of light and enhances the display in the viewfinder. This works, but only up to a point.

We already know that the live histogram doesn't relay any useful information in M mode. With a very dark subject, the live histogram also can't deliver useful information in the other exposure modes (P , A , and S). Using a third-party lens with a narrow aperture is similar to creating a very dark subject, because we've reduced the amount of light that reaches the sensor and effectively darkened the viewfinder display. This causes dusk to become night quickly in the live image, which in turn renders the live histogram useless because it relies on the live image for its data.

Keep these relationships in mind when you want to expose precisely with third-party lenses in aperture-priority mode, A , with the help of the histogram. A simple solution for this problem is to use a very large aperture when setting the exposure for your shot. Then you can use the histogram and the exposure compensation dial to optimize your exposure settings. You can stop the aperture down once you're satisfied—this will change the aperture and the shutter speed, but won't change the overall exposure of your image.

You can get the best exposure preview of images taken in poor lighting conditions in the EVF or on the LCD monitor by pressing the **shutter button** halfway. The camera then enhances the live image display as much as possible.

SPECIAL FEATURES OF THE FUJIFILM M ADAPTOR

In principle, Fujifilm's own M adaptor functions in the same way as other third-party adaptors, but it offers a few additional functions that are contained in the camera's firmware and unlocked only when you attach Fuji's adaptor to the camera.

Since Fuji's M adaptor features X-mount signal contacts, it's not compatible with some M lenses for reasons of space. You can find a list of compatible lenses at:

http://www.fujifilm.com/products/digital_cameras/accessories/lens/mount/fujifilm_m_mount_adapter/compatibility_chart/index.html.

Fujifilm also includes a small template that you can use to determine whether your M lens will fit mechanically or not.

When you use the Fuji M adaptor with your camera, the adaptor menu for each of the six lenses expands to include three additional settings:

• DISTORTION CORRECTION corrects pincushion or barrel distortions caused by the lens. There are three correction levels available for each of these distortion types.

- COLOR SHADING CORRECTION counteracts color shifts near the edges of an image, which occur most often with wide-angle lenses. Each of the four image corners can be independently corrected.

- PERIPHERAL ILLUMINATION CORRECTION reduces (or increases) vignetting. There are five levels available to decrease or amplify vignetting effects.

You can set correction values separately for each of the six focal lengths available in the adaptor menu (SHOOTING MENU > MOUNT ADAPTOR SETTING). You'll need to handle all of these corrections manually—they aren't automatically detected. You also have to select the correction settings for each lens individually, which will require you to take test shots and compare the results.

The corrections you set in the adaptor menu are applied during the RAW conversion. In other words, the JPEGs will be corrected according to your inputs. Furthermore, some external RAW converters can recognize the correction settings in the RAW file's metadata. For technical reasons, however, they are only able to apply the distortion and the vignetting corrections when developing the RAW file. The correction for color shading unfortunately gets left by the wayside, which means you'll need to refer back to the camera's JPEGs.

QUALITY CONSIDERATIONS

If the sensors in your X-E1 or X-Pro1 were full-frame (as in 35mm), they would offer a resolution of more than 36 megapixels, just like the sensor in the Nikon D800E. Like the X-Trans sensor, it's built by Sony and doesn't use an anti-aliasing filter. In other words, if you crop a shot made with a D800E to match APS-C sensor size in

Photoshop (or by setting the D800E to DX mode), you will get a 16-megapixel image cut out from the center of the frame that will very much match the result you get when you put the same lens on an X-Pro1 or X-E1.

We all know that vintage analog full-frame lenses were not made to take advantage of the resolution of a 36-megapixel D800E. When those lenses were made, not too many (if any) people were thinking about digital photography or 36-megapixel sensors. This means that such lenses weren't engineered to take full advantage of current APS-C sensors with 16-megapixel or higher resolution, so please dial back your expectations, even when you're adapting vintage analog lenses from legendary brands like Leica or Zeiss. Some of these lenses may be works of art, but that still doesn't make them state-of-the-art.

There is another consideration to be made: analog lenses were built for 35mm film emulsions that absorb and reflect light differently from digital sensors. This means that your results can vary, depending on the particular lens you're using with a particular camera and sensor. For example, with the X-E1 and X-Pro1, users of Voigtländer's 15mmF4.5 Super Wide Heliar report some smearing in the corners of their images, while users of Voigtländer's 12mmF5.6 Ultra Wide Heliar report crisp results over the entire image frame.

My suggestion when using vintage lenses: don't examine pixels at 100% magnification, and don't hunt for maximum resolution. Use these lenses as if you still had a film camera. Embrace their colors, their bokeh, and all of their "flaws," as those are part of their distinct character. Don't show off their weaknesses; instead shoot with them in a way that emphasizes their strengths and makes them (and you) look good.

SPEED BOOSTER

With the Speed Booster, Metabones introduced quite
an innovative adaptor for APS-C and Micro Four Thirds
cameras, including Fujifilm X-mount cameras.

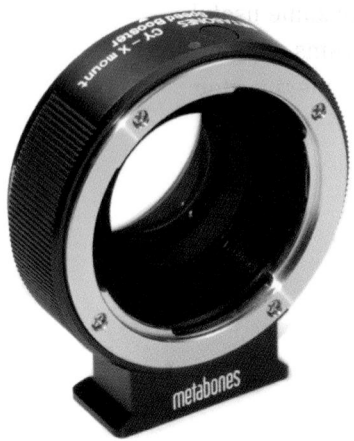

Figure 138: This image shows the Contax/Yashica
SLR-to-X-mount version of the Speed Booster. It
comes with its own tripod mount (quite practical for adapting heavier optics). However, at $399
(USD) plus shipping, it's certainly not cheap.

With its hefty price tag, the Speed Booster isn't your
regular adaptor. It converts full-frame SLR lenses into
APS-C lenses by reducing their focal length by a factor of
0.71. At the same time, it increases the maximum aperture by the same factor, which equals about 1 f-stop (EV).
With the Speed Booster, my 180mmF2.8 Zeiss Sonnar
prime for Contax cameras turns into a fast 128mmF2.0
APS-C X-mount lens.

Since you can attach a (D)SLR lens to either the
Speed Booster or a regular adaptor, you can get two
lenses for the price of one.

Due to the thickness of the adaptor and the resulting
longer flange back distance, it's not possible to adapt
Leica M lenses (or similar rangefinder-style formats)
with the Speed Booster. However, there are versions for
several SLR formats. For Fuji X-mount, you can currently
get Speed Boosters for Leica R, Contax/Yashica (Zeiss),
Contarex, and Alpa lenses.

APPENDIX

I hope this book has answered your questions, solved a few concrete problems, and provided a slew of useful information. However, since even a wide-ranging book can't cover every possible topic, I'd like to share some useful links for online sources and discussion forums where you can gather more information about your camera system.

MY OWN FREE X-PERT CORNER BLOG
🌐 www.fujirumors.com/category/x-pert

FORUMS
🌐 www.fujix-forum.com
🌐 www.fujixseries.com
🌐 www.fujixspot.com
   (I have my own Q&A section in this forum.)

OFFICIAL SOURCE
🌐 www.fujifilm.com/products/digital_cameras

VIDEOS FROM THE FUJI GUYS
🌐 www.youtube.com/user/fujiguys

ACCESSING EXIF DATA AND MAKER NOTES
Your camera saves a wealth of information in your RAW and JPEG files about your exposure settings as EXIF (Exchangeable Image File) metadata. To access the metadata as well as a lot of information specific to individual vendors (i.e., Maker Notes), such as the camera serial number, date of manufacture, dynamic range extension, film simulation, etc., and to read this information on your computer, it's advisable to use an image viewing or editing program that relies on the utility ExifTool.

In Windows, for example, the program ExifTool GUI enables this. On a Mac OS, you can use GraphicConverter.

```
                    Make:  FUJIFILM
     Camera Model Name:  X-Pro1
            Orientation:  Horizontal (normal)
           X Resolution:  72
           Y Resolution:  72
        Resolution Unit:  inches
               Software:  Digital Camera X-Pro1 Ver1.10
            Modify Date:  2012:06:08 11:01:00
    Y Cb Cr Positioning:  Co-sited
              Copyright:
                         ---- ExifIFD ----
          Exposure Time:  1/120
               F Number:  2.0
       Exposure Program:  Program AE
                    ISO:  800
       Sensitivity Type:  Standard Output Sensitivity
           Exif Version:  0230
     Date/Time Original:  2012:06:08 11:01:00
            Create Date:  2012:06:08 11:01:00
 Components Configuration:  Y, Cb, Cr, -
  Compressed Bits Per Pixel:  3.2
     Shutter Speed Value:  1/122
          Aperture Value:  2.0
        Brightness Value:  1.13
    Exposure Compensation:  0
      Max Aperture Value:  2.0
           Metering Mode:  Multi-segment
            Light Source:  Unknown
                   Flash:  Off, Did not fire
            Focal Length:  18.0 mm
        Flashpix Version:  0100
             Color Space:  sRGB
         Exif Image Width:  4896
        Exif Image Height:  3264
  Focal Plane X Resolution:  2092
  Focal Plane Y Resolution:  2092
 Focal Plane Resolution Unit:  cm
          Sensing Method:  One-chip color area
             File Source:  Digital Camera
              Scene Type:  Directly photographed
         Custom Rendered:  Normal
           Exposure Mode:  Auto
           White Balance:  Auto
 Focal Length In 35mm Format:  27 mm
      Scene Capture Type:  Standard
               Sharpness:  Normal
   Subject Distance Range:  Unknown
               Lens Info:  18mm f/2
               Lens Make:  FUJIFILM
              Lens Model:  XF18mmF2 R
       Lens Serial Number:  21A00660
                         ---- FujiFilm ----
                 Version:  0130
    Internal Serial Number:  FPX 21128392     593130323434 2012:02:10 FD903011198E
                 Quality:  FINE
               Sharpness:  Normal
           White Balance:  Auto
              Saturation:  Normal
  White Balance Fine Tune:  Red +0, Blue +0
         Noise Reduction:  n/a
   High ISO Noise Reduction:  Normal
         Fuji Flash Mode:  Off
      Flash Exposure Comp:  0
                   Macro:  Off
             Focus Mode:  Auto
             Focus Pixel:  4151 1632
               Slow Sync:  Off
            Picture Mode:  Program AE
         Auto Bracketing:  Off
         Sequence Number:  0
            Blur Warning:  None
           Focus Warning:  Good
        Exposure Warning:  Good
           Dynamic Range:  Standard
               Film Mode:  F0/Standard (PROVIA)
   Dynamic Range Setting:  Auto (100-400%)
        Min Focal Length:  18
        Max Focal Length:  0
  Max Aperture At Min Focal:  2
  Max Aperture At Max Focal:  0
      Auto Dynamic Range:  400%
          Faces Detected:  0
```

Figure 139: **EXIF data with maker notes:** This screen grab of the Mac OS program Graph-icConverter shows a snippet of the EXIF data for an image taken with my X-Pro1. You can see that in addition to a vast amount of information about the exposure parameters, there are also general details such as the camera's serial number, its date of manufacture, and the serial number for the lens used to take the shot.

INDEX